To Mummy

Love Jamie

In memory of Dad.
Who taught me right from wrong but loved me
just the same, regardless of which path I took.
Still miss you every day.

COOKING
WITH BALLS

First published in 2010 by Network Book Publishing Ltd.

Network House, 28 Ballmoor, Celtic Court, Buckingham MK18 1RQ, UK

www.networkpublishingltd.com

© NETWORK BOOK PUBLISHING LTD.

ISBN NO: 978-0-9562661-5-6
PRINTER: Printed in China by CT Printing Ltd.
PUBLISHER: Peter Marshall
MANAGING EDITOR: Shirley Marshall
EDITOR: Katy Morris
ASSISTANT EDITORS: Sue Christelow, Hilary Mayes
DESIGN DIRECTOR: Philip Donnelly
GRAPHIC DESIGNER: Duncan Boddy
PHOTOGRAPHER: Myburgh du Plessis. With the assistance of Hugh Adams.
Rugby photography courtesy of Getty Images®.

With special thanks to Claire Koffmann & Simon Martin of QV Foods without whose help this book would not have been possible.

Page 125 Recipe kindly reproduced from 'Foolproof French Cookery' by Raymond Blanc, published by BBC Books.

↘ FOREWORD

**RUGBY AND COOKING –
NOT NECESSARILY AN OBVIOUS PAIRING
BUT WHEN I HEARD ABOUT THIS COOKBOOK
I THOUGHT "WHAT A GREAT IDEA!"**

Such a unique opportunity to bring together well-known rugby players who are at the top of their game with great chefs who are the highlight of some of the most well-known kitchens throughout England.

The control and skill demanded by rugby is very similar to that involved in high standard cooking so it was no surprise that the chefs and rugby players hit it off brilliantly.

Working with both the chefs and rugby players was such a great experience, it was fantastic to meet some of the best players of the game and a delight to work with chefs old and new on this project.

Our greatest thanks go to all for being involved.

Happy kicking and happy cooking!

PETER MARSHALL
Publisher of Yes Chef! Magazine

↘ THE LINE UP

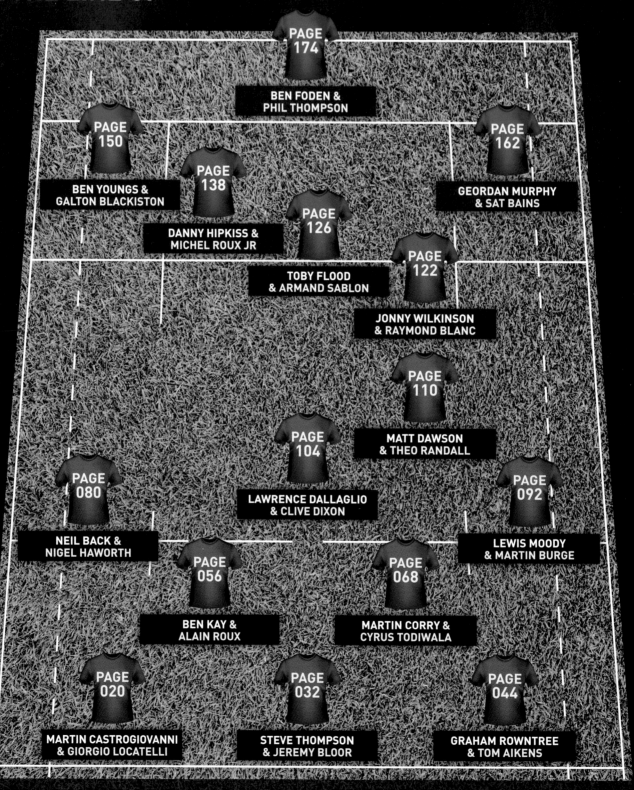

↘ THE MANAGEMENT

PAGE 186

MARTIN JOHNSON & PIERRE KOFFMANN

PAGE 282

MATT LOVELL ENGLAND RUGBY NUTRITIONIST

↘ ON THE BENCH

PAGE 198

LEE MEARS & HYWEL JONES

PAGE 210

TOM CROFT & ALAN MURCHISON

PAGE 222

NICK EASTER & MARCUS WAREING

PAGE 234

JAMES HASKELL & FRANCESCO MAZZEI

PAGE 246

JOE WORSLEY & JONAS KARLSSON

PAGE 258

ANDY GOMARSALL & ANDRE GARRETT

↘ IN THE SIN BIN

PAGE 270

BEN KAY & MARK JORDAN

↘ CONTENTS

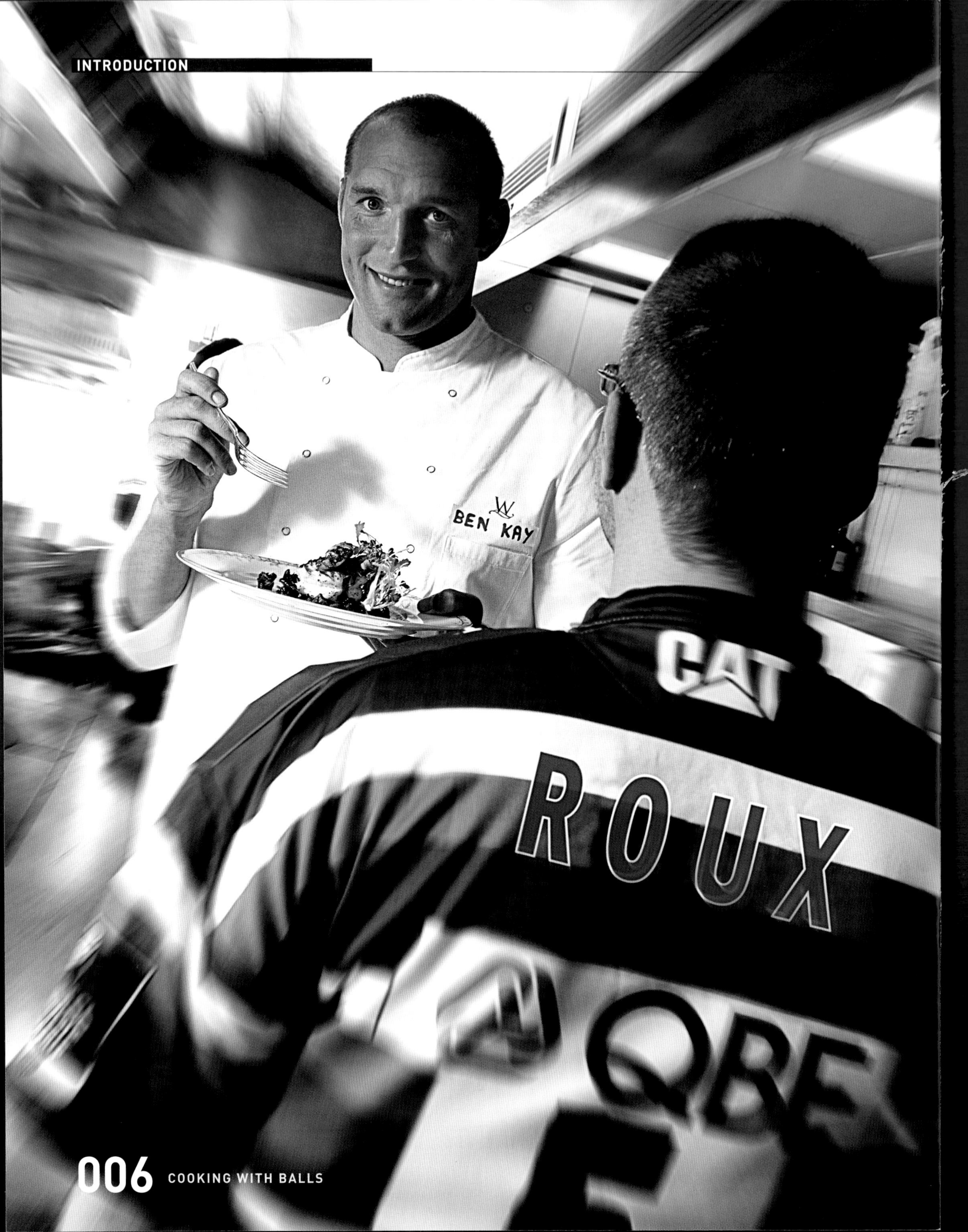
BEN KAY
CAT
ROUX
QBE

⬂ INTRODUCTION
COOKING WITH BALLS
BY BEN KAY LEICESTER TIGERS & ENGLAND

RUGBY PLAYERS ARE SIMPLE BEASTS AND AS A RESULT MOST OF US HAVE ONE PRIMARY CONCERN – WHERE IS MY NEXT MEAL GOING TO COME FROM?

When the idea of producing a book together with some of my former team mates, to celebrate my testimonial year and career, was proposed I thought one sure fire way of ensuring they all turned up was to appeal to that Neanderthal basic instinct and constant rumbling in a rugby player's stomach. The idea of a cookery book was born.

Obviously the stereotypical rugby player, through history, may occasionally have garnered a reputation that might not be all that attractive to sane members of society wishing to purchase a cookery book. So I thought it might be an idea to match our rugby stars with heroes of the professional kitchen and let them teach us how to cook or at least wash our hands properly!

As I have worked upon this book I have grown to realise how fascinating it can be to learn the favourite meals of people you admire and think you know really well. It also became apparent that a chef's attitude to only using the best ingredients for flavour was matched, with all joking aside, by the modern day professional rugby player demanding only the highest quality for his nutrition. At the top level at least, gone are the days of the beer swilling pot-bellied amateur player, replaced by a highly trained machine. And as our trainers and nutritionists constantly tell us "a machine only runs as well as the fuel you put into it – you wouldn't put diesel into a Ferrari!"

To begin each player passed his favourite dish onto his paired chef so they could put their mercurial spin on it. The chef then 'wowed' the player with one of his signature dishes. Next we asked the chefs to produce a healthy option, the sort of meal we might eat in our training week leading up to a game or even as our pre-match meal and finally a sin bin, a treat for Saturday night after the game to replenish some calories!

England rugby team's nutritionist Matt Lovell also has dedicated a selection of recipes at the back of the book, with

a range of nutritional dishes perfect for starters, main courses or desserts. Covering healthy eating together with advice and recipes, this section gives an invaluable insight into the importance of the food we eat and how it affects our physical and mental performance.

Finally, I would like to whole-heartedly thank all the chefs and players for finding the time in their extremely busy schedules to make this book possible. The quality of the line-ups for both squads and their enthusiasm – which I'm sure you'll agree the photographs portray – is testament to the fact that there is obviously a deeply rooted respect for each profession and that this idea was one to capture the imagination. I hope it captures yours and you enjoy the book as much as we have making it!

BEN KAY

MARTIN CASTROGIOVANNI

TEAM: Leicester Tigers/Italy

POSITION: Tight Head Prop

AGE STARTED PLAYING: 18

INTERNATIONAL CAPS: 59

FAVOURITE FOOD: Asado (Argentinian flamed beef BBQ).

FAVOURITE FOOD AS A CHILD: Asado – it's always been the same and I still love it!

EAT BEFORE A MATCH: I am very superstitious and always go to Timo's restaurant in Leicester to have pasta and chicken salad.

AFTER A MATCH: Burgers and pizza.

FAVOURITE RUGBY MOMENT: My first cap for Italy at 22, being named player of the season in my first year with Leicester Tigers and finally playing and winning the premiership final this year with Leicester Tigers – this year was really special.

↘ **020**

GIORGIO LOCATELLI

RESTAURANT: Locanda Locatelli, London

TITLE: Chef/Patron

SIGNATURE DISH: Rabbit with parma ham and polenta.

ACCOLADES: One Michelin Star.

FAVOURITE FOOD AS A CHILD: Risotto.

BEST FOOD MEMORY: My grandmother's polenta.

LAST SUPPER: Risotto with white truffle.

↘ **020**

STEVE THOMPSON

TEAM: Leeds Carnegie/England

POSITION: Hooker

AGE STARTED PLAYING: 16

INTERNATIONAL CAPS: England 54, British & Irish Lions 3

FAVOURITE FOOD: Sunday roast.

FAVOURITE FOOD AS A CHILD: Chicken and chips.

EAT BEFORE A MATCH: Bacon sandwiches.

AFTER A MATCH: A big take-away!

FAVOURITE RUGBY MOMENT: Playing county finals at Twickenham with my mates, winning my first England cap versus Scotland and every England lineout with Ben Kay!

↘ **032**

JEREMY BLOOR

RESTAURANT: OXO Tower, London

TITLE: Head Chef

SIGNATURE DISH: John Dory with smoked duck and pear barley, quince emulsion, barley biscuit.

ACCOLADES: 2 AA rosettes.

FAVOURITE FOOD AS A CHILD: My grandad used to take me and my brothers to a restaurant in Bradford, West Yorkshire, called Kashmir for chicken tikka – good times!

BEST FOOD MEMORY: I have too many to choose from! I think the first time I tried Tahitian vanilla ice cream it was at The Fat Duck in Bray – I will always remember that.

LAST SUPPER: My mother-in-law's red wine braised rabbit, smoked bacon and parsley with roast baby new potatoes from her garden. It's always a winner and I love it.

↘ **032**

GRAHAM ROWNTREE

TEAM: Leicester Tigers/England

POSITION PLAYED: Prop

AGE STARTED PLAYING: 10

INTERNATIONAL CAPS:
England 54;
British & Irish Lions 2

FAVOURITE FOOD: Fish and chips.

FAVOURITE FOOD AS A CHILD:
Fish and chips.

EAT BEFORE A MATCH:
Carbonara.

AFTER A MATCH: Anything with beer but normally a big curry!

FAVOURITE RUGBY MOMENT: Winning the 2001 European Cup.

↘ **044**

TOM AIKENS

RESTAURANT:
Restaurant Tom Aikens and Tom's Kitchen, London

TITLE: Chef/Patron

SIGNATURE DISH: Poached lobster tail with pork belly and apple consommé.

ACCOLADES: One Michelin Star; AA Five Rosettes.

FAVOURITE FOOD AS A CHILD:
My mum's apple pie and custard, with apples straight from the garden.

BEST FOOD MEMORY: Eating at a Two Michelin Star restaurant when I was younger which was booked by complete accident. The tastes and flavours were stunning!

LAST SUPPER: Perfectly thick medium rare côte de boeuf with big chips and béarnaise sauce all washed down with a nice Côte Rôtie – heaven!

↘ **044**

BEN KAY

TEAM: Leicester Tigers/England

POSITION: Second Row Forward

AGE STARTED PLAYING: 5

INTERNATIONAL CAPS:
England 62,
British & Irish Lions 2

FAVOURITE FOOD: There are so many but definitely steak, lobster and crème brûlée.

FAVOURITE FOOD AS A CHILD:
Spaghetti bolognese.

EAT BEFORE A MATCH: For breakfast a big omelette; for lunch: steak, rice and vegetables.

AFTER A MATCH: A huge Chinese take-away.

FAVOURITE RUGBY MOMENT: Winning the European Cup with Leicester Tigers in 2001.

↘ **056**

ALAIN ROUX

RESTAURANT:
The Waterside Inn, Bray

TITLE: Chef/Patron

SIGNATURE DISH: Émietté de tourteau du Devon aux effluves de melon, amandes fraîches et crevettes roses marinées.

Flaked Devon crab with melon and fresh almonds, served with marinated prawns.

FAVOURITE FOOD AS A CHILD:
Mum's rabbit stew with prunes.

BEST FOOD MEMORY: Eating le soufflé Suissesse.

LAST SUPPER: One of my wife's specials – a chicken 'curry style' with rice, broccoli and almonds.

↘ **056**

MARTIN CORRY

TEAM: Leicester Tigers/England

POSITION: No 8; Flanker; Prop

AGE STARTED PLAYING: 6

INTERNATIONAL CAPS:
England 64;
British & Irish Lions 7

FAVOURITE FOOD: Curry.

FAVOURITE FOOD AS A CHILD:
My mum's shepherd's pie.

EAT BEFORE A MATCH:
Ham and leek pasta.

AFTER A MATCH: Fish and chips from Grimsby Fisheries in Leicester or a curry.

FAVOURITE RUGBY MOMENT: Playing in the first test of the 2001 Lions Tour against Australia.

↘ **068**

CYRUS TODIWALA

RESTAURANT:
Café Spice Namasté, London

TITLE: Chef/Patron

SIGNATURE DISH:
Parsee Dhaansaak.

ACCOLADES: Mood Food 2009 Restaurant of the Year

FAVOURITE FOOD AS A CHILD:
Dhaan Daar Nay Kharu Gos (steamed surti kolum rice, parsee-style lentils and whole spice flavoured lamb).

BEST FOOD MEMORY: Eating sesame and peanut brittle that is made only during the winter months.

LAST SUPPER: Dhaan Daar Nay Vaghaar – Rice parsee daal or lentils and drizzled with crisp caramelised onions, fried sliced garlic and papadams.

↘ **068**

NEIL BACK

TEAM: Leicester Tigers/England

POSITION: Flanker

INTERNATIONAL CAPS:
England 66;
British & Irish Lions 5

AGE STARTED PLAYING: 5

FAVOURITE FOOD AS A CHILD:
Sunday roast beef, Yorkshire pudding, roasted and mashed potatoes, plenty of vegetables and gravy.

EAT BEFORE A MATCH: Pre-match meal was a little pasta, broccoli, poached eggs, sea salt and black pepper.

AFTER A MATCH: Over the next 24 hours I would eat up to 10,000 calories to replenish energy stores, usually curry or Chinese.

FAVOURITE RUGBY MOMENT: Plucking my 4-year-old daughter Olivia from the crowd in 2003 and sharing the World Cup Winners' platform with her and my mates while my wife Alison and 14-month-old son, Finley, looked on from the crowd.

↘ **080**

NIGEL HAWORTH

RESTAURANT:
Northcote, Blackburn; Ribble Valley Inns, Lancashire

TITLE: Chef/Patron

SIGNATURE DISH:
Lancashire hotpot.

ACCOLADES: One Michelin Star

FAVOURITE FOOD AS A CHILD:
Queen of puddings by Granny Ish.

BEST FOOD MEMORY: Visiting the Festival of Food and Wine in California and working with some amazing people – it was that that inspired me to start the Obsession festivals at Northcote.

LAST SUPPER: Anything fresh from our local area – it has so many great dishes to choose from, I'd have a selection of everything Lancashire!

↘ **080**

LEWIS MOODY

TEAM: Bath Rugby/England

POSITION: Open Side Flanker

AGE STARTED PLAYING: 5

INTERNATIONAL CAPS:
England 63;
British & Irish Lions 3

FAVOURITE FOOD: Cottage pie.

FAVOURITE FOOD AS A CHILD:
Spaghetti bolognese.

EAT BEFORE A MATCH: Pasta with tuna, sweetcorn and pickle.

AFTER A MATCH: Sushi or BBQ ribs.

FAVOURITE RUGBY MOMENT: Winning the 2003 World Cup.

↘ 092

MARTIN BURGE

RESTAURANT: The Dining Room at Whatley Manor, Bath

TITLE: Head Chef

SIGNATURE DISH: Braised snails set in garlic cassonade and topped with red wine sauce infused with veal kidney.

ACCOLADES: Two Michelin Stars; 4 AA Rosettes.

FAVOURITE FOOD AS A CHILD: Rice pudding.

BEST FOOD MEMORY: Dining at Per Se – four hours passed so very quickly.

LAST SUPPER: A good curry.

↘ 092

LAWRENCE DALLAGLIO

TEAM: London Wasps/England

POSITION: No 8, Flanker

AGE STARTED PLAYING: 8

INTERNATIONAL CAPS:
England 85;
British & Irish Lions 3

FAVOURITE FOOD: Italian.

FAVOURITE FOOD AS A CHILD: Italian.

EAT BEFORE A MATCH: Spaghetti bolognese, sandwiches and fruit.

AFTER A MATCH: Anything put in front of me!

FAVOURITE RUGBY MOMENT: Winning the World Cup in 2003 in Sydney and the British & Irish Lions tour of South Africa 1997.

↘ 104

CLIVE DIXON

RESTAURANT: Koffmann's, London

TITLE: Head Chef

SIGNATURE DISH: Twice-cooked blade of beef with foie gras sauce.

ACCOLADES: One Michelin Star.

FAVOURITE FOOD AS CHILD: Chips, mushy peas and gravy.

BEST FOOD MEMORY: The Menu Dégustation at Le Champignon Sauvage in Cheltenham.

LAST SUPPER: Côte de boeuf.

↘ 104

MATT DAWSON

TEAM: Northampton Saints, London Wasps/England

POSITION: Scrum Half

AGE STARTED PLAYING: 5

INTERNATIONAL CAPS:
England 77,
British & Irish Lions 7

FAVOURITE FOOD: Japanese.

FAVOURITE FOOD AS A CHILD: My mum's Chicken à la Crème – delicious!

EAT BEFORE A MATCH: Porridge and scrambled egg on toast.

AFTER A MATCH: Loads of tasty stuff!

FAVOURITE RUGBY MOMENT: Winning the 2003 World Cup. Actually it would have been scoring the winning try in the 2003 World Cup final, but instead of running the ball over the line myself, I passed it to Ben Kay who then dropped it!

↘ **110**

THEO RANDALL

RESTAURANT: Theo Randall at the InterContinental Hotel, London

TITLE: Chef/Patron

SIGNATURE DISH:
Calamari in padella – pan-fried squid with fresh canellini beans, chilli, anchovy, parsley and chopped rocket.

ACCOLADES: Italian Restaurant of the Year 2008.

FAVOURITE FOOD AS A CHILD: Snails in garlic.

BEST FOOD MEMORY: Eating grilled sardines on a boat in Venice.

LAST SUPPER: Poached Scottish langoustine, tagliolini with white truffles, roast grouse on bruschetta with fresh porcini mushrooms, small piece of gorgonzola and finally a big bowl of dark red chilled cherries.

↘ **110**

JONNY WILKINSON

TEAM: Toulon/England

POSITION PLAYED: Fly Half, Inside Centre

AGE STARTED PLAYING: 8

INTERNATIONAL CAPS: England 80; British & Irish Lions 6

FAVOURITE FOOD: Spicy chicken.

FAVOURITE FOOD AS A CHILD: Chicken in pastry.

EAT BEFORE A MATCH: Chicken and baked potatoes, or a chicken sandwich and an energy/protein bar.

AFTER A MATCH: I try to have one of my favourite meals as a reward for the day's efforts, at the moment this would probably be chicken fajitas.

FAVOURITE RUGBY MOMENT: The first game I played for Newcastle in the premiership alongside my brother. It was an amazing opportunity to share something very important with someone very important. I was playing number 10 and he was playing 12 in the centre. We won the game and it was a great day.

↘ **122**

RAYMOND BLANC

NAME: Raymond Blanc OBE

RESTAURANT: Le Manoir aux Quat'Saisons, Oxfordshire

TITLE: Chef/Patron

SIGNATURE DISH:
Chocolate fondant.

ACCOLADES: Two Michelin Stars; 5 AA Rosettes.

FAVOURITE FOOD AS A CHILD: Anything fresh from our garden.

BEST FOOD MEMORY:
Cooking with Maman Blanc and winning our second star.

LAST SUPPER: A hearty meal of a true Frenchman – oysters, escargot and Maman Blanc's crudities to start; then a slow cooked shoulder of wild boar steeped in a deep, vinous red-wine jus. To finish would be Maman Blanc's Floating Islands, not forgetting all the great cheese from my region of Franche-Comte.

↘ **122**

TOBY FLOOD

TEAM: Leicester Tigers/England
POSITION: Fly Half/Centre
AGE STARTED PLAYING: 6
INTERNATIONAL CAPS: 31
FAVOURITE FOOD:
Rack of lamb.
FAVOURITE FOOD AS A CHILD:
'Hash and mash' – beef in gravy with onions and potato.
EAT BEFORE A MATCH:
The night before it's important to eat carbohydrates.
AFTER A MATCH: Anything.
FAVOURITE RUGBY MOMENT: Favourite and worst would be playing in the 2007 World Cup final for England. It's one of the greatest achievements, but at the same time we lost and it will always be a bittersweet feeling. Also winning the 2009 Premiership with Leicester.

↘ **126**

ARMAND SABLON

RESTAURANT:
Bistro K, London
TITLE: Head Chef
SIGNATURE DISH:
Wild seabass and sauce vierge – because it's a very light dish the combinations work perfectly.
ACCOLADES: 2007 Roux Scholarship winner.
FAVOURITE FOOD AS A CHILD:
My mum's roast dinner.
BEST FOOD MEMORY: Winning the Roux Scholarship was a massive stepping stone in my career and it put me in contact with people I may never have got in contact with.
LAST SUPPER: It would have to be my mum's roast dinner.

↘ **126**

DANNY HIPKISS

TEAM: Leicester Tigers/England
POSITION PLAYED: Centre
AGE STARTED PLAYING: 5
INTERNATIONAL CAPS: 13
FAVOURITE FOOD:
Slow-roasted shoulder of lamb.
FAVOURITE FOOD AS A CHILD:
Fruit. In particular I loved nectarines and peaches – definitely my favourites.
EAT BEFORE A MATCH:
Protein drink and oats for breakfast, and then brown rice with chicken or fish three hours before kickoff.
AFTER A MATCH: Fish and chips followed by ice cream – it's the only time our nutritionist will let us get away with it!
FAVOURITE RUGBY MOMENT: Playing in the 2007 World Cup final, followed closely by winning the premiership with Leicester later that year.

↘ **138**

MICHEL ROUX JR

RESTAURANT:
Le Gavroche, London
POSITION: Chef/Patron
ACCOLADES:
Two Michelin Stars.
SIGNATURE DISH: Soufflé Fruit de la Passion et Glace Ivoire.
FAVOURITE FOOD AS A CHILD:
Braised sweetbreads.
BEST FOOD MEMORY:
Grilled lobster on the beach in the Seychelles.
LAST SUPPER: As above but with a bottle of Champagne Gosset.

↘ **138**

BEN YOUNGS

TEAM: Leicester Tigers/England

POSITION: Scrum Half

AGE STARTED PLAYING: 8

INTERNATIONAL CAPS: 3

FAVOURITE FOOD: Belly of pork or roast beef and Yorkshire pudding with the works!

EAT BEFORE A MATCH? The night before I have carbonara.

AFTER A MATCH? Chinese take-away.

FAVOURITE RUGBY MOMENT: Scoring the winning try for England against Australia in Sydney 2010.

↘ 150

GALTON BLACKISTON

RESTAURANT: Morston Hall, Norfolk

TITLE: Chef/Patron

SIGNATURE DISH: Grilled fillet of wild sea bass.

ACCOLADES: One Michelin Star.

FAVOURITE FOOD AS A CHILD: Toad in the hole.

BEST FOOD MEMORY: Foraging locally, and cockling and shrimping on the coast.

LAST SUPPER: Local lobster with new potatoes and mayonnaise.

↘ 150

GEORDAN MURPHY

TEAM: Leicester Tigers/Ireland

POSITION: Full Back

AGE STARTED PLAYING: 13

INTERNATIONAL CAPS: 69

FAVOURITE FOOD: Scallops.

FAVOURITE FOOD AS A CHILD: Ham and cabbage, cooked by my mum.

EAT BEFORE A MATCH: Chicken pasta or carbonara.

AFTER A MATCH: Fish and chips.

FAVOURITE RUGBY MOMENT: My first Irish International cap for Ireland against the USA.

↘ 162

SAT BAINS

RESTAURANT: Restaurant Sat Bains, Nottingham

TITLE: Chef/Patron

SIGNATURE DISH: Ham, egg and peas.

ACCOLADES: One Michelin Star; 5 AA Rosettes.

FAVOURITE FOOD AS A CHILD: Keema minced lamb curry.

BEST FOOD MEMORY: A grilled lamb chop beautifully prepared by a friend who is a chef. He tossed the salad in the lamb juices – a memorable food moment.

LAST SUPPER: Steak and chips. Keens Steakhouse in New York prepares the best steak.

↘ 162

BEN FODEN

TEAM: Northampton Saints/
England

POSITION: Scrum Half,
Full Back, or Wing

AGE STARTED PLAYING: 4

INTERNATIONAL CAPS: 6

FAVOURITE FOOD:
Anything Italian.

FAVOURITE FOOD AS A CHILD:
Pizza.

EAT BEFORE A MATCH: Usually
a pasta dish with chicken or fish.

AFTER A MATCH: Anything – the tastier the better! Our
conditioner at Northampton claims it's the only time
players can eat whatever they want and get away with it!

FAVOURITE RUGBY MOMENT: I have two, winning the
Premiership with Sale in 2006 and beating Australia in
Sydney with England!

↘ **174**

PHIL THOMPSON

RESTAURANT:
Auberge du Lac, Welwyn
Garden City

TITLE: Executive Chef

SIGNATURE DISH: I don't
believe in signature dishes
because I like to keep myself
and the kitchen constantly
evolving!

ACCOLADES: One Michelin
Star; 3 AA Rosettes.

FAVOURITE FOOD AS A CHILD:
My mum's roast dinner.

BEST FOOD MEMORY: Nan's roast potatoes – she used to
part-boil them, score them with a fork and then roll them
in flour for the crispiest skin!

LAST SUPPER: Spaghetti bolognese, fresh parmesan
and freshly baked bread.

↘ **174**

MARTIN JOHNSON

TEAM: Leicester Tigers/England

POSITION: England Manager

AGE STARTED PLAYING: 11

INTERNATIONAL CAPS:
England 84,
British & Irish Lions 8

FAVOURITE FOOD:
Traditional English food – meat,
potatoes, sausages, bacon,
fish and chips – not a very
sophisticated palate!

FAVOURITE FOOD AS A CHILD: Food in general was my
favourite as a child, I had a big appetite.

EAT BEFORE A MATCH: Cereal or scrambled eggs or
probably pasta with a bolognese sauce.

AFTER A MATCH: Whatever you feel like and enjoy it!

FAVOURITE RUGBY MOMENT: Winning and the build up
of the 2003 World Cup.

↘ **186**

PIERRE KOFFMANN

RESTAURANT:
Koffmann's, London

TITLE: Chef/Patron

SIGNATURE DISH:
Pig's trotters stuffed with
sweetbreads and morels.

ACCOLADES:
Three Michelin Stars.

FAVOURITE FOOD AS A CHILD:
Civet of hare.

BEST FOOD MEMORY:
Bouillabaisse – a fish soup
from the south of France.

LAST SUPPER: Bouillabaisse.

↘ **186**

LEE MEARS

TEAM: Bath Rugby/England

POSITION: Hooker

AGE STARTED PLAYING: 7

INTERNATIONAL CAPS:
England 35,
British & Irish Lions 1

FAVOURITE FOOD:
Beef Wellington.

FAVOURITE FOOD AS A CHILD:
Mum's sausage wheels.

EAT BEFORE A MATCH:
Sandwiches! I love sandwiches!

AFTER A MATCH: Anything chocolate! I love chocolate as well!

FAVOURITE RUGBY MOMENT: Winning my first England cap.

↘ 198

HYWEL JONES

POSITION: Executive Chef

RESTAURANT: The 'Park' and The 'Brasserie' both at Lucknam Park, Bath

ACCOLADES: One Michelin Star

SIGNATURE DISH: Pork belly.

FAVOURITE FOOD AS A CHILD: My Mothers 'Cawl' – Welsh lamb stew.

FAVOURITE FOOD MEMORY: Dinner at Alain Ducasse, Plaza Athena in Paris closely followed lunch at the French Laundry in California.

LAST SUPPER: Simply cooked Welsh seafood and homemade bread, eaten overlooking the Pembrokeshire coastline with my wife and two boys.

↘ 198

TOM CROFT

TEAM: Leicester Tigers/England

POSITION: Flanker, Lock

AGE STARTED PLAYING: 11

INTERNATIONAL CAPS:
England 18,
British & Irish Lions 3

FAVOURITE FOOD:
Lamb with all the trimmings.

FAVOURITE FOOD AS A CHILD:
Chicken dippers, beans and chips.

EAT BEFORE A MATCH:
Carbonara.

AFTER A MATCH: Curry from my local Indian.

FAVOURITE RUGBY MOMENT: Winning my first British Lions cap.

↘ 210

ALAN MURCHISON

RESTAURANT:
L'ortolan, Reading;
La Becasse, Ludlow;
Paris House, Woburn

TITLE: Executive Chef

SIGNATURE DISH: Coq au vin.

ACCOLADES: One Michelin Star; 3AA Rosettes

FAVOURITE FOOD AS A CHILD: Full cooked breakfast.

BEST FOOD MEMORY: Eating my Nana's Yorkshire pudding.

LAST SUPPER: Steak and chips.

↘ 210

NICK EASTER

TEAM: Harlequins/England
POSITION: Number 8
AGE STARTED PLAYING: 7
INTERNATIONAL CAPS: 34
FAVOURITE FOOD: Thai curry.
FAVOURITE FOOD AS A CHILD:
Roast lamb.
EAT BEFORE A MATCH:
Spaghetti bolognese.
AFTER A MATCH:
Anything, I'm not fussy!
FAVOURITE RUGBY MOMENT: The World Cup 2007.

↘ 222

MARCUS WAREING

RESTAURANT:
Marcus Wareing at
The Berkeley, London
TITLE: Chef/Patron
SIGNATURE DISH: Custard tart
cooked for the Queen's 80th
birthday.
ACCOLADES: 2 Michelin stars;
AA chef of the Year 2009;
Harden's best London restaurant
2009 and 2010; San Pelegrino
breakthrough award 2009.
FAVOURITE FOOD AS A CHILD: Bananas and custard.
BEST FOOD MEMORY: Too many great experiences to
write, but for food as a whole it would be opening Marcus
Wareing at The Berkeley in 2008.
LAST SUPPER: Foie gras, scallops, rib of beef, cheese, our
chocolate moelleux! All matched with wines from Burgundy.

↘ 222

JAMES HASKELL

TEAM: Stade Français/England
POSITION PLAYED: No 8
AGE STARTED PLAYING: 5
INTERNATIONAL CAPS:
England 26
FAVOURITE FOOD: Almost
everything English. I love
sausages and I'm a really big
fan of fish.
FAVOURITE FOOD AS A CHILD:
Any of my mum's home cooking
and also Indian food.
EAT BEFORE A MATCH: Fish or meat and my green tea.
There is no problem in the world that can't be fixed by my
green tea!
AFTER A MATCH: I love pizza after a game, I don't know
why but I always want it!
FAVOURITE RUGBY MOMENT: Winning the Heineken Cup
with Wasps against Leicester and playing for England
against Wales in last year's 6 Nations.

↘ 234

FRANCESCO MAZZEI

RESTAURANT:
L'Anima, London
TITLE: Chef/Patron
SIGNATURE DISH: Sicilian
rabbit, Beef tagliata, Fish stew
with Sardinian fregola.
ACCOLADES: Tatler Louis
Roederer Restaurant Awards
2009 for Best Newcomer,
Harden's Remy Martin
Restaurant Award for
Excellence 2009.
FAVOURITE FOOD AS A CHILD: Sundays were always a
big celebration with lunches using the best ingredients
from our garden – everything was home-made including
the bread, the pasta and even the ice creams.
BEST FOOD MEMORY: My best food memory must be a trip
to Sardinia with Chris Corbin. We went to Gallura Restaurant
where we tasted some marvellous dishes prepared in true
'mama style'. It was undoubtedly the best meal of my life.
LAST SUPPER: My mother's rabbit stew.

↘ 234

JOE WORSLEY

TEAM: London Wasps/England

POSITION: No 8

AGE STARTED PLAYING: 7

INTERNATIONAL CAPS:
England 76;
British & Irish Lions 1

FAVOURITE FOOD: Japanese or roasts.

FAVOURITE FOOD AS A CHILD: Sausage and mash.

EAT BEFORE A MATCH: High carbs – something like pasta with tomato sauce.

FOOD TO AFTER A MATCH: Anything not allowed in the week (I call it the dirty meal) – it's delicious.

FAVOURITE RUGBY MOMENT: Winning the 2003 World Cup and equally the Wasps' first European win.

↘ **246**

JONAS KARLSSON

RESTAURANT: Fifth Floor Restaurant, Harvey Nichols, London

TITLE: Executive Chef

SIGNATURE DISH: Lobster Mimosa Salad

ACCOLADES: 2 AA rosettes

FAVOURITE FOOD AS A CHILD: My grandmother's homemade meatballs with lingonberry jam.

BEST FOOD MEMORY: Legendary Don Alfonso restaurant near Sorrento, where I sampled the tasting menu with my wife on our honeymoon. It was a very special time for us and the food, service and beautiful surroundings surpassed our expectations.

LAST SUPPER: A smorgasbord which is a typical meal in Sweden. Smorgas meaning open- faced sandwich and bord meaning table, a smorgasbord is a coming together of family and friends to share buffet-style food of cured meats, smoked and pickled fish and other typical Swedish favourites.

↘ **246**

ANDY GOMARSALL

TEAM: Leeds Carnegie/England

POSITION: Scrum Half

AGE STARTED PLAYING: 6

INTERNATIONAL CAPS: 35

FAVOURITE FOOD: Spaghetti bolognese.

FAVOURITE FOOD AS A CHILD: Bangers and mash, and Angel Delight.

EAT BEFORE A MATCH: The night before – spaghetti bolognese; my pre-match meal is always a good English breakfast and that sorts me out before a game.

AFTER A MATCH: Enjoyable food such as piri-piri chicken or a shepherd's pie. My wife makes an excellent curry.

FAVOURITE RUGBY MOMENT: Obviously winning the World Cup in 2003; my first cap in 1996; and beating Australia in the World Cup quarter final in 2007 in Marseilles and the good party afterwards.

↘ **258**

ANDRE GARRETT

RESTAURANT: Galvin at Windows, London

TITLE: Head Chef

SIGNATURE DISH: South Coast John Dory, Cauliflower Purée, Sea Aster, Raisins, Capers and Curry Oil.

ACCOLADES: One Michelin Star.

FAVOURITE FOOD AS A CHILD: Fish finger sandwiches and my mum's cakes. She makes a fantastic fruit cake and I was always around her apron strings helping her cook.

BEST FOOD MEMORY: Dinner at Michel Bras, a Three Michelin Star restaurant in Laguiole, France. His salad 'Gargouillou' was an explosion of flavour that I will always remember.

LAST SUPPER: My girlfriend, Viviana's, seafood antipasto.

↘ **258**

BEN KAY

BRITISH & IRISH LIONS APPEARANCES: 5

ENGLAND APPEARANCES: 62

WORLD CUP APPEARANCES: 13

ENGLAND TRIES: 2

ENGLAND HONOURS: World Cup winner 2003; World Cup runner-up 2007; Grand Slam winner 2003; Triple Crown 2002, 2003.

LEICESTER TIGERS APPEARANCES: 279

EUROPEAN CUP APPEARANCES: 65

LEICESTER TIGERS TRIES: 12

LEICESTER TIGERS HONOURS: European Cup Winner 2002, 2001; European Cup runner-up 2009, 2007; Premiership winner 2010, 2009, 2007, 2002, 2001, 2000; Premiership runner-up 2008, 2006, 2005; Anglo/Welsh Cup winner 2007; Anglo/Welsh runner-up 2008.

BARBARIANS APPEARANCES: 2

DROPPED BALLS OVER TRY-LINE IN WORLD CUP FINAL: 1 (Oops!)

↘ **270**

MARK JORDAN

RESTAURANT: The Atlantic, Jersey

POSITION: Head Chef

SIGNATURE DISH: Pan-roast Manor Farm Jersey beef fillet with St. Ouen's lobster ravioli, summer vegetables and beef consommé.

ACCOLADES: One Michelin Star; 3 AA Rosettes.

FAVOURITE FOOD AS A CHILD: My mum used to make the best fruit cakes!

BEST FOOD MEMORY: When I was only 16 the great late Keith Floyd, who I worked for at the time, drove me up to London in his brand new white Bentley convertible to have lunch and meet the three Michelin-star chef Marco Pierre White – just the best feeling of excitement and awe ever!

↘ **270**

MATT LOVELL

TEAM: England

POSITION: Team Nutritionist

AGE STARTED WATCHING RUGBY: 12

FAVOURITE FOOD: Vietnamese.

FAVOURITE FOOD AS A CHILD: Marmite on toast.

EAT BEFORE A MATCH: Beef stir-fry with oyster sauce.

AFTER A MATCH: A big roast dinner.

FAVOURITE RUGBY MOMENT: Winning the World Cup Final 2003 and the Finals in 2007.

↘ **282**

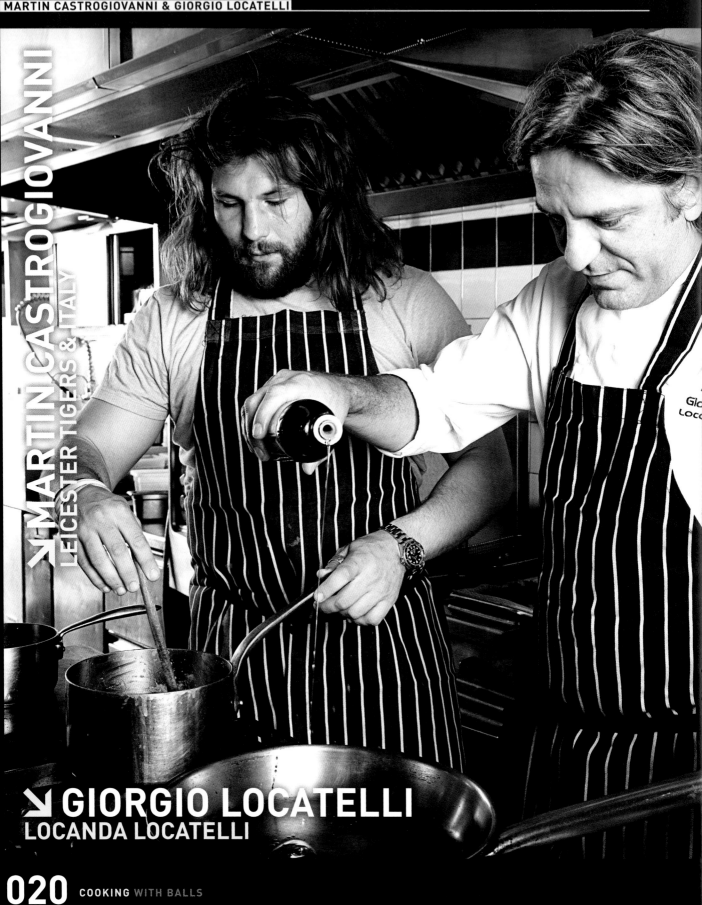

MARTIN CASTROGIOVANNI
LEICESTER TIGERS & ITALY

GIORGIO LOCATELLI
LOCANDA LOCATELLI

↘ RISOTTO DI GAMBERI E FIORE DI ZUCCHINE
PRAWN AND COURGETTE RISOTTO
BY GIORGIO LOCATELLI / SERVES 4

METHOD

STOCK: Peel the prawns, take off the heads and devein them, reserving the shells and heads. Cut the tails into pieces about 2cm long and set aside for later.

Heat the oil in a large, heavy-based pan. Take the garlic out of the oil (but keep the oil) and add to the pan with the vegetables, bay leaf, parsley and peppercorns. Cook for a minute or so, without allowing them to colour, then put in the prawn heads and shells. Crush with a wooden spoon to release the juices.

Shake the pan and, after a minute, add the wine. Continue to cook over a high heat for about 3 minutes, letting the alcohol evaporate. Add the tomato paste and cover with the water (make sure the shells are covered). Bring to the boil, then turn down the heat and simmer for about 15 minutes.

RISOTTO: To make the risotto, strain the stock into a clean pan and have it barely simmering next to where you are going to make the risotto. Melt the butter in a heavy-based pan and add the onions and the baby courgettes. Cook gently until the onions are softened, but not coloured, for around 5 minutes.

Add the rice and stir around to coat in the butter and 'toast' the grains. Make sure all the grains are warm, before adding the wine. Let the wine evaporate completely until the onions and rice are dry.

Start to add the stock a ladleful or two at a time, stirring and scraping the rice in the pan as you do so. Also add the passata with the first ladleful of stock. When each addition of stock has almost evaporated, add the next ladleful.

Carry on cooking the risotto for about 14 minutes, adding stock continuously as above, but slow up towards the end, so that the rice doesn't become too wet. Remember you don't want it to be soupy at this stage, as when you add the butter at the end it will become too sloppy. The risotto is ready when the grains are soft, but still al dente.

Season the pieces of prawn, add them to the risotto and carry on cooking for another minute. Add the garlic oil and lemon juice. Season to taste. Take off the heat and let the risotto rest for a minute without stirring.

At the mantecatura stage, vigorously beat the cold diced butter into the risotto with a woodern spoon, making sure you shake the pan energetically at the same time as you beat. Just before serving, if it is too firm, beat in a little more hot stock.

TO SERVE: Add the parsley and serve. Decorate with the courgette flower.

PLANNING AHEAD
Cut the courgette flower vertically down the middle, put it on top of a piece of parchment paper and dry it in the oven at 50ºC for 12 hours.

INGREDIENTS

STOCK:
- 1kg large prawns (Mediterranean or Tiger)
- 3 tbsp extra-virgin olive oil
- 4 garlic cloves, chopped and put into a little olive oil
- 1 carrot, roughly chopped
- 1 onion, roughly chopped
- 1 celery stalk, roughly chopped
- 1 bay leaf
- few parsley stalks
- few black peppercorns
- 150ml dry white wine
- 1 tbsp tomato paste
- 2 litres water

RISOTTO:
- 50g butter
- 1 onion, very finely chopped
- 2 baby courgettes. very thinly sliced
- 400g superfino carnaroli rice
- 125ml dry white wine
- 1 tbsp tomato passata
- salt and freshly ground black pepper
- 2 tbsp garlic oil
- juice of ½ lemon
- 75g cold butter, cut into small dice
- 2 tbsp parsley, chopped

TO SERVE:
- 1 courgette flower

↘ SALTIMBOCCA DI VITELLO E PARMIGIANA DI MELANZANE E FINFERLI

VEAL WITH PARMA HAM AND SAGE, BAKED AUBERGINE AND GIROLLES
BY GIORGIO LOCATELLI / SERVES 4

PLANNING AHEAD
The aubergines need to be salted and left over night to draw out as much water as possible.

INGREDIENTS

PARMIGIANA:
- 500g aubergines (around 4 pale egg-shaped ones)
- salt, as needed
- vegetable oil, as needed
- 300ml tomato sauce
- 300g parmesan, finely grated
- 1 bunch of basil leaves

SALTIMBOCCA:
- 600g veal loin
- 4 slices of prosciutto
- 8 sage leaves

GIROLLES:
- butter, as needed
- 1 garlic clove, finely chopped
- girolle mushrooms, cleaned
- white wine, as needed
- parsley, chopped

TO SERVE:
- salt and pepper
- flour, as needed
- vegetable oil, as needed
- 80ml marsala wine
- 20g cold butter, cubed

METHOD

PARMIGIANA: With a potato peeler, take four strips off the aubergine skin, so you have one strip of flesh, one of skin, one of flesh and so on. Cut the aubergine in rounds 0.5cm wide. Put the aubergines in a colander, sprinkle with salt and leave for a couple of hours or preferably overnight.

Preheat the oven to 180ºC.
Take the aubergines from the colander and pat them dry. Then put a few slices at a time in a very hot pan with vegetable oil, and cook them until they start to get colour on each side. Lay them in paper towels to drain off the excess oil.

In a square baking dish, around 20cm x 20cm, spread a thin ladleful of tomato sauce, then overlap the aubergine rounds into a layer, again a ladleful of tomato sauce, parmesan and basil leaves.

Repeat with another layer of aubergines and so on, finishing with tomato sauce and lots of parmesan. Cover with foil and bake in the oven for 30 minutes. Remove the foil and continue cooking for 10 more minutes.

SALTIMBOCCA: While the aubergines are in the oven, clean the veal loin and cut in eight slices of 75g. Hammer each piece very thinly until around 5mm thick. Place a slice of prosciutto on a veal escalope, put two sage leaves on top and cover it with another veal escalope. Repeat with the rest.

GIROLLES: In a sauté pan, melt a knob of butter, add the garlic and cook without allowing it to colour. Add the girolles to the pan, season and sauté for a minute. Add a drizzle of white wine, let the alcohol evaporate and turn the heat down. Add another knob of butter to the pan and cover it. Cook slowly for a couple of minutes and keep apart. Add a little parsley just before serving.

TO SERVE: Season each saltimbocca and dust with flour, then put it in a very hot pan with a little vegetable oil, and cook it through quickly on each side. Take it out and keep warm while you work your sauce in the pan. Pour the Marsala into the still hot pan and let it reduce by half, then beat in the butter.

Cut the parmigiana in squares of 10 x 10cm and if necessary warm it through. Place a square on a warmed plate, the girolles next to it and the saltimbocca laying on top of the parmigiana. Spoon the sauce on top of the meat.

↘ RAVIOLI DI ERBE CON SALSA DI NOCI

HERB RAVIOLI WITH WALNUT SAUCE

BY GIORGIO LOCATELLI / SERVES 4

▐▌ THIS IS A SPRINGTIME DISH, WHEN THE HERBS ARE IN SEASON – YOU CAN USE BORAGE OR YOUNG NETTLES AS WELL, IF YOU LIKE. YOU CAN BUY THE WALNUT PASTE FROM ITALIAN DELICATESSENS, BUT MAKE SURE IT IS GOOD QUALITY. ▐▌
- GIORGIO LOCATELLI

SPECIAL EQUIPMENT

Food processor, pasta machine, pestle and mortar, fluted ring cutter.

INGREDIENTS

FILLING:
- 2 large bunches of parsley leaves, plus a handful to garnish
- 2 large bunches of basil leaves
- 2-3 sprigs of rosemary
- bunch of sage leaves
- 125g Swiss chard leaves
- 125ml extra-virgin olive oil
- 2 handfuls of fresh spinach
- 2 handfuls young nettle leaves (optional)
- 2 handfuls of borage leaves (optional)
- 350g ricotta
- salt and freshly ground black pepper
- ¼ nutmeg, freshly grated
- 1 tbsp parmesan cheese, grated
- 1 egg
- 1 tbsp breadcrumbs
- 2 tomatoes

RAVIOLI PASTA DOUGH:
- 250g 00 flour
- 100ml warm water
- salt, to taste
- ½ tbsp extra virgin olive oil

WALNUT PASTE:
- 1kg walnuts, in the:ir shells
- 2 garlic cloves
- 3 tablespoons of olive oil
- boiling water, as needed

METHOD

FILLING: Add the herbs to the chard leaves, reserving one of the bunches of parsley for garnish.

In a separate pan, warm the olive oil, add the herbs and chard leaves, then the spinach, together with the young nettle and borage leaves if using them.

Gently 'stew' without frying for 4-5 minutes until soft (you are softening, rather than cooking, as you want everything to stay green). Drain in a colander and weight everything down for about 10 minutes to lose as much of the excess moisture as possible.

Put the contents of the colander into a food processor and whiz to a smooth paste, then transfer to a fine sieve and leave to drain for another 10 minutes.

Put the ricotta into a bowl, add the drained herbs and leaves, season and add the nutmeg, parmesan, one of the eggs and the breadcrumbs. Taste and adjust the seasoning, if necessary, then put into the fridge until needed.

Put the tomatoes into a pan of boiling water for 10 seconds. Skin them, quarter and deseed, then cut into about 1cm dice. Keep to one side.

PASTA DOUGH: Sieve the flour into a clean bowl, then turn it out into a mound on a clean surface and make a well in the middle. Sprinkle the salt into the well, warm up the water and oil and add to the flour.

Gradually incorporate the flour into the well until you have worked it enough to make a dough. Wrap each in a damp cloth and rest for about an hour before using.

Roll the ball of dough with a rolling pin until it is about 1cm thick, and will go through the pasta machine comfortably

Put the machine on the largest setting to start with, then feed the piece of pasta through the machine turning the handle with one hand, and supporting the dough as it comes through with the other. Repeat another two or three times, taking the setting down by one each time.

Fold the strip of pasta back on itself, put the machine back onto the first setting and put the pasta through. Repeat three or four more times, again taking the setting down one each time.

Cut your strip in half. Keep one half covered in a damp cloth, then fold the length of the other strip into three, bringing one end in and the other over the top of that, so that the pasta is the same width as the machine. Roll it with the rolling pin, so it is no more than half 1cm thick, then put the machine back onto the first setting and feed the pasta through widthways. Keep feeding it through this way, taking it down two or three settings as you go.

Finally, fold the pasta back on itself, then put the machine back onto the first setting, and take it down again through the settings until it is about 1.5mm thick. Then cut it into strips or use it to make filled pasta.

RAVIOLI: Mark the halfway point of your first strip of pasta and brush one half with water, then place little mounds of filling (about a teaspoonful) on the half that is brushed with water, leaving a space of about 3-4cm between each mound. You should have enough to make around 10-25 ravioli.

Fold the other half of the pasta over the top, carefully matching the long edges down one side and pressing them together, then doing the same the other side. Gently press down around each parcel.

Using a fluted ring cutter about 1cm bigger in circumference than the filling, cut out each parcel and discard all the trimmings. Seal each one and press out any air trapped inside.

WALNUT PASTE: Crack the walnuts, keeping them as intact as possible. Put them on a tray, toast them in the oven at about 170°C, for 4-5 minutes until golden. While they are still warm, wrap them in a cloth and rub them to pull off as much of the skins as possible. Peel off any remaining skin with a small knife.

Leave to cool down and, in the meantime, crush the garlic cloves in a mortar, add the walnuts and pound everything into a smooth paste. Stir in 2 tablespoons of olive oil – just enough to make a thick paste.

In a sauté pan warm the walnut paste with a little of the boiling water and 1 tablespoon of olive oil.

TO SERVE: Put the ravioli into a large pan of boiling water and cook for 3-4 minutes, then drain them using a slotted spoon and transfer to the pan containing the 1 tablespoon of oil and water. Toss gently for a minute or so, then add the diced tomato and chopped reserved parsley.

Spoon some walnut sauce onto each of your plates, arrange the ravioli on top and serve.

CHEF'S TIP: Have a bowl of water on one side, so you can dip your hands into it and wet them, to help bring the dough together if it is being stubborn towards the end of kneading. When dispelling the air hold each parcel up to the light to see where the filling is, and whether or not you have smoothed out all the air pockets.

You can keep the walnut sauce in a sterilized jar covered with at least a finger depth of extra-virgin olive oil – it should keep for around 4 weeks.

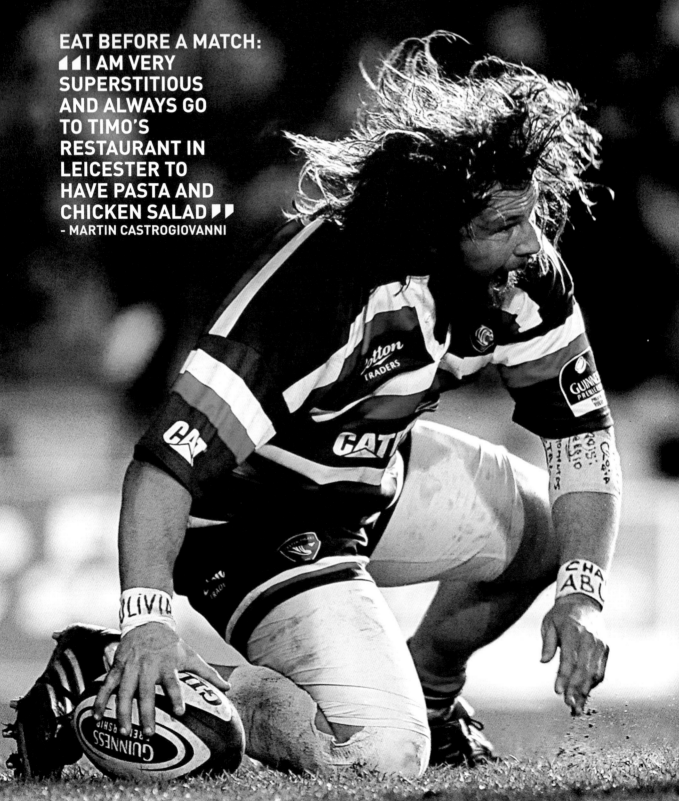

EAT BEFORE A MATCH:
◀◀ I AM VERY
SUPERSTITIOUS
AND ALWAYS GO
TO TIMO'S
RESTAURANT IN
LEICESTER TO
HAVE PASTA AND
CHICKEN SALAD ▶▶
– MARTIN CASTROGIOVANNI

↘ CATALAN CREAM FOAM WITH BERRIES
BY GIORGIO LOCATELLI / SERVES 4

METHOD

CATALAN CREAM FOAM: Place the cream and milk in a pan, with the vanilla pod, cinnamon stick and the orange and lemon peel. Bring to the boil. Take from the heat and leave for 30-40 minutes to infuse. Pass through a fine sieve.

Place the egg yolks, cornflour and sugar into a bowl and whisk together, then add 50g of the milk and cream mixture, and whisk again. Have a large bowl of iced water ready. Put the rest of the cream and milk mixture back on the hob and, when it is almost boiling, add the egg yolk mixture and whisk very quickly.

When you see the first bubbles appearing around 85°C, quickly remove from the heat and place the base of the pan into the iced water to cool it down as quickly as possible.

Before it is completely cold, blend with a hand blender until completely smooth, then put in the fridge until cold. Put through a fine sieve and then into the siphon. Charge it, and then put the siphon into the fridge for 2 hours.

TO SERVE: Arrange some berries on each plate, then the foam on top, and some tuile biscuits on the side, which you can use like spoons for the foam. Sprinkle the foam with caster sugar and use a blow torch to caramelise it quickly.

SPECIAL EQUIPMENT

½ litre siphon plus one CO_2 charge, thermometer, bowl of ice water, blow torch.

INGREDIENTS

CATALAN CREAM FOAM:
- 180ml whipping cream
- 180ml milk
- ½ vanilla pod
- ½ cinnamon stick
- peel of ½ orange
- peel of ½ lemon
- 80g egg yolks (about 4 large eggs)
- 6g cornflour
- 55g caster sugar

TO SERVE:
- 200g mixed red berries
- 8 tuile biscuits

STEVE THOMPSON
LEEDS CARNEGIE

↘ **JEREMY BLOOR**
OXO TOWER, LONDON

↘ JOHN DORY
WITH SMOKED DUCK AND PEAR BARLEY, QUINCE EMULSION, BARLEY BISCUIT
BY JEREMY BLOOR / SERVES 4

"THE SMOKED DUCK AND PEAR BARLEY RISOTTO IS AMAZING AND MARRIES WELL WITH THE JOHN DORY. THE BISCUIT GIVES A BIT OF CRUNCH, WHILE THE QUINCE GIVES A SWEET AND SOUR ELEMENT."

INGREDIENTS
- 2 x 600g John Dory, filleted

RISOTTO:
- 160g pearl barley
- 500ml chicken stock
- 120g smoked duck breast, diced
- ½ quince, diced
- 2g chopped parsley
- 120g whipped double cream
- salt and pepper, to taste
- juice of 1 lemon

QUINCE EMULSION:
- 25g butter
- 1 shallot
- ½ quince, core removed
- 1 sprig of thyme
- 1 garlic clove
- 1 sprig of rosemary
- 100ml white wine
- 100ml fish stock
- 100ml homogenized milk
- 100ml double cream
- 25g quince paste
- 15ml sherry vinegar
- salt and pepper, to taste

BARLEY BISCUIT/TUILE:
- 65g pearl barley
- 150g egg whites
- 65g flour
- 90g sugar
- 7g salt
- 125g butter

METHOD

RISOTTO: Cook the barley in the chicken stock until tender (by this time the barley should have absorbed the chicken stock), then add the duck, quince and parsley. Finish with the cream, salt, pepper and a squeeze of lemon and stir in gently. Keep warm.

QUINCE EMULSION: Melt the butter in a thick-bottomed pan, sweat the shallots and the quince, thyme, garlic and rosemary. Add the wine and reduce to a syrup, then add the fish stock and reduce by half. Add the milk and cream, bring to a simmer then add the quince paste and vinegar, and correct the seasoning. Pass through a fine conical strainer.

BARLEY BISCUIT/TUILE: Preheat the oven to 150ºC.

Blend the barley in a blender until it forms a powder, then mix in the rest of the ingredients.

Spread thinly on a non-stick baking sheet and cook in the oven for 15 minutes. When warm shape around metal rings.

TO SERVE: Pan fry the John Dory fillets skin-side down in a hot pan for 3 minutes.

On four large plates serve the risotto in the middle then place the John Dory on top. Spread the emulsion over the fish and around the plate, then finish with the barley tuile.

WHEN PAN FRYING THE JOHN DORY PUT A PAN ON TOP OF THE FISH SO THAT IT DOESN'T CURL UP
- JEREMY BLOOR

**THIS IS NOT AN EASY DISH
TO PREPARE – THE TRICK IS
TO WATCH THE TIMING**
- JEREMY BLOOR

↘ VENISON, ROAST
AND 'CHOU FARCI' SALSIFY AND SCOTTISH GIROLLES, CUMIN-SCENTED QUINOA
BY JEREMY BLOOR / SERVES 4

"THIS IS A DEFINITE 'MAN'S' DISH WITH THE EMPHASIS ON PROTEIN. THE CUMIN-SCENTED QUINOA IS HIGH IN PROTEIN ALSO."

SPECIAL EQUIPMENT
Steamer, mincer.

PLANNING AHEAD
You could make the stuffed cabbage balls the day before – chill them after steaming then heat up in a microwave to serve.

INGREDIENTS

VENISON:
- 1 shallot, finely chopped
- 1 clove of garlic, finely chopped
- 40g duck fat
- 10g powdered dried cepes
- salt and pepper, to taste
- 150g diced venison
- 50g salted pork fat
- 75g pork belly
- 30g bread soaked in milk
- 4 Savoy cabbage leaves, blanched
- 2 x 400g venison haunch steaks, tied

QUINOA AND CUMIN:
- 125g butter
- 1 small shallot, chopped
- 1 tbsp ground cumin
- 300g quinoa
- 1 litre chicken stock
- salt and pepper, to taste

SALSIFY:
- 500g salsify
- 200g girolle mushrooms
- 5g parsley
- 25g unsalted butter

PORT AND JUNIPER SAUCE:
- 1 large banana shallot
- 1 garlic clove
- 20g butter
- 1 sprig of thyme
- 75ml port
- 100ml beef stock
- 5 juniper berries

METHOD

VENISON: Preheat the oven to 165ºC.

In a pan on a medium heat cook the shallot and garlic in the duck fat, then add the cepes. Season and leave to cool.

Mince the diced venison, pork fat and belly together with the bread and the shallot mix. Form four balls from the mix then cover each with a cabbage leaf and wrap in cling film. Steam for 10 minutes, remove from the steamer and keep warm.

Seal the venison steaks in a hot pan then roast in the oven for 9 minutes, remove and leave to rest.

QUINOA AND CUMIN: Melt the butter in a thick-bottomed pan, add the shallot and the cumin and cook for 3 minutes. Add the quinoa and stir in well, then add the chicken stock and cook out until most of the quinoa has absorbed the chicken stock, season if needed.

SALSIFY: Wash, peel and re-wash the salsify, cook in boiling salted water and when tender remove from the pan and cut into 5cm pieces.

Melt the butter in a pan on a stove, add the salsify and sauté gently, add the girolle mushrooms then the chopped parsley, season with salt and pepper.

PORT AND JUNIPER SAUCE: Sweat the chopped shallot and garlic in the butter in a pan, add the thyme and the grated juniper berries. Add the port and reduce by half then add the beef stock and reduce by half again.

Pass the sauce through a fine strainer.

TO SERVE: Serve together with the salsify and port and juniper sauce.

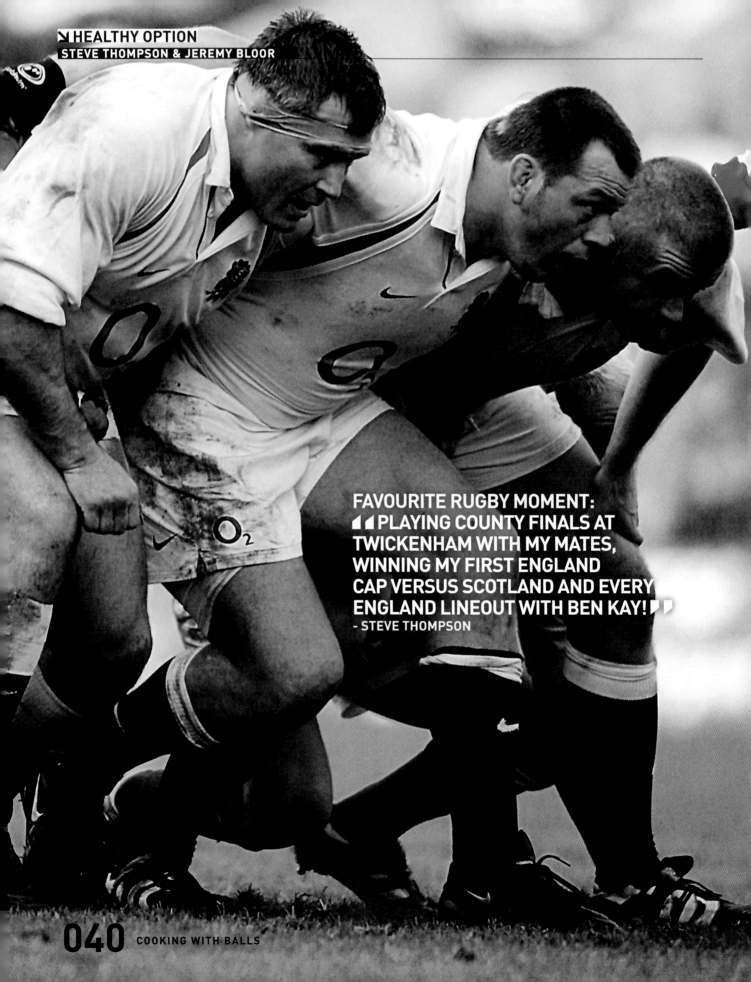

FAVOURITE RUGBY MOMENT:
❝❝PLAYING COUNTY FINALS AT TWICKENHAM WITH MY MATES, WINNING MY FIRST ENGLAND CAP VERSUS SCOTLAND AND EVERY ENGLAND LINEOUT WITH BEN KAY! ❞❞
- STEVE THOMPSON

⬐ GRILLED ENGLISH SQUID,
WATERCRESS, CRISP KALE AND BLOOD ORANGE
BY JEREMY BLOOR / SERVES 4

"WE HAVE THIS ON THE MENU WHEN BLOOD ORANGES ARE IN SEASON. THERE IS NOTHING BETTER THAN FRESHLY GRILLED SQUID. THE BLOOD ORANGES AND CRISP KALE ARE DIFFERENT BUT WORK REALLY WELL TOGETHER – IT'S LIGHT AND REALLY FLAVOURSOME."

METHOD

Score the squid and cut into manageable pieces, add a little olive oil and the garlic clove, then season with salt and pepper.

Cut the bread into crouton shapes then grill under a low heat until crisp. Tear the kale into bite-sized pieces then shallow fry in the sunflower oil. When crisp remove and place on a tray with a cloth underneath to drain any excess oil, then season with the sugar, salt and five spice.

Segment the blood oranges and put the extra juice into a small bowl, then add the rest of the olive oil to create a dressing.

Grill the squid on a very hot grill pan for around 2-3 minutes, remove then slice into thin strips. Add the lemon zest and parsley.

TO SERVE: Place all the ingredients together with the watercress into a large mixing bowl, add the dressing then mix gently, making sure to keep the crispy kale intact. Serve in four salad bowls.

INGREDIENTS
- 500g fresh squid
- 75ml extra virgin olive oil
- ½ garlic clove, chopped
- salt and pepper, to taste
- 2 slices seaweed bread
- 200g curly kale
- 500ml sunflower oil
- sugar, as needed
- ½ tsp Chinese five spice
- 2 blood oranges
- 1 lemon, zest finely grated
- 5g flat leaf parsley, chopped
- 2 bunches of watercress

ONCE THE SALAD IS DRESSED IT HAS TO BE SERVED IMMEDIATELY
- JEREMY BLOOR

DESIGNED BY OUR
PASTRY CHEF TO
COMPLEMENT THREE
DIFFERENT COGNACS –
XO, PARADIS AND LOUIS
TREIZE – WHICH ARE
SERVED ON THE SIDE
OF THIS DISH
- JEREMY BLOOR

↘ RICHARD'S LAST WISH

BY JEREMY BLOOR / SERVES 4

SPECIAL EQUIPMENT
Sugar thermometer, 4 x metal rings lined with baking parchment.

PLANNING AHEAD
The meringues and parfait can be made in advance.

INGREDIENTS

LEMON BALM AND MILK CHOCOLATE PARFAIT:
- 300ml double cream
- 100g lemon balm
- 500g chocolate, 41% cocoa
- 8 egg yolks
- 8 egg whites
- 100g sugar
- 400ml water

CHOCOLATE CARAMEL TUILE:
- 1000g sugar
- 200g white chocolate

COCOA NIB MOUSSE BASE:
- 200g milk chocolate
- 200g feuilletine

GANACHE:
- 300ml double cream
- 50g sugar
- 5g rosemary
- 300g chocolate, 70% cocoa

MOUSSE:
- 600g double cream
- 50g cocoa nibs
- 2 egg whites
- 120g sugar
- 2 gelatine leaves, soaked
- 16 raspberries

THYME MERINGUES:
- 200g egg whites
- 400g sugar
- 5g thyme, finely chopped

VANILLA WHITE CHOCOLATE GANACHE:
- 200ml double cream
- 10g sugar
- 1 vanilla pod
- 500g white chocolate, melted

STRAWBERRIES:
- 10 strawberries
- 20ml balsamic vinegar
- pinch of pink peppercorns

METHOD

LEMON BALM AND MILK CHOCOLATE PARFAIT: Boil the cream with the lemon balm and leave the infusion to rest overnight.

Melt the chocolate. Reboil the cream mix, whisk in the egg yolks and pass through a sieve. Mix this custard into the chocolate.

Boil the sugar together with the water to make a soft ball.

Whisk the egg whites, then add the sugar ball and continue whisking until the mixture is warm. Fold into the chocolate mix then pour into pre-lined metal rings.

CHOCOLATE CARAMEL TUILE: Caramelise the sugar in a pan over a medium heat. Cool down and add the chocolate to the pan a little at a time, mix and leave to cool.

COCOA NIB MOUSSE BASE: Mix the ingredients together and press into bottom half of the ring.

GANACHE: Boil together the cream, sugar and rosemary and leave to infuse for 1 hour, then add the melted chocolate and pour over the base of the cocoa nib mousse.

MOUSSE: Boil the cream together with cocoa nibs, stirring constantly until the cream is reduced by half. Leave to cool. Lightly whisk the egg whites. Boil the

sugar to 140ºC soft ball and pour onto the egg whites. Add the gelatine and whisk until warm, then fold into the cocoa nib cream and pour over the ganache.

Leave to set overnight then top with the raspberries.

THYME MERINGUES: Preheat the oven to 100ºC.

Whisk the egg whites with the sugar until firm then whisk in the thyme.

Spread the mixture onto a lined baking tray into the shape of triangles (draw on the underneath of the baking paper to use as a guide). Cook in the oven until crisp.

VANILLA WHITE CHOCOLATE GANACHE: Boil the cream together with the sugar and vanilla. Leave to infuse for 1 hour. Re-boil, pour into the melted chocolate and mix until smooth.

STRAWBERRIES: Chop up the strawberries mix with balsamic vinegar and pink peppercorns.

TO SERVE: Pipe white chocolate ganache around the edge of two triangle meringues, fill the centre with strawberries and continue until you have three layers. Assemble the lemon balm parfait with a caramel tuile and cocoa nib mousse on a long plate, then finally add the meringue.

↘ TOM AIKENS
TOM AIKENS RESTAURANT/ TOM'S KITCHEN

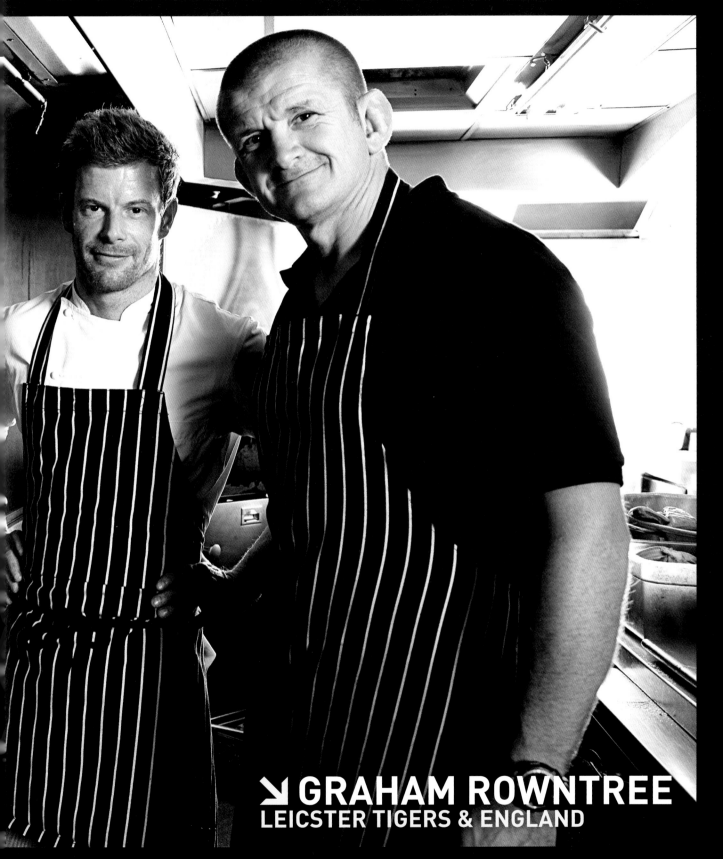

↘ GRAHAM ROWNTREE
LEICSTER TIGERS & ENGLAND

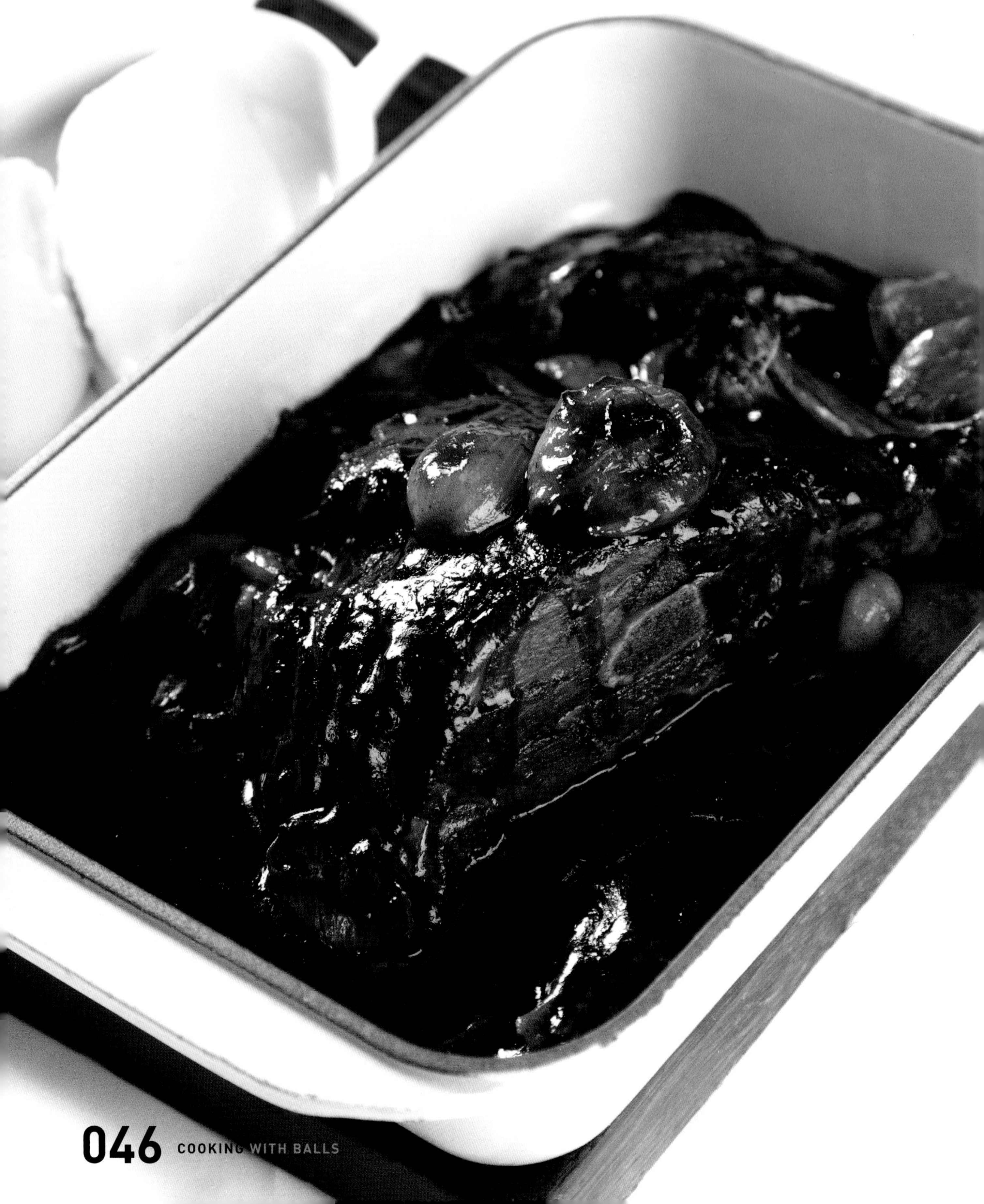

⬊ SLOW ROAST SHOULDER OF LAMB
WITH ONIONS AND THYME, BALSAMIC VINEGAR, MASHED POTATO
BY TOM AIKENS / SERVES 6-8

METHOD

LAMB: Before you cook the lamb leave it out of the fridge for a good hour or two so that the meat is at room temperature. Pre-heat the oven to 180°C. Rub on a little olive oil and season with salt and pepper. Place a little olive oil into the bottom of the casserole pot with the onions, add the lamb on top, then put it into the oven for 15-20 minutes until the lamb and onions have coloured.

Remove the pot from the oven, then add about 8 sprigs of thyme along with the garlic, turn the oven down to 100-110°C and cook for 5 hours with the lid on. Remove the garlic and onions from the pan and place onto a tray. Add the balsamic vinegar to the pot and continue to cook without the lid for a further 1-1½ hours, basting the shoulder in the vinegar every 20 minutes. Remove the pan from the oven and place onto a low heat to reduce any excess liquid that is in the bottom and baste the lamb in this while it is reducing.

MASHED POTATO: Cut the potatoes into 5cm pieces and rinse in cold water, place into a pan with the water and 16g of salt, place onto the heat and bring to a slow simmer. Simmer for 25-35 minutes till the potatoes are just tender, then tip into a colander to drain well. Place the potatoes into a moulis or mash with a potato masher, adding the butter. Place back into the pan, adding the remaining salt and pepper, and the milk, and mix together.

TO SERVE: Add the onions and garlic back to the casserole pot for 10 minutes to reheat and serve with the mashed potato.

SPECIAL EQUIPMENT

Large casserole pot with lid to fit the shoulder of lamb.

INGREDIENTS

LAMB:
- 1 x 2.5kg shoulder of lamb
- 150ml olive oil
- 2g sea salt
- freshly milled black pepper
- 8 whole peeled medium-sized onions
- 1 small bunch washed thyme
- 2 peeled bulbs garlic
- 350ml balsamic vinegar

MASHED POTATO:
- 1kg peeled potatoes
- 2 litres water
- 20g salt
- 350g butter
- 12 turns of freshly milled black pepper
- 400ml milk, warmed

DEPENDING ON WHEN YOU ARE GOING TO BE EATING THIS DISH – EITHER LUNCH OR DINNER – YOU WANT TO PUT IT INTO THE OVEN FOR LUNCH AT 8AM AND FOR THE EVENING AT AROUND 2PM. IT WILL TAKE BETWEEN 6-7 HOURS TO COOK, BUT IT IS ONE OF THOSE DISHES THAT DOES NOT NEED ANY ATTENTION AT ALL.
- TOM AIKENS

↘ BATTERED POLLOCK
OR LINE-CAUGHT COD WITH THICK-CUT CHIPS
BY TOM AIKENS / SERVES 4

METHOD

THICK-CUT CHIPS: Peel the potatoes and cut them into 1cm square batons the length of the potato, so they are all the same size. Wash the starch off the potato with cold running water, place into a pan of slightly salted cold water and bring to a rapid boil. Cook for 1 minute at a simmer then drain and chill in ice-cold water in a bowl, which will cool them straightaway and stop them cooking any further. Dry them off very well on a tea towel and plunge into the hot oil at 140ºC to blanch for 2-3 minutes then drain. Heat the oil back up to 180ºC, then plunge the chips back into the oil till they are golden brown, approximately 4-5 minutes, then season with salt.

FISH: Place the flour, pepper, cornflour, sugar and salt into a bowl. Make a well then place the yeast into the well, then also add the sparkling water and beer into the well and leave for a good 10 minutes. Whisk to a smooth consistency and leave for 15-20 minutes.

Place the fish into the batter and hold it by the tail end, let the excess drip off then fry for approximately 8 minutes till golden and crispy.

TARTARE SAUCE: Whisk the mustard, salt, pepper and egg yolks in a bowl then slowly pour the oil onto the mixture, whisking well, keep adding all the oil – you may need to add a little water to the mayonnaise as it may become too thick. Once all the oil has been added mix the rest of the ingredients into the mayonnaise to make it into a tartare sauce.

TO SERVE: Serve on plates with 150g cut chips per serving and season to taste.

SPECIAL EQUIPMENT
Bowl of ice-cold water, deep fat fryer.

INGREDIENTS

THICK-CUT CHIPS:
- 2kg large potatoes (Maris Piper or Desiree Red)
- 4 litres vegetable oil or ground nut oil
- sea salt, to taste

FISH BATTER:
- 300g high gluten bread flour (T55)
- ¼ tsp white pepper
- 60g cornflour
- 15g sugar
- 1½ tsp salt
- 30g yeast
- 300ml sparkling water
- 300ml Heineken

FISH:
- 4 x 140g pollock or cod fillets

TARTARE SAUCE:
- 10g English mustard
- 5g salt
- ¾g milled black pepper
- 4 egg yolks
- 750ml vegetable oil
- 2 tbsp water
- 8g lemon juice
- 15g white wine vinegar
- 75g gherkins, chopped
- 75g capers, chopped
- 10g parsley, chopped
- 75g shallots, finely chopped

COOKING THE CHIPS THREE TIMES MEANS THEY WILL TAKE ON SOME OF THE WATER WHEN THEY ARE FIRST BLANCHED, WHICH NOT ONLY HELPS THE FLUFFINESS OF THE POTATO, BUT ALSO HELPS THE POTATOES TO BECOME CRISP AS OPPOSED TO SOGGY AS THEY HAVE STARTED TO COOK FROM THE INSIDE. SO WHEN THE CHIPS HIT THE OIL FOR THE FIRST TIME THEY ARE COOKING INSTEAD OF BEING BLANCHED. FOR THE LAST FRY THEY WILL BE CRISPY.
- TOM AIKENS

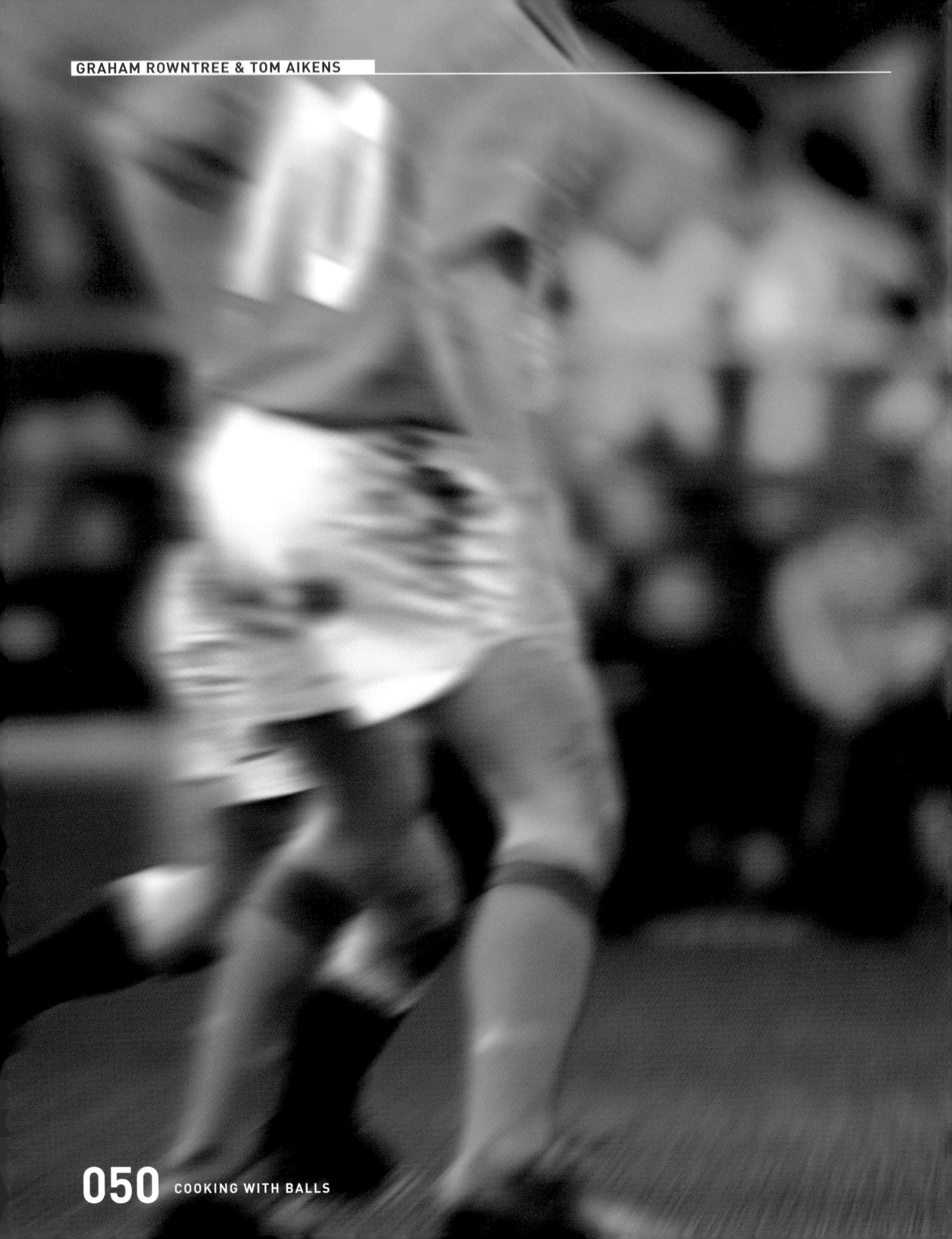

FOOD TO EAT AFTER A MATCH: ❝❝ANYTHING WITH BEER BUT NORMALLY A BIG CURRY! ❞❞
– GRAHAM ROWNTREE

↘ BAKED LOCH DUART SALMON
WITH CITRUS FRUITS, FRESH HERBS, SAFFRON FENNEL
BY TOM AIKENS / SERVES 4

METHOD

BRAISED SAFFRON FENNEL: Cut the fennel in half then each half into four pieces depending on what size the bulbs are. Place a shallow pan onto a medium heat, add the butter and once melted add the shallots, salt, sugar, pepper, thyme, bay leaf and coriander seeds. Cook for 2-3 minutes, till semi-soft. Add the wine and saffron and reduce by two-thirds, then add the fish stock and reduce by one-third, keeping the side of the pan clean. Add the lemon juice, olive oil and fennel and cook, covered with parchment paper and a lid, for approximately 20 minutes at a simmer till they are tender, then cool. Cut each piece of fennel in half (the reason we do this after they are cooked is so the fennel is not over cooked).

SALMON: Pre-heat the oven to 180°C. Take the salmon fillet and brush with some of the olive oil on both sides, season with salt and pepper, and then take the square pieces of parchment paper and brush them with olive oil. Next place four to six pieces of fennel inside with half the herbs and half the orange and lemon segments, then put the seasoned salmon fillets on top. Dab the fish with the butter and place the remaining segments of orange and lemon and the zests on top of each fillet along with the rest of the herbs. Squeeze over the orange and lemon juice, drizzle in olive oil and carefully fold the paper over to the other side and either secure with staples or paper clips – it should look like a little rectangle with the fish inside. Place the salmon on a baking tray and bake for 6 minutes.

TO SERVE: Remove from the oven, carefully tear open the paper – be careful of the steam coming out – and turn out onto a plate.

SPECIAL EQUIPMENT
10 x 30cm squares of parchment paper.

INGREDIENTS

BRAISED SAFFRON FENNEL:
- 2 medium bulbs fennel
- 30g butter
- 100g sliced shallots
- 2g salt
- 4g caster sugar
- 14 turns of freshly milled black pepper
- 6g thyme
- 1 bay leaf
- 10 coriander seeds
- 150ml white wine
- 2 large pinches saffron
- 300ml fish stock
- 50ml lemon juice
- 350ml olive oil

SALMON:
- 1 x 180g Loch Duart salmon
- juice and fine zest of 1 lemon
- juice and fine zest of 1 orange
- 5 orange segments
- 5 lemon segments
- 80ml olive oil
- 20g unsalted butter
- 3g coarse sea salt
- 10 turns of freshly milled black pepper
- 6 pieces dill, freshly picked
- 6 pieces chervil, freshly picked
- 6 pieces tarragon, freshly picked

↘ BAKED ALASKA
BY TOM AIKENS / SERVES 6

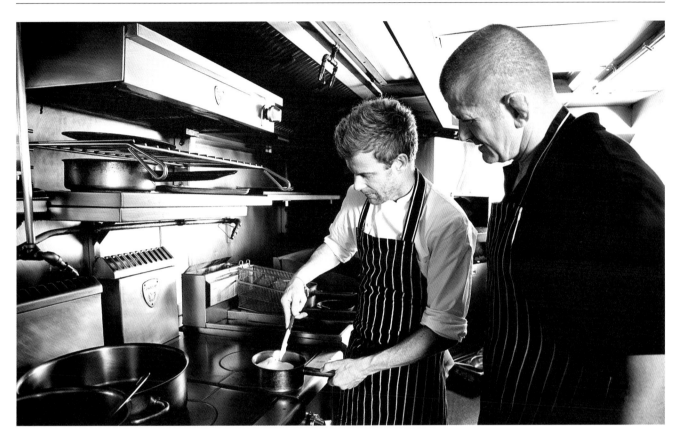

METHOD

MERINGUE: Boil the sugar, water and glucose to a soft ball. Semi-whip the egg whites and add the sugar ball, then whip on a slower speed till cool.

VANILLA ICE CREAM: Simmer the milk, cream, vanilla pods and seeds, vanilla essence, salt and half the sugar together. Remove from the heat then cover with cling film and leave for 30 minutes to infuse. Bring back to the boil. In the meantime whisk the egg yolks and remaining sugar together, then pour the hot cream onto the yolks, whisking all the time. Return to the stove to cook out the custard till it coats the back of a spoon. Pass through a fine sieve into a bowl set over iced water to cool. Place in a freezer and whisk every 5-10 minutes or beat with a wooden spoon until frozen and set. Alternatively use an ice cream machine following the manufacturer's instructions.

TO SERVE: Pre-heat the oven to 180°C. Place the panettone into the bottom of a dish, add three scoops of ice cream then top with the meringue. Bake in the oven for approximately 5 minutes.

INGREDIENTS

MERINGUE:
- 400g caster sugar
- 100ml water
- 40g glucose
- 200g egg whites

PANETTONE:
- 1 large piece of panettone (thick cut 1.5cm)

VANILLA ICE CREAM:
- 1 litre milk
- 500ml double cream
- 2 vanilla pods, scraped
- 15g vanilla essence
- ½ tsp salt
- 300g sugar
- 15 egg yolks

TO SAVE TIME USE READY-MADE VANILLA ICE CREAM
- TOM AIKENS

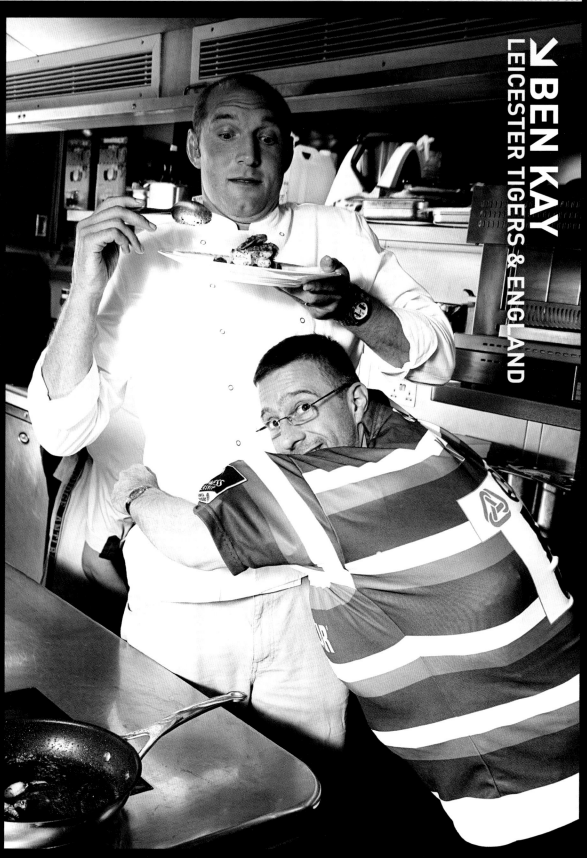

BEN KAY
LEICESTER TIGERS & ENGLAND

↘ EMIETTE DE TOURTEAU DU DEVON
AUX EFFLUVES DE MELON, AMANDES FRAICHES ET CREVETTES ROSES MARINEES

FLAKED DEVON CRAB WITH MELON AND FRESH ALMONDS, SERVED WITH MARINATED PRAWNS
BY ALAIN ROUX / SERVES 4

METHOD

MARINATED MELON BALLS: In a saucepan, bring the water and sugar to the boil.Take the pan off the heat, add the mint and leave to cool.

Using a 2cm melon baller, scoop out eight balls of flesh from each variety of melon. Place them in the cold syrup and marinate 1-2 hours.

MELON COULIS: Place the ingredients in a small mixing bowl. Whiz using a hand-held stick blender until completely smooth. Adjust the seasoning.

MELON DRESSING: Follow the same method as for the coulis above. Dress the salad leaves at the last minute.

MARINATED PRAWNS: Peel the prawns, leaving the tip of the tail intact. Using a sharp knife, cut down the back to remove the intestine.

In a non-stick pan smeared with olive oil cook the prawns over high heat for 1 minute on each side. Drain on kitchen paper and season with salt. Leave to cool.

For the marinade, combine in a bowl all remaining ingredients, stir with a whisk and season. Roll the prawns in the marinade just before serving.

CRAB: In a bowl mix the crab meat gently with the mayonnaise and lime juice. Season to taste.

TO SERVE: On a plate, pile the crab and rest two prawns on top. Arrange the melon balls, almonds and dressed salad leaves. Pour some coulis and marinade around. Serve.

SPECIAL EQUIPMENT
Hand-held stick blender.

PLANNING AHEAD
Marinate the melon balls in the cold syrup 1-2 hours.

INGREDIENTS

MARINATED MELON BALLS:
- 100ml water
- 15g caster sugar
- 10-12 mint leaves
- 8 watermelon balls
- 8 charentais melon balls
- 8 honeydew melon balls

MELON COULIS:
- 150g chatentais melon flesh
- 10ml olive oil
- ¼ lime, juiced
- salt, to taste

MELON DRESSING:
- 100g honeydew melon flesh
- 10ml olive oil
- 1 tbsp Chardonnay vinegar
- salt and pepper, to taste

MARINATED PRAWNS:
- 8 medium-sized tiger prawns
- 50ml olive oil
- juice and zest of 1 lime
- juice and zest of ½ lemon
- pinch of espelette chilli flakes
- salt, to taste

CRAB:
- 300g flaked white crab meat
- 2 tbsp of mayonnaise
- ½ lime, juiced
- pinch of cayenne pepper
- salt, to taste

TO SERVE:
- 16-20 fresh almonds
- purslane or lamb's lettuce leaves, as needed

⬊ QUEUE DE HOMARD ROTIE

FLAMBEE GRANDE-CHARTREUSE, SERVIE SUR UNE FRICASSEE DE MANGE-TOUT ET SON CORDON D'ESCARGOTS DE BOURGOGNE EN PERSILLADE

ROASTED LOBSTER TAIL, FLAMED WITH 'GRANDE-CHARTREUSE' ON A FRICASSEE OF MANGE TOUT BEANS, SERVED WITH BURGUNDY SNAILS IN PARSLEY AND GARLIC BUTTER

BY ALAIN ROUX / SERVES 4

METHOD

LOBSTER: Place the live lobsters in a plastic bag in the freezer 2 hours before cooking them.

GRANDE-CHARTREUSE SAUCE: In a saucepan combine the shallots, the Grande-Chartreuse, the white wine and the parsley stalks. Reduce by two-thirds. Add the fish stock and the cream. Reduce the sauce until it coats the back of a spoon. Stir in the lemon juice and chopped parsley. Season to taste.

GARLIC BUTTER: Crush the peeled garlic to a paste with a pestle and mortar.

In a bowl, place the garlic paste and all other ingredients. Mix with a whisk and season with cayenne pepper and salt.

COURT-BOUILLON: In a large saucepan, place the ingredients and bring to the boil over high heat. Take the lobsters out of the freezer. Remove them from the bag and plunge the lobsters in the boiling court-bouillon. Cook for 4 minutes. Drain and place them in a large bowl of cold water with ice cubes added. After 5 minutes, drain the lobsters.

Break off the heads, remove the claws and the pincers from the claws. Crack the claws and joints and remove the meat. For the tails, use scissors, to remove the shell/carapace, but keeping the tip of the tail intact and still attached to the tail's meat.

Using a sharp knife cut down along the back to remove the intestine.

In a pan smeared with clarified butter, start roasting the lobster tails over high heat. Add the snails, the lobster claws, the knuckles and the garlic butter.

Finish cooking the lobsters and snails, basting with the cooking juices. Flame with a generous splash of Grande-Chartreuse, taking care not to burn yourself or set fire to the kitchen. Add the chopped parsley.

TO SERVE: Arrange the mange tout and butternut squash on a warm plate, in a star shape. Place the lobster tail on top with the knuckles and claws in the middle. Dress the snails around and drizzle the sauce. Finish with the baby cress salad and serve.

SPECIAL EQUIPMENT

Pestle and mortar.

PLANNING AHEAD

Place the live lobsters in a plastic bag in the freezer 2 hours before cooking them.

INGREDIENTS

LOBSTER:
- 4 x 450g live lobsters

GRANDE-CHARTREUSE SAUCE:
- 2 shallots, sliced
- 20ml Grande-Chartreuse
- 25ml dry white wine
- parsley stalks, as needed
- 70ml fish stock
- 40ml double cream
- ¼ lemon, juiced
- 2 tbsp parsley, chopped
- salt and pepper, to taste

GARLIC BUTTER:
- 2 small garlic cloves
- 100g butter, softened
- 20ml Grande-Chartreuse
- juice of ½ lemon
- cayenne pepper, as needed
- salt, as needed

COURT-BOUILLON:
- 5 litres water
- 50g coarse salt
- 1 bouquet garni
- 300ml white wine vinegar
- 1 tsp white peppercorns

SNAILS:
- 24 Burgundy snails, cooked
- 1 tbsp parsley, chopped

TO SERVE:
- 20 mange tout, cut in triangles and steamed
- 20 butternut squash slices, cut in triangles and steamed
- baby cress salad

FAVOURITE FOOD:
❝ THERE ARE SO MANY BUT DEFINITELY STEAK, LOBSTER AND CREME BRULEE ❞
- BEN KAY

↘ PAVE DE SAUMON SAUVAGE

DELICATEMENT POCHE AU COURT-BOUILLON, GARNI D'UN PILAF DE TROIS RIZ, VINAIGRETTE TIEDE VERDURETTE

FILLET OF WILD SALMON GENTLY POACHED IN AN AROMATIC STOCK, SERVED WITH A SELECTION OF PILAF RICE AND WARM HERB VINAIGRETTE

BY ALAIN ROUX / SERVES 4

INGREDIENTS

COURT-BOUILLON:
- 2 carrots, cut into rounds
- 1 leek, white part only, sliced
- 1 celery stick, sliced
- 1 fennel bulb, sliced
- 1 onion, sliced
- 1 garlic clove
- ½ lemon, sliced
- 2 tomatoes, sliced
- 10 white peppercorns, crushed
- 1 bouquet garni
- 2 litres water
- 250ml dry white wine
- 100ml white wine vinegar

PILAF RICE:
- 25g butter
- 1 tbsp onion, finely chopped
- 150g mixed rice
- 350ml fish stock
- salt and pepper, to taste

VINAIGRETTE VERDURETTE:
- 100g shallots, finely chopped
- 1 lemon, juiced
- 20ml red wine vinegar
- 50ml grape seed oil
- 80ml olive oil
- 1 tsp Dijon mustard

TO FINISH THE VINAIGRETTE:
- 4 tbsp of mixed chopped herbs; parsley, tarragon, chervil, sorrel and watercress
- 4 hard boiled egg yolks, chopped

SALMON:
- 4 x 160g salmon pavés, skin removed

TO SERVE:
- 4 tbsp creamed cauliflower purée
- 4 tbsp French beans, cut in julienne and steamed
- 12-16 pak-choi leaves, steamed

METHOD

COURT-BOUILLON: In a large saucepan, place all the ingredients.

Bring to the boil and cook at bare simmer for 30 minutes, skimming as necessary. Strain through a fine meshed conical sieve into a bowl and set aside.

PILAF RICE: Preheat the oven to 160ºC.

Melt 15g of butter in a casserole, add the onion and sweat it gently for 1 minute. Add the rice, cook for 2 minutes, stirring with a spoon. Pour the stock, season with salt and pepper. Cover and cook in the oven for 18 minutes.

When cooked, add the remaining 10g of butter and with a fork fluff up the rice. Adjust the seasoning.

VINAIGRETTE VERDURETTE: Combine all the ingredients in a saucepan and mix with a whisk.

Add the herbs and egg yolks. Mix with a spoon and season with salt and pepper. Just before serving, warm the vinaigrette to about 30-40ºC

SALMON: Pour some court-bouillon in a wide shallow saucepan, season with salt, pepper and bring to the boil.

Reduce the heat and add the 4 salmon pavés.

Poach gently for 8-10 minutes. Lift out and drain the salmon on a kitchen paper, season with salt and pepper.

TO SERVE: On a warm plate, spoon some cauliflower purée and the pilaf rice. Place the salmon pavé partly on top.

Arrange the French beans and pak-choi leaves around. Spoon the sauce and serve.

↘ CREME BRULEE A LA VANILLE,
CERISES RAFRAICHIES A LA VODKA ET GLACE AUX PISTACHES

VANILLA CREME BRULEE AND CHERRIES CHILLED WITH VODKA, PISTACHIO ICE CREAM
BY ALAIN ROUX / SERVES 4

SPECIAL EQUIPMENT
4 x 15cm gratin dishes, cherry stoner, thermometer, pestle and mortar, ice cream machine, blowtorch, pastry piping bag with a star nozzle, 4 shot glasses.

PLANNING AHEAD
If using fresh pistachios for the ice cream, soak them in cold water for 24 hours.

INGREDIENTS

CREME BRULEE:
- 350ml double cream
- 350ml milk
- 2 vanilla pods, split
- 8 egg yolks
- 80g caster sugar

CHERRIES:
- 36 cherries
- 80g caster sugar
- 80ml vodka

PISTACHIO ICE CREAM:
- 350ml milk
- 4 egg yolks
- 80g caster sugar
- 30g pistachio paste or 200g shelled pistachios, skinned

TO SERVE:
- 70g demerara sugar
- a few pistachios, chopped
- a few cherries

METHOD

CREME BRULEE: Preheat the oven to 100ºC.

In a saucepan, heat the cream, the milk and the vanilla pods, then bring slowly to the boil.

In a bowl whisk the egg yolks and caster sugar until pale. Gradually pour the boiling mixture onto the egg mixture, whisking all the time. Pass this custard through a fine chinois into a bowl.

Place the gratin dishes on a baking tray and ladle the custard into them. Cook in the oven for 40-50 minutes, or until just set. Transfer the dishes to a wire rack until cool and then chill until ready to serve.

CHERRIES: Rinse the cherries in a bowl of cold water and drain.

Remove the stalks and stone the fruit using a cherry stoner.

In a hot frying pan put the cherries and sugar. Keep tossing the pan and cook for about 2 minutes. Off the heat, add the vodka, return to the heat and bring to the boil, then transfer into a bowl. When cool, chill until ready to serve.

PISTACHIO ICE CREAM: If using fresh pistachios, soak them in cold water for 24 hours. The following day, drain them and crush to a paste using a pestle and mortar.

Put the milk in a saucepan and bring to the boil.

In a bowl, whisk the egg yolks and sugar until pale and of a ribbon consistency.

Pour the boiling milk onto the egg mixture, whisking continuously.

Pour the mixture back into the saucepan and heat gently, stirring continuously with a spoon until about 80ºC (check with a thermometer) and thick enough to coat the back of the spoon.

Off the heat whisk in the pistachio paste. Pass the custard through a fine chinois into a bowl, set over crushed ice.

Stir occasionally with a spoon. When cold, churn in an ice cream machine.

TO SERVE: Shortly before serving, sprinkle each crème brûlée with the demerara sugar and caramelise with a blowtorch.

Fill each shot glass with some cherries and pistachio ice cream using a pastry piping bag with a star nozzle.

Arrange some cherries with the chopped pistachio nuts on top and serve.

MARTIN CORRY
LEICESTER TIGERS & ENGLAND

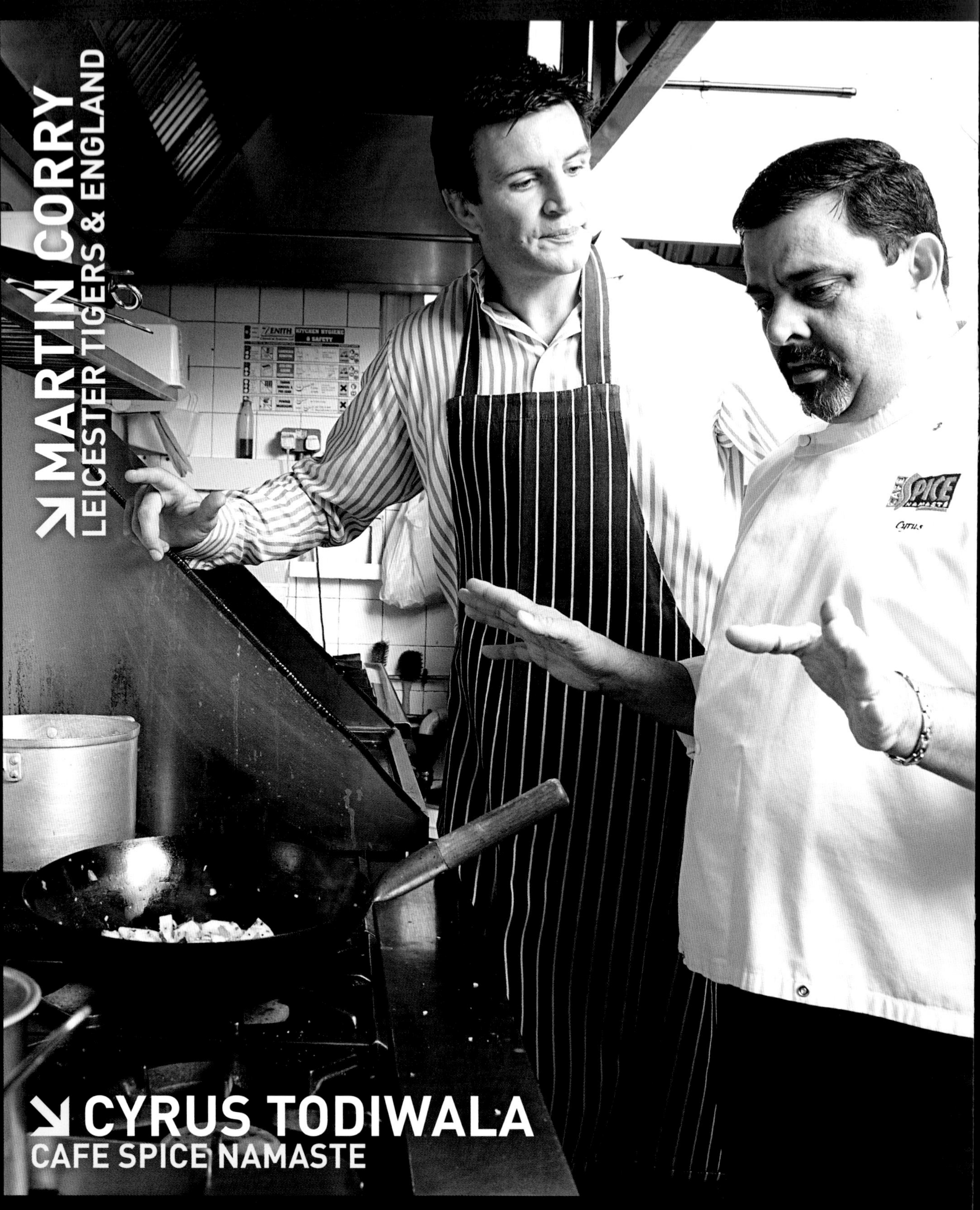

CYRUS TODIWALA
CAFE SPICE NAMASTE

↘ MASALA NU ROAST GOS

BY CYRUS TODIWALA / SERVES 4-6

"THIS IS A PARSEE-STYLE ROASTED JOINT OF LAMB. ONCE ROASTED THE LAMB MAY BE SLICED AND SERVED COLD AS A SANDWICH FILLER OR SERVED HOT WITH GRAVY AS SHOWN, WITH BOILED RICE OR A LIGHT CUMIN PULAO."

SPECIAL EQUIPMENT

Blender.

INGREDIENTS

- 1.25kg leg of lamb, trimmed for roasting
- 1 tsp cumin
- 1 tbsp coriander seeds
- 50g ginger
- 50g garlic
- water, as needed
- 12 small potatoes
- 2-3 tbsp sunflower oil
- 2 x 2.5cm piece cinnamon or cassia bark
- 3-4 green cardamom pods
- 2-3 cloves
- 3-4 peppercorns
- 3 medium onions, chopped
- 1 tsp salt
- 200g chopped tomatoes
- lamb stock, as needed

METHOD

Preheat the oven to 150°C.

Trim the leg of lamb for roasting.

Roast the cumin and coriander on a low heat until they change colour slightly and cool.

In a blender grind together the ginger, garlic and the roasted cumin and coriander to a fine paste (masala) with a little water.

Peel the potatoes, remove any spots, wash and keep them soaked in water.

In a large ovenproof casserole dish add the oil and heat on a medium heat until a light haze forms on the surface. Reduce the heat a little and add the leg of lamb. Brown well on all sides until the meat is well sealed.

Remove the lamb from the casserole dish and add the whole spices: cinnamon/cassia bark, cardamom, cloves and peppercorns. Sauté for a minute or so on a low heat until the cloves swell a bit, then deglaze the casserole with a little water to release the residue from the lamb stuck at the base. Scrape with a wooden spatula until the base is clean, then add the onions.

Continue cooking until the liquid evaporates and the onions start becoming sautéed. Sauté until they are soft, then add the ground masala. Add water to the container to release any stuck masala and add this to the pan too.

Continue cooking for 5-6 minutes, then put the lamb joint back into the casserole dish. Coat it well with the masala mixture, check the seasoning and add salt as desired. Then place the covered casserole dish into the oven. After about 15 minutes remove from the oven, turn the meat and put it back into the oven. Ensure that the contents do not dry out, adding more water if necessary.

In another 15 minutes the lamb should be approximately half cooked. At this stage add the tomatoes and potatoes and, if necessary, some water or lamb stock, cover and continue cooking for another 10-15 minutes.

When the lamb is done remove it onto a tray and also remove any gravy stuck to it. Remove the potatoes and set these aside. Check the gravy and, if necessary, add enough liquid to make a pouring consistency.

TO SERVE: Either serve the lamb sliced hot with the gravy and the potatoes or serve it later by slicing it when cold.

For the heated dish, heat the gravy and the lamb with the potatoes, covered with a lid in a hot oven for 10 minutes and after plating pour the gravy over the meat. For a touch of magic add coriander to the gravy and serve with chunks of deep fried par-boiled potatoes and steamed rice.

CHEF'S TIP: If not using a thermometer the best way to test the lamb would be to notice the cooking process and the shrinkage accordingly. When the lamb is almost cooked the muscles at the shin will have retracted and the lamb will feel soft to the touch. If in doubt insert a thin skewer or a roasting fork and check to see if the fluid released is running clear.

↳ DHAANSAAK
BY CYRUS TODIWALA / SERVES 4-6

❝❝ **THE BEST KNOWN OF GREAT PARSEE COOKING. DHAAN MEANS RICE AND SAAK STANDS FOR THE LENTILS AND LAMB THAT GO WITH IT. IT IS NOT COMPLETE AS A MEAL UNLESS ACCOMPANIED WITH CACHUMBAR OR ONION SALAD AND DEEP-FRIED LAMB KEBABS.** ❞❞
- CYRUS TODIWALA

PLANNING AHEAD

Cooking Dhaansaak is a painstaking affair, but very simple and can be started the day before for lunch the following day. The end result can be a sheer achievement and if done well will go down as a masterpiece.

INGREDIENTS

DHAN THE PULAO:
- 5 tbsp sunflower oil
- 1 x 2.5cm piece of cinnamon
- 4 cardamom pods
- 4 cloves
- 4 star anise
- 2 medium-sized onions, finely sliced with the centre stub removed
- 100g basmati rice, per person
- salt, to taste

MASALA 1 (FOR COOKING LAMB):
- 5cm piece cinnamon
- 6 cardamom pods
- 6-8 cloves
- 2 tsp whole cumin
- 10 peppercorns
- 1 heaped tbsp coriander seeds
- 8-10 large-sized red chillis
- 3 x 2.5cm pieces ginger, cut into coarse chunks
- 10-12 cloves garlic, cut into coarse chunks
- 40g fresh coriander, with stalks
- 1 tsp water

MASALA 2 (FOR FINAL FLAVOURING):
- 3-4 cardamom pods
- 3-4 cloves
- 3-4 badian or star anise
- 1 heaped tsp cumin
- 8-10 peppercorns
- 2-3 red chillis
- 2 tsp dry fenugreek

DAAL:
- 100g massor daal (pink lentils)
- 100g toover daal (toor)
- 50g channa daal (split chickpeas)
- 50g moong daal (yellow mung)
- 1 small-sized aubergine, cut into small pieces
- 100g red pumpkin, skinned and sliced
- 2 tbsp fresh dill, coarsely cut
- 1 leaf colcasia leaves (arbi), if available
- 50g fresh methi leaves or 1 tbsp dry methi leaves)
- salt, to taste
- 1 tbsp tamarind paste
- 100g jiggery (cane molasses)

- 2 tbsp coriander stalks, washed and chopped without the root ends
- 2 tbsp mint stalks, washed and chopped without the root ends
- water, as needed

LAMB (SAK):
- 2-3 tbsp sunflower oil
- 500g lamb leg, cut into 2cm pieces
- 150ml water
- salt, to taste

CACHUMBER:
- 1 large onion, finely sliced
- 10-15 leaves of mint, chopped
- 2 heaped tbsp coriander, chopped
- 1 medium green chilli, finely chopped
- 1 small tomato, deseeded and shredded
- 1 tsp cider vinegar
- salt, to taste

TO SERVE:
- oil, as needed
- 1-2 onions
- mint, chopped
- coriander, chopped

METHOD

DHAN THE PULAO: Heat the oil in a casserole dish and add the spices. When they are well browned add the onions and sauté, gently stirring regularly until they are a deep brown.

Add the rice and sauté for 5-6 minutes on a medium heat, add salt to taste and turn regularly so that all the grains cook evenly.

Add hot water to 2.5cm above the level of the rice, stir for a minute, cover and allow to cook. Reduce the heat to low so that the pulao cooks gently.

Check from time to time, stirring from the bottom with a flat wooden spatula, adding more water if necessary, a little at a time. Leave to cook for approximately 15-20 minutes. When the grains are cooked, set aside but do not uncover the pot.

MASALA 1 (FOR COOKING LAMB): Add all the ingredients to a skillet or wok, except the fresh coriander and water, and roast gently. Stir regularly.

When the chillis and the spices have changed colour, but are not discoloured, remove from the wok and transfer to a blender.

Add the fresh coriander and a little water, grind the mixture to a fine paste in a blender.

MASALA 2 (FOR FINAL FLAVOURING): Add all the ingredients to a skillet or wok and roast gently. Stir regularly and then cool and powder the masala in a blender.

DAAL: Wash the lentils and transfer to a large casserole dish. Add water to 2.5cm over the level of the lentils, add all the remaining ingredients and boil. Cook on a low flame once it has started to boil until the lentils are fully cooked, soft and easily mashed.

While cooking scrape the bottom regularly with a wooden spatula. When the lentils are fully cooked, purée everything together, cover and set aside.

LAMB (SAK): In a casserole dish heat the oil and sauté the lamb on a high heat. Once the lamb has sealed and is well coloured add masala number 1 and sauté until you see the oil escaping along the sides.

Add the water and salt, cover and cook on a medium heat for around 20-25 minutes. Stir at regular intervals and add more water, a little at a time, if required. When there is a thick rich gravy, blend the lamb with the lentil purée. Check the seasoning and adjust if required.

Just before serving sprinkle over some chopped coriander and chopped mint and blend.

KEBABS: Preheat the oven to 200°C . Make the seasoned mince into balls about 2.5cm in size, place them on a greased baking sheet and cook for approximately 20 minutes.

CACHUMBER: Add together the onion, mint, coriander, chilli, tomato, vinegar and salt and mix well.

TO SERVE: Heat the oil. Slice the onions and brown to a light golden colour. Drain and remove onto a paper towel to remove any excess oil. If well fried these will be crisp and should be sprinkled over the rice just before serving. Sprinkle with some chopped mint and coriander.

Arrange all the elements of the dish on plates as pictured.

CHEF'S TIP: Both masalas can be prepared in larger quantities and kept for future use, masala 1 in the refrigerator in an air-tight jar and masala 2 in an air-tight jar in a cool dark place. Each recipe can be used on its own. Lentil papadams go best with this dish.

↘ DAHI MANCHH
A FISH CURRY FROM BENGAL IN EAST INDIA
BY CYRUS TODIWALA / SERVES 4-6

"THIS IS ONE OF THE MOST POPULAR OF ALL BENGALI FISH DISHES."

METHOD

Rub the salt and turmeric into the fish and set aside for a few minutes.

MARINADE: Pureé together the yogurt, sugar, onions, chilli, ginger and garlic and mix well into the fish, then transfer to a bowl, cover and leave to rest for a couple of hours. Then take out the pieces of fish from the marinade, remove as much of the marinade as possible and set aside.

CURRY: Mix the rapeseed oil and mustard together and heat in a frying pan on a low heat. When nearly smoking add the whole spices: cassia, cloves, cardamom pods (making sure to crack them first), bay leaves and peppercorns and heat until the cardamom changes colour and the cloves have swollen up. Remove from the pan and set aside.

Increase the heat to medium, scrape off all excess coating from the fish and fry the fish, being careful not to let the pieces brown (this process is simply to seal the fish). Set aside.

Sauté the onion until soft and pale. Add the yogurt mix to the onions, add the fried spices, bring slowly to bubbling point and then add the fish into it. Simmer for 2-3 minutes and switch off the burner. Cover and let the fish cook in the latent heat.

TO SERVE: Remove the fish and serve with plain steamed rice.

PLANNING AHEAD
Allow 2 hours for the fish to marinade.

INGREDIENTS
- 500g Rohu or River perch, cut into small pieces
- 1 level tsp ground turmeric
- salt, to taste

MARINADE:
- 250g thick yogurt
- 1-2 tsp sugar
- 2 medium onions, roughly chopped
- level tsp ground red chilli
- 5cm piece of ginger
- 5-6 garlic cloves

CURRY:
- 4-5 tbsp cold pressed virgin rapeseed oil
- 1 level tbsp hot English ground mustard
- 1-2 piece cassia bark
- 2 cloves
- 2 green cardamom pods
- 2 bay leaves
- 4-5 black peppercorns
- 1 medium onion, chopped

TO SERVE:
- plain steamed rice
- mixed leaves, as needed

TO MAKE THIS DISH HEALTHIER USE LOW-FAT YOGURT
- CYRUS TODIWALA

FOOD TO EAT AFTER A MATCH:
◀◀**FISH AND CHIPS FROM
GRIMSBY FISHERIES IN
LEICESTER OR A CURRY**▶▶
- MARTIN CORRY

PARSEE PAV MAKHAN NU PUDDING
A RICH PARSEE-STYLE BREAD AND BUTTER PUDDING
BY CYRUS TODIWALA / SERVES 8

INGREDIENTS
- 2 litres full-cream milk
- 8 eggs
- 150g sugar
- 1½ tbsp Iranian rose water
- ½ tsp vanilla extract
- ½ tsp cardamom powder
- ½ tsp nutmeg powder
- 6 medium slices of white bread
- butter, as needed
- 1 heaped tbsp sultanas
- 1½ tbsp mixed dried fruits
- 15 almonds, skins removed
- 1 tbsp charoli (if not available use chopped pistachios)

METHOD

Heat the milk in a casserole pan and bring to boiling point. Then lower the heat and simmer the milk gently for approximately 1 hour and 30 minutes or until reduced to 1½ litres. Keep the sides of the pan clean at all times by removing any milk with a pastry brush and water every few minutes (do not use a dripping brush as that will dilute the milk). Heat until the milk turns a darker colour and gives off a caramelised aroma, stirring regularly so that the bottom of the pan does not burn.

Beat the eggs and sugar together until light and foamy. Allow the milk to cool slightly before adding it gradually to the egg and sugar mix and whisking constantly. Add more sugar if desired, then add the rose water, vanilla, cardamom and nutmeg powders to this batter.

Butter a baking dish liberally and sprinkle with sugar to coat the entire dish.

Apply butter to the bread slices (without crusts if preferred) on both sides and arrange a layer at the bottom of the dish, trimming the edges to fit. Over this sprinkle the sultanas and the mixed fruit. Place the remaining bread over this and pour over the batter. Let it soak well into the bread for around an hour.

Preheat the oven to 200ºC. Sprinkle the dish with sliced almonds and charoli/pistachios and bake for 10 minutes, then reduce the temperature to 180ºC and bake for a further 4-5 minutes or until a knife comes out clean. Finally, to create a crisp, golden top, place under a grill on a low heat and turn from time to time until you achieve the desired colour.

TO SERVE: Serve warm or cold with fresh cream.

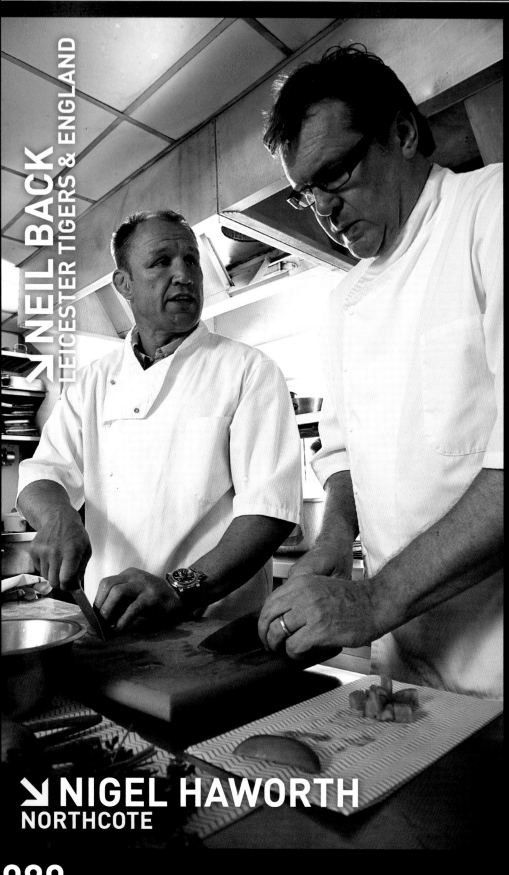

NEIL BACK
LEICESTER TIGERS & ENGLAND

↘ NIGEL HAWORTH
NORTHCOTE

⬎ CONFIT SHOULDER OF LAMB
STUDDED WITH ROSEMARY AND GARLIC, POACHED PLUM TOMATOES, FRENCH BEANS, PUREE POTATOES
BY NIGEL HAWORTH / SERVES 10

SPECIAL EQUIPMENT
Tammy cloth.

PLANNING AHEAD
The lamb must be salted a day in advance and left overnight.

INGREDIENTS

LAMB CONFIT:
- 2.4kg boneless shoulder of lamb
- 110g coarse sea salt
- 10g picked small plushes of rosemary
- 25g sliced peeled garlic, cloves sliced into 3, lengthways
- duck fat, as needed

ROAST GRAVY:
- 250g banana shallots, sliced
- 350ml Madeira
- 1litre lamb stock
- 750ml chicken stock
- 50g butter

PUREED POTATOES:
- 1.6kg potatoes, peeled and chopped (Maris Piper or Desiree)
- 300ml milk
- 100g butter
- salt, to taste

POACHED PLUM TOMATOES:
- 10 medium-size plum tomatoes
- 100ml white wine
- 200ml olive oil
- 30 slices of garlic clove
- rosemary, as needed
- salt, to taste
- pepper, to taste

FRENCH BEANS:
- 500g extra fine French beans, topped and tailed
- 50g butter
- sea salt, to taste
- black pepper, to taste

METHOD

LAMB CONFIT: Take the shoulder of lamb and salt overnight.

Preheat the oven to 140°C.

Wash off the excess salt under cold running water then dry thoroughly with a kitchen cloth. Make small incisions on both sides of the shoulder and stud with the rosemary and garlic. Slow cook the shoulder in duck fat in the oven for 3-3½ hours – make sure the lamb is completely covered in the duck fat, then cover with silicon paper and tin foil.

When the lamb is ready remove from the oven and allow to cool a little before moving from the pan and placing on to a tray to cool. Allow the shoulder to set, then place onto a carving board and, with a very sharp knife, cut the shoulder into 10 pieces.

When ready to serve place the shoulder pieces under the bottom of a salamander or in a hot oven (200°C) until crispy on the outside.

ROAST GRAVY: Sweat off the shallots lightly to caramelise, add the Madeira and reduce by three-quarters, then add the stocks. Reduce down to the desired consistency and pass through a tammy cloth, blend in the butter and reserve.

PUREED POTATOES: Place the potatoes into a pan of water and boil until cooked. Then strain away the water, add the milk, butter and salt and beat until smooth. Put the mash into a piping bag and keep warm.

POACHED PLUM TOMATOES: Gently poach the tomatoes in the wine, oil, garlic and rosemary. Season with salt and pepper, reserve until ready.

FRENCH BEANS: Boil the French beans in lightly salted water until al dente, take them out and refresh in iced water. When the beans are cold pour off the ice and water and keep them on a small tray ready for use. Reheat in a little butter and a few drops of water seasoned with salt and pepper just before serving.

TO SERVE: Take a large white pasta bowl and place a quenelle of hot mash to one side. Put the shoulder of lamb at the side of the mash then the poached tomato. Place the French beans on top, pour over the gravy and serve.

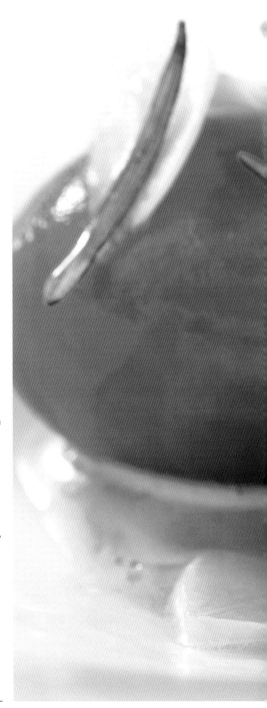

↘ NATIVE LOBSTER
AND MUNCASTER CRAB RISOTTO
BY NIGEL HAWORTH / SERVES 4

METHOD

LOBSTER: Take the live lobster and quickly pierce with a sharp knife through the head, boil gently or steam for 8 minutes.

Remove the lobster and allow to cool. When the lobster is cold remove the claws and tail – carefully take all the meat from the tail and claws.

Cut the tail in half lengthways and remove the waste pipe portion in each half tail. Cut into four pieces, then cut the claws equally in half and store in the fridge.

Discard the stomach sack from the head of the lobster, leaving the coral and liver in the shell to give a good flavour to the lobster stock.

LOBSTER STOCK: In a hot heavy-bottomed pan place your lobster shell and bash with the back of a rolling pin. Roast in the pan for a minute or two.

Flame with the brandy then add the wine and burn off quickly, add the vegetables, parsley stalks and spices, and stir quickly for a few minutes. Add the garlic, tomatoes and tomato purée, mix in well and cook until the tomatoes start to break down. Pour in enough cold water to cover your lobster mix, bring to the boil and then simmer for 20 minutes. Pass through a fine sieve and reserve.

RISOTTO: In a small, hot, heavy-bottomed pan pour in the oil and gently fry off the shallots until translucent, add the rice and stir for a minute, being careful not to colour the shallots.

Add the garlic and chilli and stir in well. Pour in the and reduce until completely absorbed.

Over the next 10 minutes carefully add your hot lobster and vegetable stocks – between 50ml and 100ml, stirring as you go until the rice is nearly cooked but still al dente.

When the risotto is nearly cooked slow the cooking process down by removing the pan from the heat and allowing to cool, but continuing to stir the rice.

TO SERVE: Add 50g of butter to the risotto and stir in well. Add the parmesan and a little more stock, then the crab, broad beans, girolles, tomatoes and basil, check the seasoning and finally add the lobster, leaving a piece to garnish.

Make a sauce with the lobster stock using the remaining butter and a little olive oil and blend until smooth and add to the plate. Plate up as pictured.

SPECIAL EQUIPMENT
Blender.

INGREDIENTS

LOBSTER:
- 1 x 550-600g native lobster

LOBSTER STOCK:
- 1 lobster shell
- 25ml light olive oil
- brandy, to taste
- 25ml white wine
- 20g fennel, sliced
- 20g onions, chopped
- 20g leeks, finely sliced
- few parsley stalks
- 3 pink peppercorns, crushed
- ¼ star anise
- 1 small garlic clove, crushed
- 3 tomatoes, roughly chopped
- 1 dsp tomato purée
- water, as needed

RISOTTO:
- 100ml good quality virgin olive oil
- 60g shallots, chopped
- 120g arborio rice
- 1 garlic clove, crushed
- hot red chilli flakes, as needed
- 150ml white wine
- 200ml vegetable stock

TO SERVE:
- 100g butter
- 50g parmesan, grated
- 100g Muncaster crab, picked
- 60 broad beans, cooked and shelled
- 50g small girolle mushrooms, sautéed in butter
- 2 ripe plum tomatoes, blanched, seeded and diced
- 1 small bunch of basil
- sea salt, as needed
- 300-400ml lobster stock

↘ GOOSNARGH CORNFED CHICKEN
AND CRACKED WHEAT SALAD
BY NIGEL HAWORTH / SERVES 4

SPECIAL EQUIPMENT
Steamer, liquidiser, stainless steel ring.

INGREDIENTS

CHICKEN:
- 4 cornfed Goosnargh chicken breasts

HERB SALSA:
- 90g mixed herbs (basil, parsley and chervil, roughly chopped)
- 3 large garlic bulbs, roasted
- 125ml extra virgin olive oil
- 40g parmesan, grated
- 30g ground almonds
- 2.5g salt
- pepper, to taste

CRACKED WHEAT SALAD:
- 100g cracked wheat
- 4 tsp fresh mint, finely cut with scissors
- 4 tsp parsley, finely chopped
- 50g peas, blanched
- 50g broad beans, blanched and shelled
- 90g red onion, diced and washed in hot and cold water 3 times, and then dried on a kitchen cloth
- 30g spring onions. finely sliced
- 20 red and yellow cherry tomatoes, roasted in olive oil
- salt and pepper
- 250ml vegetable bouillon
- 1 garlic clove, crushed
- rapeseed oil, as needed

YOGHURT CUCUMBER DRESSING:
- 7 fresh mint leaves
- 50g yoghurt
- $1/8$ lemon
- salt, to taste
- pepper, to taste

TO SERVE:
- juice of ½ lemon
- salt and pepper

METHOD

CHICKEN: Steam the chicken breasts for 12 minutes.

HERB SALSA: Place all the dry ingredients in a good liquidiser, add a little of the oil and blitz, then add the remainder gradually – if you add the oil too fast it may split the mixture. Liquidise the mixture well, then remove and store in a small jar.

CRACKED WHEAT SALAD: Put the cracked wheat, mint, parsley, peas, broad beans, onion, spring onions and 12 of the roasted cherry tomatoes together in a bowl and dress with the herb salsa and a small amount of the oil from the tomatoes. Season with salt and pepper.

Add the cracked wheat salad, vegetable bouillon, garlic and rapeseed oil together in a bowl. Cover the bowl with cling film and cook in a microwave on full power for approximately 2½ minutes until dry and fluffy.

Allow the cracked wheat to cool and then fluff up with a fork.

YOGHURT CUCUMBER DRESSING: Mix all the ingredients together until combined.

TO SERVE: Place the stainless steel ring in the centre of the bowl and spoon the cracked wheat salad into the ring then remove. Carve the chicken breast and arrange around the salad garnish with the salsa and the remaining cherry tomatoes. Season with lemon juice, salt and pepper. Serve the cucumber dressing separately.

⬊ BLACKCURRANT SLICE,
WHITE CURRANT JELLY, CROMWELL STOUT ICE CREAM
BY NIGEL HAWORTH / SERVES 4

SPECIAL EQUIPMENT
Food mixer, ice cream machine, blender

PLANNING AHEAD
The pastry is best made 4 days in advance. The ice cream should also be made in advance.

INGREDIENTS

PUFF PASTRY:
- 900g white bread flour
- 165g unsalted butter, softened and diced
- 500g unsalted butter
- 12g salt
- 6g caster sugar
- 45ml lemon juice
- 210ml water
- 30g icing sugar

VANILLA CREAM:
- 75g sugar
- 25g cornflour
- 25g plain flour
- 160g egg yolks
- 500g milk
- 1 vanilla pod
- 150g whipped cream

BLACKCURRANT COMPOTE:
- 250g blackcurrants
- 350g sugar

CROMWELL STOUT ICE CREAM:
- 250g Cromwell stout
- 360ml whole milk
- 150g whipping cream
- 50g milk powder
- 3g ice cream stabiliser
- 80g pasteurised egg yolk
- 180g caster sugar

WHITE CURRANT JELLY:
- 200g white currants
- 200ml water
- 10g lemon juice
- 75g sugar
- 2½ leaves gelatine, soaked

TO SERVE:
- icing sugar, as needed
- blackcurrant sorbet, as needed

METHOD

PUFF PASTRY: Place the flour and the 165g butter into a food processor and mix until it resembles fine breadcrumbs. Add the 500g of butter and mix for 2-3 minutes until just combined. Whisk together the salt, sugar, lemon juice and water. Gradually add this to the flour and butter mix, and continue mixing until just combined.

Remove the mix from the machine, lightly kneed for 2-3 minutes, then form the pastry into a flat square. Wrap the pastry in cling film and leave in the fridge overnight to rest.

Once the pastry has rested, roll into a long rectangle of around 1cm thick, then turn the pastry to landscape then turn both sides to meet in the middle, and fold one on top of the other. Repeat this process four times turning the pastry clockwise each time.

Preheat the oven to 170ºC.

For the layers roll out 500g of the puff pastry on a clean surface to 1cm thick, dusting with icing sugar 3 or 4 times when rolling out.

Place the pastry onto a flat tray covered with greaseproof paper. Put a heavy weight on top to get a flat flaky pastry.

Bake in the oven for 15 minutes until golden, then remove from the oven. Cut the pastry immediately into 2½ x 6cm rectangle pieces.

VANILLA CREAM: Mix together the sugar, cornflour, flour and egg yolk to a smooth paste.

Place the milk and split vanilla pod in a pan and bring to the boil. Once boiled, remove from the stove, pass through a fine sieve onto the egg yolk mix bit by bit, whisking all the time to prevent lumps forming. When all is incorporated, place back into the pan on a low heat and cook out for 5-8 minutes, whisking continuously until thick. Remove from the pan, put into a food processor and whisk until cold.

Semi-whisk the cream and fold through the custard mix – this is to get a light custard.

Place into a piping bag and reserve.

BLACKCURRANT COMPOTE: Preheat the oven to 160ºC.

Place the blackcurrants and sugar into a deep tray. Put into the oven and cook for 10 minutes until the currants are just cooked and starting to burst. Remove from the oven and leave to cool.

CROMWELL STOUT ICE CREAM: In a large pan reduce the beer by two-thirds over a medium heat. To the reduced beer add the milk, cream and milk powder and bring to the boil. Once boiled, add the stabiliser and reboil for a further 2 minutes. Mix together the egg yolks and sugar until light and fluffy. Pour the cream and milk mix onto the egg yolks bit by bit, whisking all the time.

Place the mix back into a non-stick pan and cook out on a low heat for 2-3 minutes, stirring all the time until the liquid coats the back of a spoon – be careful not to scramble the mix.

Pass through a fine sieve into a bowl set over ice and leave to cool. Once cooled, churn in a ice cream machine to the manufacturer's instructions.

WHITE CURRANT JELLY: Place the white currants, water, lemon juice and sugar into a pan. Cover with cling film or place a tight lid on top of the pan and bring to the boil. Once boiled, remove from the stove and leave to infuse for 1 hour.

Pour the currants through a fine sieve, discard the currant mixture and return the liquor back into a pan. Bring to the boil and whisk in the soaked gelatine. When the gelatine has completely dissolved, pour the liquid back through a fine sieve into a flat metal tray (you want the jelly about 1cm deep). Place into a fridge to set. Cut into cubes just before serving.

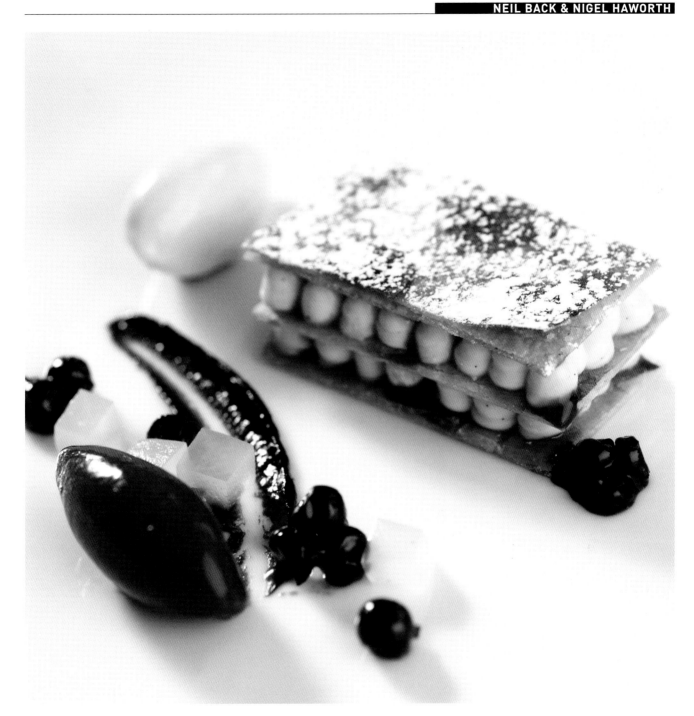

TO SERVE: On two rectangles of puff pastry evenly pipe vanilla cream around the edges, then fill the centres with blackcurrant compote. Place them carefully on top of each other and finish with the third rectangle. Dust with icing sugar.

Place the slice into the middle of the plate. Onto each side of the slice place a quenelle of sorbet and ice cream. Garnish with cubes of white currant jelly and a small amount of compote scattered around the plate.

IT'S IMPORTANT TO CUT THE PASTRY WHEN IT IS HOT IN ORDER TO GET A PERFECT SHAPE
- NIGEL HAWORTH

⤦ SNAILS SET IN GARLIC CASSONADE

AND TOPPED WITH RED WINE SAUCE INFUSED WITH VEAL KIDNEY, ACCOMPANIED WITH PARSLEY PUREE AND GARLIC CROUTONS

BY MARTIN BURGE / SERVE 4

"THE SNAIL'S DISH HAS BEEN ON THE MENU FROM THE OPENING OF THE DINING ROOM. IT IS AN INNOVATIVE, TIMELESS AND DELICIOUS WAY IN WHICH TO SERVE SNAILS."

SPECIAL EQUIPMENT

Vac-pac machine and vac-pac bags, muslin cloth, 24 small pots.

PLANNING AHEAD

Prepare the cassonade the day before.

INGREDIENTS

SNAILS:
- 350g snails, blanched
- 25g carrots
- 15g celery
- 15g onions
- 10g leeks
- 15ml pernod
- 12g garlic
- 10g parsley stalks

GARLIC CASSONADE:
- 30g garlic, peeled
- 250ml double cream
- 100ml whole milk
- 2 whole eggs
- 4 egg yolks
- 15g salt
- ½g freshly milled white pepper
- 5ml lemon juice

RED WINE SAUCE INFUSED WITH VEAL KIDNEY:
- 75g rendered veal suet
- 250g shallots, sliced
- 20g garlic, peeled
- 7g thyme
- 1 bay leaf
- 135ml red wine vinegar
- 500ml ruby port
- 1 litre red wine
- 200g button mushrooms, sliced
- 3.5 litres chicken stock
- 750ml water
- 75g veal glace (reduced veal stock)
- 200g veal kidney, diced

PARSLEY PUREE:
- 200g picked flat parsley leaves
- 2 litres water
- 50g salt
- 75g unsalted butter

- ¼g freshly milled white pepper
- ½g salt

GARLIC CROUTONS:
- 150g unsalted butter
- 20g garlic, peeled
- 1g salt
- 24 bread croutons

METHOD

SNAILS: Wash the snails in cold water and dry them on a cloth or paper towel. Dice the carrots, celery, onions and leeks into approximately 1cm cubes. Place all of the ingredients into a vac-pac bag and vac-pac on full power.

Place the sealed bag into another vac-pac bag and seal again. Place the bag into a water bath set at 75ºC for 7 hours. After 7 hours remove the vac-pac bag and plunge the bag into iced water, allowing to cool completely.

Once chilled open the vac-pac bags, pick out the snails and gently wash and dry them. Store the snails in the fridge until ready to use.

GARLIC CASSONADE: Blanch the garlic three times, this should be done by placing the garlic in a pan of cold water and bringing up to the boil, drain off the hot water and replace with cold – repeat this process three times.

In a saucepan bring up to a gentle simmer the blanched garlic with the cream and milk, and allow to cool to room temperature, infusing the cream with the garlic. Place the infusion with the garlic in a food blender with the eggs and egg yolks and blend until smooth. Add the salt, pepper and lemon juice and allow the mix to rest in the fridge for 24 hours prior to use.

The next day, using a small ladle, skim the foam from the top of the mixture and then the mix is ready to use.

RED WINE SAUCE INFUSED WITH VEAL KIDNEY: In a saucepan sweat the shallots with the garlic, thyme and bay leaf in the veal fat until the shallots soften slightly.

Add the vinegar and reduce until all of the vinegar disappears. Add the port and reduce until a syrup is formed. At this stage add the red wine and mushrooms and continue reducing until there is only one-eighth of the original amount of wine.

Add the rest of the ingredients apart from the veal kidney and bring up to the boil, at this stage using a small ladle to skim off any impurities. Turn the sauce down to a gentle simmer and cook for 2 hours, taking care to regularly remove any impurities from the top by skimming – this will prevent any cloudiness.

Pass the stock through a muslin cloth and reduce until a sauce consistency is achieved. Sauté the veal kidney until golden brown and drain the fat off on paper. Add this to the reduced sauce and gently simmer for 10 minutes, then allow to stand for a further 10 minutes to infuse the kidney flavour.

PARSLEY PUREE: Boil the water and salt together, cook the parsley leaves in the salted water until soft. Using a chinois pass off the parsley leaves and place into iced water to cool them down quickly.

Set up a blender and blend the parsley leaves until smooth. Pass the purée, using a chinois, and ladle into a saucepan. Add the butter, salt and pepper, and stir over a low heat until the butter has emulsified into the purée.

GARLIC CROUTONS: Preheat the oven to 180ºC.

Melt the butter with the garlic and salt, and allow to stand for 30 minutes to infuse. Using a pastry brush, apply a thin coat of butter to each side of the crouton.

Bake on a flat tray in the oven, until golden brown. Place the croutons on tissue paper – this draws out the excess butter and prevents the croutons being greasy.

TO SERVE: Preheat the oven to 100ºC. Place a snail in each pot totalling 24, and cover each one with the garlic cassonade mixture. Place these on a 2.5cm deep tray, and fill the tray with boiling water until the level of water is three-quarters covering the sides of the pots.

Cling film the top of the tray and place in the oven for approximately 45 minutes, until the cassonades are set. Remove from the tray and dry off any excess water on the pots.

On top of each pot pour a teaspoon of sauce to finish.

Serve the warm croutons and parsley purée in suitable dishes.

CHEF'S TIP: Snails can be purchased online. First purge them in salted water then blanch

in boiling water for a few minutes. Then remove their shells and cook them in a court bouillon. You can also buy them pre-cooked in their own court bouillon.

We make the croutons from breadsticks sliced on an angle, but they can be made using any shaped bread as long as they are the same thickness.

At the restaurant we cook a small amount of the cassonade as a tester before use to check the texture and seasoning.

↘ COTTAGE PIE

BY MARTIN BURGE / SERVES 6

"LEWIS CHOSE THIS DISH AND COTTAGE PIE IS CLASSIC COMFORT FOOD. THE INGREDIENTS WERE CHOSEN FOR THEIR NUTRITIONAL CONTENT AND THE PREPARATION REQUIRED FOR THIS DISH SUITS THE LIFESTYLE OF A RUGBY ATHLETE. THIS VEGETARIAN COTTAGE PIE IS MADE WITH QUORN (A MYCROPROTEIN – A MUSHROOM DERIVATIVE) AND IS HIGH IN PROTEIN AND LOW IN FAT. IT'S HIGH IN DIETARY FIBRE (IMPORTANT FOR YOUR DIGESTIVE SYSTEM) AND HAS THE ESSENTIAL AMINO ACIDS YOUR BODY NEEDS, WITH NO CHOLESTEROL OR TRANS-FATS AT ALL."

SPECIAL EQUIPMENT

Water bath, vac-pac bags and vac-pac machine, fine sieve.

PLANNING AHEAD

You can prepare the cottage pie one day in advance or alternatively prepare the cottage pie base and store in a fridge to top with the mashed potatoes the following day.

INGREDIENTS

MASHED POTATOES:
- 2kg Maris Piper or Red Desiree potatoes
- 200ml warm milk
- 20g butter
- salt and pepper, to taste

VEGETABLES:
- 3 large carrots
- 1 large celeriac
- 2 medium onions
- 60ml olive oil
- salt and pepper, to taste
- 150g garden peas, blanched
- 20g tomato purée
- 30g plain flour

VEGETABLE STOCK:
- good quality vegetable bouillon
- 1 bay leaf

MINCE:
- 700g Quorn mince
- 7g thyme petals, chopped (reserve the stalks for the vegetable stock)
- salt and pepper, to taste

METHOD

MASHED POTATOES: Wash and peel the potatoes. Cut them into slices of about 1cm thick. Lay the potatoes into two vac-pac bags and vacuum on full power, making sure the potatoes do not overlap.

Place each bag into another bag and repeat the vac-pac process to double vac them.

Place the two bags into a preheated water bath set at 72ºC for 30 minutes. After 30 minutes take the bags out and plunge them into a bowl of iced water, allowing them to cool for 10 minutes.

Remove the bags from the iced water and place them into a pan of simmering water until the potatoes become soft. Once the potatoes are soft, remove from the bags and place onto a tray, allowing the steam to evaporate for 1-2 minutes. To mash the potatoes take a fine sieve and, using a spatula, push the potatoes through the sieve into a bowl. Gradually add the warm milk and butter, and mix well. Season to taste with salt and pepper. Do not overwork the mashed potatoes as they will become starchy. Keep the mashed potatoes warm until ready to use.

Alternatively prepare the mashed potatoes in the traditional way making sure that the mash potatoes are dry and fluffy.

VEGETABLES: Peel the carrots and celeriac. Square them off using a sharp knife and dice into 1cm pieces. Peel and finely chop the onions. Reserve the remaining vegetable trimmings for the vegetable stock and throw away the peel.

In a suitable sized heavy-based saucepan heat the olive oil over a medium heat. Add the carrots, celeriac and onions to the pan. Season with salt and pepper to release the flavours from the vegetables. Cook the vegetables until they have softened and slightly caramelised. Add the tomato purée and plain flour and mix thoroughly. Set the heat to a low setting and cook the mixture for a further 8-10 minutes, stirring continuously.

VEGETABLE STOCK: Make up 600ml of vegetable stock using a good quality vegetable bouillon. In a pan add the thyme stalks, the bay leaf and vegetable trimmings to the bouillon. Bring the liquid to the boil, then remove the pan from the heat and allow the ingredients to infuse. Set aside until required.

MINCE: Preheat the oven to 170ºC.

Strain the vegetable stock through a fine sieve into a jug. Gradually add the stock to the mixture, stirring continuously so that the flour does not go lumpy. Add the thyme petals, the mince, blanched garden peas and continue to cook for a further 5 minutes. Season with salt and pepper to taste. Place the ingredients into a suitably sized oven-proof dish and allow to stand for 10 minutes. Evenly top the pie with the mashed potatoes. Run a fork over the top – this will give the top a crispy 'golden brown' finish when cooked in the oven. Cook in the oven for 30-40 minutes until the mashed potatoes are golden brown on top and the cottage pie is piping hot.

CHEF'S TIP: It is important to source a good quality vegetable bouillon as this will improve the depth and flavour of the cottage pie and other vegetarian recipes. Alternatively, try making your own vegetable stock to get the depth of flavours that you wish to achieve. Alternatively a beef stock may used for a non vegetarian option however keep in the quorn mince as this will ensure the cottage pie is high in protein and low in fat.

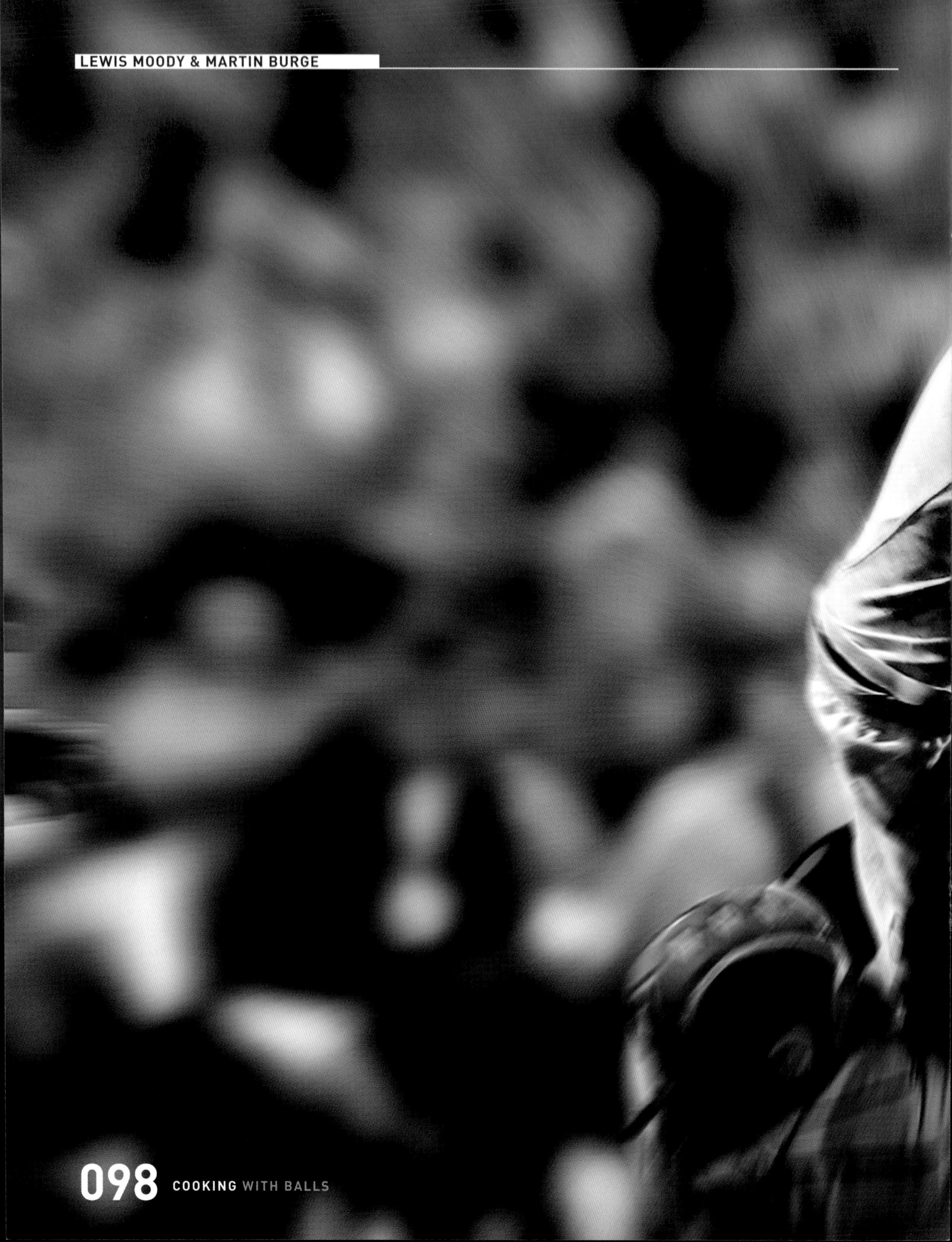

FOOD TO EAT BEFORE A MATCH:
**▮▮PASTA WITH TUNA,
SWEETCORN AND PICKLE▮▮**
- LEWIS MOODY

↘ SOY GLAZED MACKEREL
RESTING ON AN ORIENTAL SALAD
BY MARTIN BURGE / SERVES 4

"THIS DISH IS SERVED IN THE BRASSERIE AT WHATLEY MANOR. IT HAS BEEN CHOSEN BECAUSE OF ITS NUTRITIONAL CONTENT AND IS AN EXTREMELY HEALTHY DISH MAINLY DUE TO THE OILY FISH MACKEREL. MACKEREL IS HIGH IN ESSENTIAL OMEGA OILS AND VITAMIN B, HIGH IN PROTEIN AND LOW IN CARBOHYDRATES. THE HEALTH BENEFITS ASSOCIATED WITH EATING OILY FISH INCLUDE: PREVENTS CARDIOVASCULAR DISEASE, IMPROVES BRAIN ACTIVITY, ENHANCES MEMORY AND STRENGTHENS THE IMMUNE SYSTEM. THE EDAMAME BEANS IN THE ORIENTAL SALAD ARE HIGH IN PROTEIN, VITAMIN C AND FIBRE."

SPECIAL EQUIPMENT
Mandolin.

PLANNING AHEAD
The oriental dressing must be made a day in advance.

INGREDIENTS

PICKLED GINGER:
- 1 lemon
- 75g ginger, peeled and sliced
- 700ml cold water
- 85g caster sugar
- 200ml rice wine vinegar

ORIENTAL DRESSING:
- 75ml honey
- 75ml rice wine vinegar
- 100ml peanut oil

SOY GLAZE:
- 100ml Ketjap manis
- 10ml light soy sauce

SALAD:
- 50g mix:ed baby leaf lettuce
- ½ cucumber
- 150g frozen edamame beans
- 4 red radishes
- 20g pickled ginger

MACKEREL:
- 5g toasted sesame seeds
- 2 whole mackerel, filleted, pin boned and skinned

METHOD

PICKLED GINGER: Cut the lemon into four equal quarters, then peel and slice the ginger thinly on a mandolin or with a sharp knife. Squeeze the juice from one quarter of the lemon onto the ginger to stop it from oxidising. In a saucepan, place the ginger, 350ml of the cold water, 12.5g of the sugar and squeeze the juice from another quarter of the lemon. Repeat this who process once more.

Bring the mixture up to the boil and strain through a colander. Repeat the process once more.

In a separate pan mix the rice wine vinegar and the remaining 60g sugar, then add the strained ginger and bring to the boil. Once boiled take off the heat and allow to cool. Place in the fridge until ready to use.

ORIENTAL DRESSING: Place the honey and vinegar into a bowl and whisk together until completely mixed. Slowly add the oil until incorporated. Set aside until ready for use.

SOY GLAZE: Mix the two ingredients together. Set aside until ready to use.

SALAD: Remove the edamame beans from the pods and the skin from around the beans. Remove the sprout and take the bottom off the radishes with a sharp knife. Slice them thinly on a mandolin or with a sharp knife.

Peel the cucumber and cut in half. Using a teaspoon scrape out the cucumber seeds and discard. Cut the cucumber into 5cm batons, about the thickness of a pencil. Set aside until ready to use. Wash the baby leaf salad in a bowl of cold water and allow to drain in a colander.

In a large bowl mix the salad leaves, radish slices, drained pickled ginger, edamame beans and cucumber batons. Lightly dress the salad with the oriental dressing.

MACKEREL: Lightly toast the sesame seeds under a preheated grill and set aside.

Place the mackerel onto a non-stick tray flat-side facing up. Using a pastry brush heavily brush the soy glaze over the fish ready to cook.

Place the mackerel under a preheated grill for 4 minutes and brush more soy glaze onto the mackerel every 20-30 seconds so that the glaze starts to thicken.

TO SERVE: Arrange the salad leaves and vegetables in the centre of the plate. Once the mackerel is cooked gently lift from the tray and place on top of the salad. To finish the dish sprinkle the toasted sesame seeds over the mackerel.

SOURCE YOUR MACKEREL FROM A REPUTABLE FISHMONGER MAKING SURE THAT THE FISH IS TOP QUALITY. LOOK FOR A FIRM TEXTURE, FRESH SMELL, AND BRIGHT RED GILLS. A FISHMONGER WILL FILLET AND PIN BONE THE MACKEREL FOR YOU.
- MARTIN BURGE

↘ CHICORY MOUSSE
LAYERED WITH BITTER COFFEE AND MASCARPONE CREAM
BY MARTIN BURGE / SERVES 4

"THE COMBINATION OF FLAVOURS IN THIS DESSERT MAKE IT SINFUL, FROM THE LAYERING OF THE DARK CHOCOLATE, THE BOOZINESS OF THE KAHLUA AND SHERRY FOLLOWED BY THE RICH CREAMY MASCARPONE MOUSSE."

SPECIAL EQUIPMENT
Spray gun, blow torch, water bath, vac-pac machine, food mixer, 4 x 50mm diameter hexagonal mould for the mascarpone mousse, 4 x 50mm diameter sphere moulds for the chicory mousse, 60cm x 40cm tray, thermometer.

PLANNING AHEAD
The chicory mousse and the joconde sponge may be prepared ahead of time.

INGREDIENTS

CHICORY MOUSSE:
- 75g chicory beans
- 75ml full fat milk
- 185ml whipping cream
- 2 medium egg yolks
- 20g sugar
- 15g milk chocolate
- 2.5g gelatine

COFFEE SYRUP:
- 75g espresso coffee
- 50g Kahlua
- 50g Pedro Ximenez sherry
- 20g caster sugar

JOCONDE SPONGE:
- 187g icing sugar
- 187g almonds, ground
- 5 medium eggs, beaten
- 35g unsalted butter, melted
- 50g caster sugar
- 6 medium egg whites
- 50g plain flour, sieved
- 15g dark chocolate, 70% cocoa, melted

MASCARPONE MOUSSE:
- 55g caster sugar
- 10ml water
- 2 medium egg yolks
- 85g mascarpone cheese
- 2g gelatine leaf
- 80ml whipping cream

CHOCOLATE SPRAY:
- 300g cocoa butter
- 300g dark chocolate, 70% cocoa

TO SERVE:
- 25g dark chocolate
- 24 tempered chocolate leaves (4cm x 3cm)
- 4 pieces of gold leaf
- 5g gold dust

METHOD

CHICORY MOUSSE: In a frying pan toast the chicory beans on a medium heat.

Pour the milk and 75ml of whipping cream into a vac-pac bag with the toasted chicory beans. Seal the bag and place in a water bath set at 75ºC for 30 minutes.

Remove the bag from the water bath and pass the mixture through a fine sieve or chinois.

Measure out the infusion to 125ml and discard the remaining infusion.

Whisk together the egg yolks and sugar. Meanwhile bring the infusion to the boil then pour over the egg yolks and sugar. Return to the heat, continuously stirring with a spatula or wooden spoon. The mixture will thicken to make an anglaise. Pass this chicory anglaise through a chinois or fine sieve. Add the chocolate and set aside until required. Take a glass bowl and soften the gelatine in cold water for about 10 minutes.

Squeeze the gelatine to remove any excess water. In a pan add 10ml of whipping cream and the gelatine, heat the mixture up gently until the gelatine has dissolved. Take the gelatine cream off the heat and then pour onto the chicory anglaise and whisk until well mixed. Whisk the remaining cream to form soft ribbons and then fold into the chicory anglaise. Mix well. Pour the mixture into half-sphere moulds and freeze.

COFFEE SYRUP: Dissolve the sugar into the coffee. Add the rest of the ingredients. Set aside until required.

JOCONDE SPONGE: Preheat the oven to 220ºC.

Place the icing sugar, almonds and half of the beaten eggs into a food mixer. Whisk on high speed for 8 minutes. Add the remainder of the eggs and whisk on high speed for another 10 minutes. Add the butter into the mix and set aside.

Line a tray 60cm x 40cm with silicone paper.

Meanwhile make a meringue by whisking the caster sugar and the egg whites until soft peaks are formed. Fold the almond mixture into the meringue. Fold the flour into the mixture. With a palate knife spread the mixture gently and evenly over the tray. Bake in the oven for 10-12 minutes, until firm to the touch.

Leave to cool and then spread a thin layer of melted dark chocolate over the top. Cut the sponge into eight hexagons using the mould as a cutter. Set aside. Discard any remaining sponge.

MASCARPONE MOUSSE: Dissolve the sugar and water in a pan and boil to 118ºC to make a sugar syrup.

Meanwhile in a mixing bowl add the egg yolks then pour on the sugar syrup and whisk the mixture to form a sabayon. Set aside. In a separate bowl whisk the mascarpone cheese until soft and smooth. Fold the sabayon into the mascarpone.

In a glass bowl soften the gelatine in cold water for about 10 minutes. Squeeze the gelatine to remove any excess water. In a pan heat up 5ml of cream and add the gelatine until dissolved. Take the melted gelatine off the heat and then pour into the mascarpone sabayon and whisk until combined. In a bowl whisk 75ml of cream to form soft peaks and then fold into the mascarpone sabayon.

Place the joconde sponge on the bottom of the hexagonal mould and soak the sponge with a tablespoon of the coffee syrup. In the mould pipe the mascarpone mousse up to half way. Repeat the layering of the joconde sponge, coffee syrup and the mascarpone mousse. Leave to set in the fridge for 2 hours.

CHOCOLATE SPRAY: Set up a bain marie and melt the cocoa butter and chocolate together until it reaches 50-55ºC. Pass the chocolate through a chinois into a spray gun.

TO SERVE: Remove the chicory mousse from the freezer. Turn the mousse out of the mould by heating the outside of the mould with a blow torch. Meanwhile melt some dark chocolate over a bain marie. Brush the bottom of each mousse with the melted chocolate. Place the mousse back in the freezer for 10 minutes.

Set up the spray gun. The temperature of the chocolate must be about 50ºC so that the gun works efficiently. Remove the frozen mousses from the freezer and spray all over, except the base, making sure they remain frozen while spraying. Lay the sprayed mousses on a tray lined with silicone paper and place in the fridge to defrost naturally (around 1 hour).

Light the blow torch and heat the outside of the hexagonal mould to assist with removing the mousse from the mould.

Place the chicory mousse carefully on top of the mascarpone mousse. Arrange the chocolate leaves around the outside of the mascarpone mousse to form a hexagon. Then place the pieces of gold leaf on top of the dome and sprinkle with a light dusting of gold dust on the edge of the plate.

CHEF'S TIP: Place the spherical moulds for the chicory mousse in the freezer a few hours before filling them. This will ensure that the mousse does not separate during the freezing process.

↳ **LAWRENCE DALLAGLIO**
LONDON WASPS & ENGLAND

↘ **CLIVE DIXON**
KOFFMANN'S

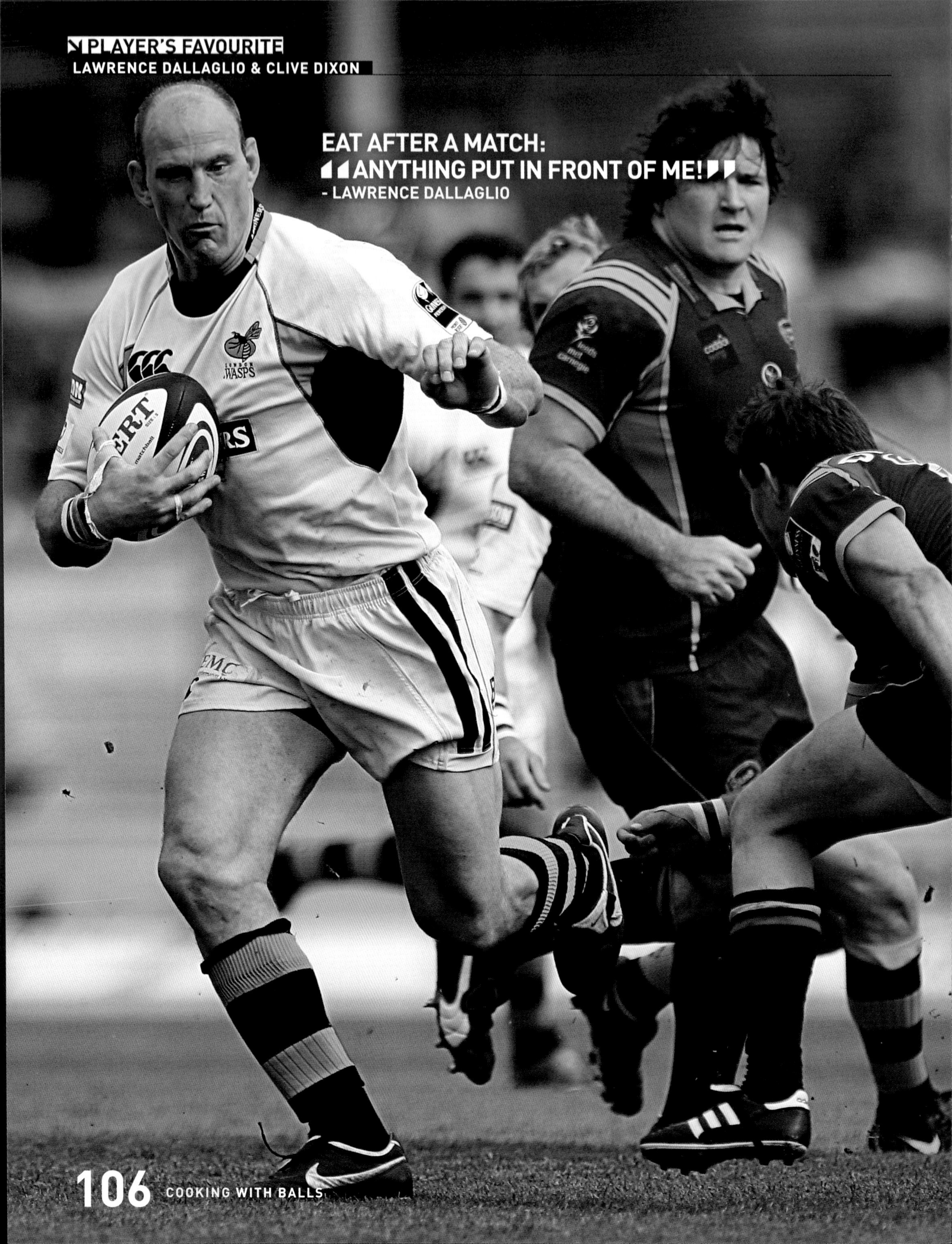

EAT AFTER A MATCH:
❝ ANYTHING PUT IN FRONT OF ME! ❞
- LAWRENCE DALLAGLIO

↘ SPINACH AND RICOTTA GNUDI
WITH CRISPY LAMB BREAST
BY CLIVE DIXON / SERVES 2

METHOD

GNUDI: Mix all the ingredients together and form small balls, size as desired. Submerge them all in 00 flour and leave, covered, for a minimum of 4 hours.

CRISPY LAMB: Add the lamb to a pre-heated non-stick pan over a high heat and fry for 5 minutes until crispy – it will cook in its own fat so keep stirring to avoid the lamb clumping together.

Drain the fat and leave to the lamb to cool for 5 minutes. Chop through the lamb again with a sharp knife and then return to the pan and cook on a high heat for 5 minutes for final crispness.

TO SERVE: Add the gnudi to a pan of boiling water for 2 minutes. Meanwhile, melt down the butter in a separate pan adding the sage, chives and lemon juice. After 2 minutes add the gnudi to the melted butter mixture, then add in the lamb and cook for a further minute.

Place on to a serving bowl, drizzle with oil and sprinkle with the grated parmesan.

PLANNING AHEAD
The gnudi must be left to rest for a minimum of 4 hours before cooking.

INGREDIENTS

GNUDI:
- 200g good quality ricotta cheese
- 100g cooked spinach, drained and chopped
- zest of ½ a lemon
- 50g parmesan, grated
- salt, pepper and nutmeg, to taste
- 00 flour, as needed

CRISPY LAMB:
- 100g lamb breast, finely diced

TO SERVE:
- 75g unsalted butter
- few sprigs of sage
- small bunch of chives, finely chopped
- juice of ½ a lemon
- olive oil, Tuscan if possible, as needed
- grated parmesan, as needed

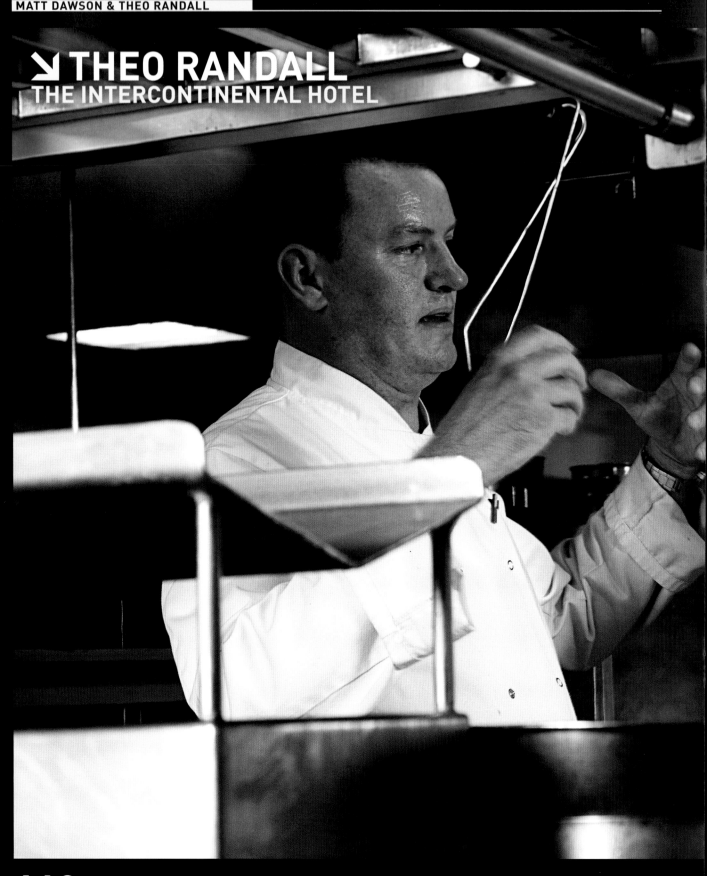

↘ THEO RANDALL
THE INTERCONTINENTAL HOTEL

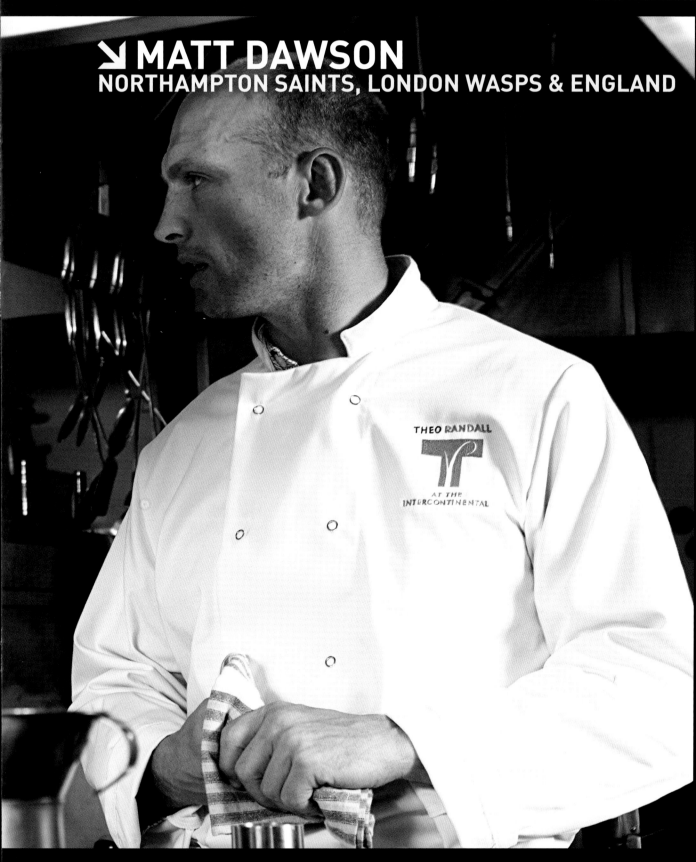

⬊ MATT DAWSON
NORTHAMPTON SAINTS, LONDON WASPS & ENGLAND

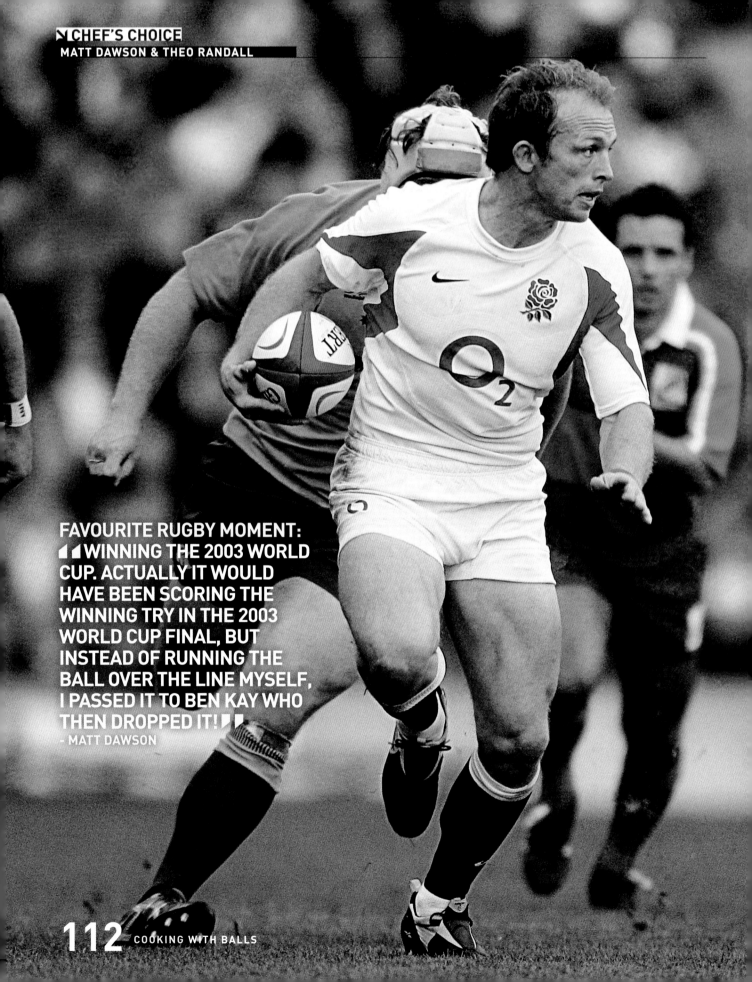

FAVOURITE RUGBY MOMENT:
❝WINNING THE 2003 WORLD
CUP. ACTUALLY IT WOULD
HAVE BEEN SCORING THE
WINNING TRY IN THE 2003
WORLD CUP FINAL, BUT
INSTEAD OF RUNNING THE
BALL OVER THE LINE MYSELF,
I PASSED IT TO BEN KAY WHO
THEN DROPPED IT!❞
- MATT DAWSON

↘ **TURBOT ON THE BONE**
WITH ROASTED RED PEPPERS AND CHARD
BY THEO RANDALL / SERVES 6

METHOD

Preheat the oven to 160ºC.

Cut the wings off the turbot and remove the head. Cut down the centre bone so you have two halves, cutting horizontally through the bone into 180g steaks.

Cut the peppers into quarters and remove any seeds.

Cover the surface of the peppers with a dash of olive oil, season with salt, garlic and a the oregano. Cook on a wire rack for approximately 30 minutes at 160ºC.

Season the steaks with the chilli and fennel seeds, and seal in a hot pan on the flesh side, then turn over and add the parsley and capers. Cook in the oven for about 10 minutes on 200ºC. After the turbot has cooked leave it to rest for at least 3 minutes before serving.

TO SERVE: Serve on the Swiss chard with peppers to the side.

INGREDIENTS
- 1 x 3kg turbot
- 1 dried chilli
- 1 tsp fennel seeds, crushed
- 2 tbsp parsley, chopped
- 75g capers
- 2 red peppers
- salt, as needed
- olive oil, as needed
- 1 garlic clove, thinly sliced
- 1 tsp dried oregano

TO SERVE:
- 250g Swiss chard, cleaned, stalks removed and blanched in salted water.

↘ PAPPARDELLE
WITH BEEF FILLET AND ROSEMARY
BY THEO RANDALL / SERVES 4

"WHEN THE PASTA HAS COOKED TOSS TOGETHER IN THE SAUCE AND COOK FOR A FURTHER 2 MINUTES SO THE PASTA ABSORBS THE FLAVOUR OF THE SAUCE."

METHOD

In a pan soften the chopped onion, celery and garlic together with the olive oil on a low heat. Turn up the heat and add the beef fillet strips and rosemary. Cook for a few minutes then add the wine and tomatoes. Cook on a low heat for 20-25 minutes or until the sauce is thick and rich in consistency, season to taste.

In a large pot of boiling salted water cook the pappardelle until al dente. Toss together with the sauce and fold in the butter and season to taste.

INGREDIENTS

- 1 small red onion, finely chopped
- 2 sticks of celery, finely chopped
- 1 garlic clove, finely chopped
- 2 tbsp olive oil
- 1 tsp chopped rosemary
- 150g beef fillet, cut into fine strips
- 150ml Chianti or good quality red wine
- 1 x 400g tin chopped plum tomatoes
- 250g fresh pappardelle
- 50g unsalted butter
- salt, to taste

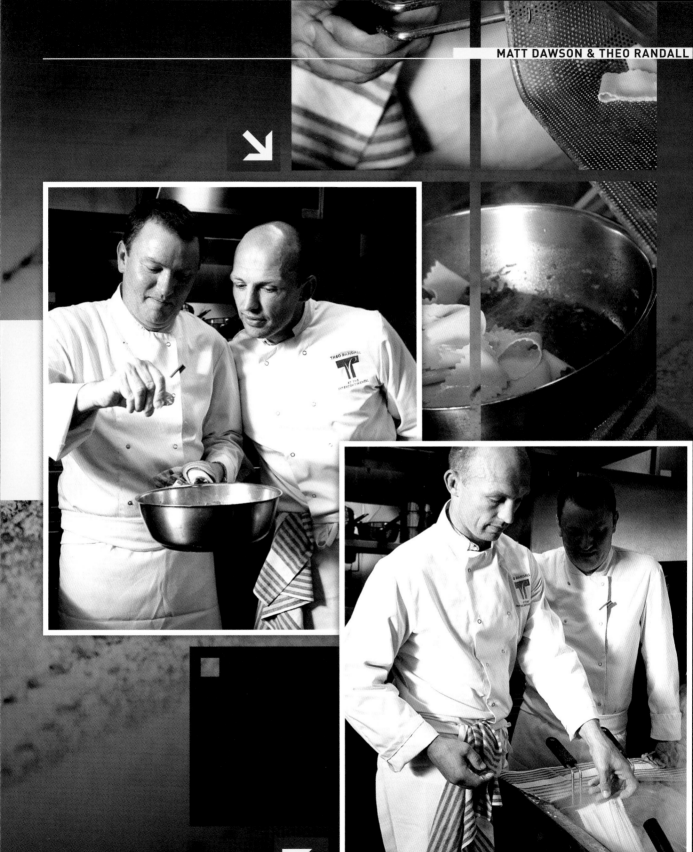

↘ SMOKED EEL

WITH DANDELION, BEETROOT AND ROCKET

BY THEO RANDALL / SERVES 6

"ALWAYS SCRAPE OFF ANY EXCESS FAT ON THE EEL FILLET OTHERWISE THE FLAVOUR CAN BE BITTER."

INGREDIENTS

EEL:
- 1 x 1kg smoked eel
- 300g beetroot, boiled
- 3 tbsp olive oil
- juice of ½ lemon
- 1 head dandelion
- 2 heads wild rocket

HORSERADISH CREAM:
- 1 stick horseradish, grated
- 100ml crème fraîche
- 1 tsp red wine vinegar

METHOD

EEL: Slice the eel thinly and peel the beetroot, dress both eel and beetroot with some oil and lemon. Dress the dandelion and rocket with the remaining oil and lemon.

HORSERADISH CREAM: Combine all the ingredients together.

TO SERVE: Place the eel on the plate together with the horseradish cream.

↘RICOTTA CHEESECAKE
BY THEO RANDALL / SERVES 8

"TRY TO USE SHEEP'S RICOTTA CHEESE AS THIS IS LIGHTER AND MAKES A CREAMIER CHEESECAKE."

SPECIAL EQUIPMENT
Food processor.

PLANNING AHEAD
Soak the raisins in the marsala for 2 hours or overnight if possible.

INGREDIENTS

SWEET PASTRY BASE:
- 100g unsalted butter
- 1 egg yolk
- 150g plain flour
- 50g icing sugar

FILLING:
- 80g raisins
- 3 tbsp sweet Marsala
- 450g sheep's ricotta
- 100g caster sugar
- 1 tbsp plain flour
- 3 eggs, separated
- 60ml double cream
- 60ml crème fraîche
- 1 vanilla pod
- ¼ tsp salt

METHOD

SWEET PASTRY BASE: Preheat the oven to 160°C.

Blend all the ingredients together in a food processor until a dough is formed and chill for 30 minutes. Roll out and cut to the size of a spring form dish. Bake for 20 minutes. Cool down, then add the filling.

FILLING: In a separate bowl add the sugar and flour to the ricotta and beat until smooth. Add the egg yolks, cream and crème fraîche, marsala and raisin mix and add the seeds of the vanilla pod.

In separate bowl beat together the egg whites with the salt. Fold in the ricotta mixture and pour into the springform tin with the cooked sweet pastry on the base.

Bake in the oven for about 50 minutes at 160ºC.

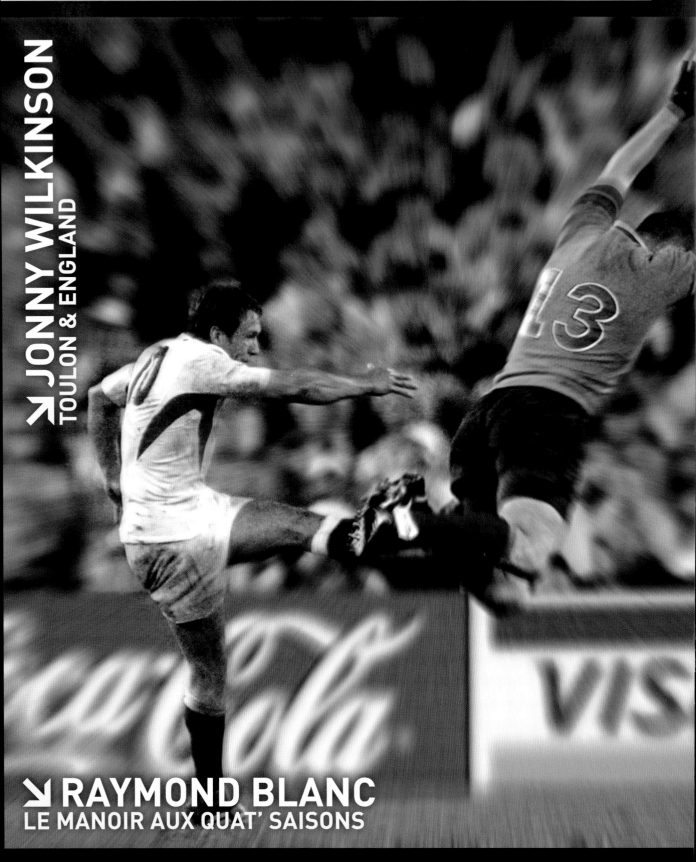

JONNY WILKINSON
TOULON & ENGLAND

RAYMOND BLANC
LE MANOIR AUX QUAT' SAISONS

EAT AFTER A MATCH:
❝I TRY TO HAVE ONE OF MY FAVOURITE MEALS AS A REWARD FOR THE DAY'S EFFORTS❞
– JONNY WILKINSON

⬊ SUPREME DE POULET AUX MORILLES –
BREAST OF CHICKEN WITH MORELS AND VIN JAUNE SAUCE
BY RAYMOND BLANC / SERVES 4

Photography by Jean Cazals.

PLANNING AHEAD
Soak the morels in water 6 hours before cooking or overnight.

INGREDIENTS

MORELS:
- 30g dried morel mushrooms, soaked in 150ml water

CHICKEN AND MUSHROOMS:
- 4 x 180g chicken breasts, skin off
- sea salt, to taste
- freshly ground black pepper, to taste
- 30g butter
- 120g button mushrooms, very firm, washed quickly and quartered
- 120ml Vin Jaune, boiled for 30 seconds to remove the alcohol
- 100ml liquor from the soaked morels
- 400ml double cream

LEEKS:
- 100ml water
- sea salt, to taste
- white pepper, to taste
- 20g butter
- 2 leeks, medium size, outer leaves removed, cut across into 1cm slices then washed

METHOD

MORELS: Pass the soaking liquor through a fine sieve or muslin, then reserve. Wash the morels quickly under running water to remove as much sand as possible.

CHICKEN AND MUSHROOMS: Season the chicken breasts with salt and pepper. In a frying pan on a medium heat, foam the butter. Caramelise the chicken breasts for 2 minutes on each side and reserve on a

small tray. Cook the morels and the button mushrooms in the same pan for 1 minute, add the boiled wine, morel juice and double cream and bring to the boil, then lower the heat to simmering point. Return the chicken to the pan and finish cooking for 6 minutes with the lid on.

LEEKS: While the chicken is cooking bring the water, salt, pepper and butter to the boil, add the sliced leeks, cover with a lid and cook on full heat for 3-4 minutes.

TO SERVE: Place the chicken on a serving dish and reduce the sauce until it has acquired both texture and richness. Taste and correct the seasoning if required. Pour the morel sauce over the chicken and either spoon the leeks around or serve them separately.

ARMAND SABLON
BISTRO K

TOBY FLOOD
LEICESTER TIGERS & ENGLAND

↘ SEABASS,
GREEN ASPARAGUS SAUCE VIERGE
BY ARMAND SABLON / SERVES 4

"THIS DISH REMINDS ME OF THE SOUTH OF FRANCE."

INGREDIENTS

ASPARGUS:
- 20 asparagus spears
- salt, to taste
- butter, as needed

POTATOES:
- 12 large new potatoes
- salt, to taste
- 100g butter
- 1 bunch chives, chopped

SAUCE VIERGE:
- 200ml olive oil
- 2 tomatoes, chopped
- 30 black olives
- 4 chopped chives
- juice of 1 lemon
- salt, to taste

SEABASS:
- 4 wild seabass fillets, scaled and pin boned
- vegetable oil, as needed

METHOD

ASPARAGUS: Peel the asparagus, cook in boiling salted water and cool in iced water. Then trim the asparagus and heat up in a little water and butter.

POTATOES: Peel the potatoes, place in cold salted water and bring to the boil. Simmer until cooked.

Once cooked, drain and crush with a fork, add the butter and chives, then mix and check the seasoning.

SAUCE VIERGE: Put the olive oil into a bowl, add the tomatoes, olives, chopped chives, the juice of one lemon and a pinch of salt, then mix.

SEABASS: Place a little vegetable oil into a pan, add the sea bass fillets and cook till crisp and golden brown.

TO SERVE: Place the crushed potatoes in the centre of the plate, arrange the asparagus on the potato with the sea bass fillet on top and finish by sprinkling the dressing around the plate.

ASK A FISHMONGER TO SCALE AND PIN BONE THE FISH FILLETS
- ARMAND SABLON

↘ ROAST LAMB RACK,
CREAMY POLENTA, SWEET AND SOUR TOMATOES, LAMB JUS
BY ARMAND SABLON / SERVES 4

"THE COMBINATIONS OF THE DISH ALL GO TOGETHER."

PLANNING AHEAD

Marinate the tomatoes 24 hours in advance. Ask your butcher to French trim the lamb. Make the lamb jus 24 hours in advance.

INGREDIENTS

LAMB JUS:
- 1kg lamb bones and trimmings from the rack
- 1 onion, peeled
- 1 carrot, peeled
- 2 garlic cloves
- ½ bunch rosemary
- 1 stick celery
- 200ml white wine
- 500g chicken stock
- 500g veal stock

SWEET AND SOUR TOMATOES:
- 10 cherry tomatoes
- 100g honey
- 1 garlic clove
- 1 vanilla pod
- 1 tsp green anise or star anise
- 100ml sherry vinegar
- 2 tbsp olive oil

LAMB RACK:
- 2 racks of lamb French trimmed
- 30g butter

CREAMY POLENTA:
- 300g milk
- 100g water
- 50g butter
- 4g salt
- 100g polenta
- 20g grated parmesan
- 50g double cream

ROCKET:
- 200g rocket
- 1 tbsp olive oil

METHOD

LAMB JUS: Brown the bones in the oven till dark golden brown at 180°C for approximately 2 hours.

Cut the vegetables into a mirepoix. Place the bones in a large pan, add the wine, mirepoix and rosemary, then fill with the stock, bring to the boil, skim the fat off and ice the stock if needed. Then cook for 24 hours and pass through a strainer.

SWEET AND SOUR TOMATOES: Cut out the eye of the tomatoes and cross the bottom, place in boiling, salted water for 10 seconds, then place in iced water. Once cooled, take out and peel off the tomato skins.

Bring the rest of the ingredients to the boil, take off the hob, add the tomatoes and leave to marinate for 24 hours. Remove the tomatoes, reduce the marinade to a glaze and then roll the tomatoes in the glaze to cover.

LAMB RACK: Pre-heat the oven to 200°C. Season the lamb, in a pan seal in butter to colour all around and cook in the oven for 8 minutes. Leave to rest for 15 minutes. Place back in the oven for 3 minutes to heat up, then carve the meat between each bone.

CREAMY POLENTA: Bring the milk, water, butter and salt to the boil then add the polenta and whisk until stiff. Cover with cling film and leave to cool. Put into a blender, add the parmesan and cream and blitz. Then place into a pan and heat up.

ROCKET: Heat up the oil in a pan and toss the rocket through the oil to wilt it.

TO SERVE: Take a spoon, put the creamy polenta purée on the plate, place the rocket in one corner and the tomatoes in a line on one side of the plate. Then place the lamb on the rocket and drizzle the jus around.

FAVOURITE RUGBY MEMORY:
❝ **PLAYING IN THE 2007 WORLD CUP FINAL FOR ENGLAND. IT'S ONE OF THE GREATEST ACHIEVEMENTS, BUT AT THE SAME TIME WE LOST AND IT WILL ALWAYS BE A BITTERSWEET FEELING** ❞
- TOBY FLOOD

↘ CRAB SALAD,
AVOCADO PUREE
BY ARMAND SABLON / SERVES 4

"THIS IS A LIGHT LOW-FAT DISH WHICH BRINGS OUT THE BEST OF THE SUMMER INGREDIENTS."

METHOD

CRAB MIX: Pick the crab meat to remove any shell.

Place the tomatoes in boiling salted water for 10 seconds and then put in iced water. Peel the skins, deseed and dice.

Peel the celery and cut into a small dice.

Then place the crab, tomato, celery and basil leaves into a bowl, add the juice of one lemon and 80ml of olive oil and mix, adding salt and pepper to taste.

AVOCADO PUREE: Peel the avocado, remove the stone and place the flesh into a blender, add the juice of one lemon, blitz to a smooth purée and then season to taste

ASPARAGUS (OPTIONAL): Peel the asparagus and tie into two bundles, then blanch in salted boiling water until tender (1 minute), then place in iced water to cool. Once cooled, take out and cut so that you have 12 spears 5cm long.

TO SERVE: Place the crab mix into a ring in the centre of the plate, place a spoonful of the purée on top, put the salad leaves into a bowl and dress with the remaining 20ml of olive oil and place around the crab with the asparagus spears on top.

IF MAKING THE PUREE BEFOREHAND ADD LEMON JUICE TO STOP IT DISCOLOURING
- ARMAND SABLON

SPECIAL EQUIPMENT
Blender.

INGREDIENTS

CRAB MIX:
- 200g white crab meat
- 2 plum tomatoes
- 1 stick celery
- 4 leaves basil, chopped
- juice of 1 lemon
- 100ml olive oil
- salt and pepper, to taste

AVOCADO PUREE:
- 1 ripe avocado
- juice of 1 lemon
- salt and pepper, to taste

ASPARAGUS (OPTIONAL):
- 12 spears English asparagus

TO SERVE:
- 100g salad leaves

↘ APPLE TATIN,
CALVADOS CREME FRAICHE
BY ARMAND SABLON / SERVES 4

"THIS IS A CLASSIC AND ONE OF MY FAVOURITE FRENCH DISHES."

METHOD

PUFF PASTRY: First make the puff pastry by sifting together the flour and the salt. Stir in enough of the water to make a soft dough, wrap in cling film and chill for 20 minutes.

Put the butter between two pieces of greaseproof paper and flatten out with a rolling pin until it is a rectangle 10cm x 7.5cm.

Unwrap th pastry dough and roll out the dough to another rectangle that measures 12.5cm x 25cm.

Take the butter out of the paper and put on the dough rectangle. Bring the corners of the dough together to make an envelope. Chill for 10 minutes.

Roll out the envelope on a floured surface to make a rectangle that is three times longer than it is wide. Fold one-third into the middle and then the other third on top. Seal the edges lightly with a rolling pin and turn the pastry 90 degrees. Repeat this and chill for 30 minutes.

Repeat this again, rolling and folding twice more and then chill for another 30 minutes and then do two more – the pastry will have been rolled and folded six times altogether.

Now roll out and use as required. It is important that the pastry is well chilled otherwise it will become greasy and tough when baked. Also the butter might come through the surface. If this happens, dab on a little flour.

APPLE TATIN: Peel the apples and leave to dry. Take the sugar and caramelise in a pan, add the butter and whisk in, then pour onto an oiled tray and leave to set. Then break up.

Pre-heat the oven to 200°C. Take the tatin mould, add 80g of caramel to it and melt in the oven. Then take the dry apples and cut into four pieces, removing the core, and place around the pan. Then add the puff pastry, fold the edges down, make a hole in the centre and brush with clarified butter. Place in the oven and cook for 40 minutes, pushing the pastry down every 10 minutes. Then take out and turn out.

CALVADOS CREME: Mix all the ingredients together.

CARAMEL SAUCE: Caramelise the sugar, once golden brown add the cream to stop cooking, bring to the boil and then cool.

TO SERVE: Serve with the Calvados crème and caramel sauce on the side.

SPECIAL EQUIPMENT
Non-stick frying pan, tatin mould 30cm in diameter.

PLANING AHEAD
The pastry will need to be started at least 3½ hours in advance.

INGREDIENTS

PUFF PASTRY:
- 225g plain flour
- pinch of salt
- 150ml cold water
- 150g butter

APPLE TATIN:
- 4 Braeburn apples
- 100g all butter puff pastry
- 80g caster sugar
- 40g butter
- clarified butter, as needed

CALVADOS CREME:
- 200g crème fraîche
- Calvados, to taste
- Icing sugar, to taste

CARAMEL SAUCE:
- 100g sugar
- 100ml double cream

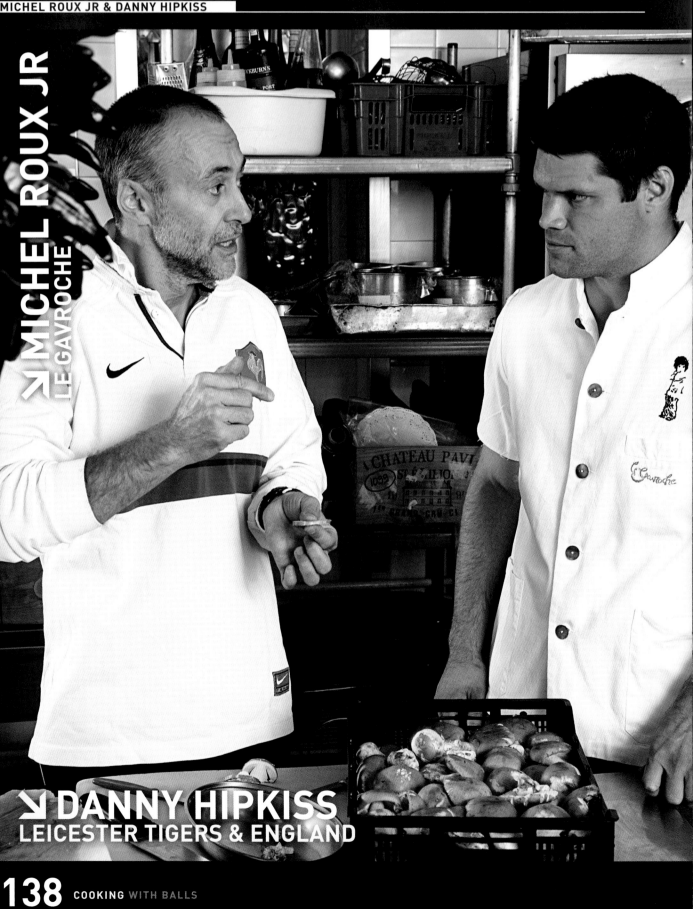

MICHEL ROUX JR
LE GAVROCHE

DANNY HIPKISS
LEICESTER TIGERS & ENGLAND

EAT AFTER A MATCH:
FISH AND CHIPS
FOLLOWED BY ICE
CREAM – IT'S THE
ONLY TIME OUR
NUTRITIONIST WILL
LET US GET AWAY
WITH IT!
-DANNY HIPKISS

↘ SOUFFLE SUISSESSE
BY MICHEL ROUX JR / SERVES 4

METHOD

SOUFFLE: Preheat the oven to 200ºC.

Melt the butter in a thick-based saucepan, whisk in the flour and cook, stirring continuously, for about 1 minute.

Whisk in the milk and boil for 3 minutes, whisking all the time to prevent any lumps from forming. Beat in the yolks and remove from the heat, then season with salt and pepper. Cover with a piece of buttered greaseproof paper to prevent a skin from forming.

Whisk the egg whites with a pinch of salt until they form firm, not stiff, peaks. Add a third of the egg whites to the yolk mixture and beat with a whisk until evenly mixed, then gently fold in the remaining egg whites. Spoon the mixture into four well-buttered 8cm diameter tartlet moulds and place in the oven for 3 minutes, until the tops begin to turn golden.

TO SERVE: Season the cream with a little salt, warm it gently and pour into a gratin dish. Turn the soufflés out into the cream, sprinkle the grated cheese over the soufflés, then return to the oven for 5 minutes. Serve immediately.

SPECIAL EQUIPMENT
4 x 8cm tartlet moulds.

INGREDIENTS

SOUFFLE:
- 45g butter
- 45g plain flour
- 500ml milk
- 5 egg yolks
- salt and freshly ground white pepper
- 6 egg whites

TO SERVE:
- 600ml double cream
- 200g Gruyère or Emmental cheese, grated

↘ SPAGHETTI WITH RAZOR CLAMS,
PARSLEY AND GARLIC
BY MICHEL ROUX JR / SERVES 4

METHOD

Rinse the razor clams in cold water. Finely chop the shallots and sweat in a large saucepan with half a tablespoon of olive oil. Add the clams and turn up the heat. Pour in the wine and cover tightly. After 3 or 4 minutes shake the pan and check the clams. The exact time they take to cook will depend on the variety used.

As soon as all the clams are open, take the pan off the heat – they go chewy if overcooked. Drain into a colander set over a bowl so you collect all the juices. Pick out the flesh of the clams – leave a few in their shells for decoration – and remove the little sand bag or intestine at the base of each meaty mollusc. Pass the cooking juices through a fine sieve and boil until reduced by half.

Cook the pasta in plenty of boiling, salted water, drain and put back in the pan. In another pan reheat the clams in the reduced juice and add the remaining oil, parsley, garlic and chillis. Pour this mixture into the drained pasta and toss everything together. Season to taste.

TO SERVE: Decorate each bowl with some clams in the shell and serve immediately.

INGREDIENTS

- 1kg fresh live razor clams
- 2 shallots
- 4 tbsp olive oil
- 200ml dry white wine
- 300g dried spaghetti
- 1 bunch of flat-leaf parsley, chopped
- 2 garlic cloves, peeled and chopped
- 1 or 2 red chillis to taste, chopped
- salt and pepper, to taste

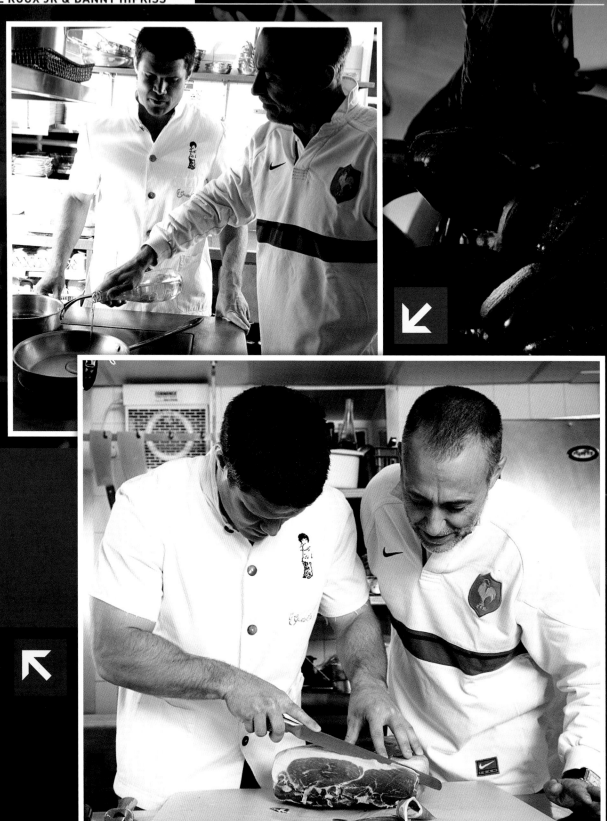

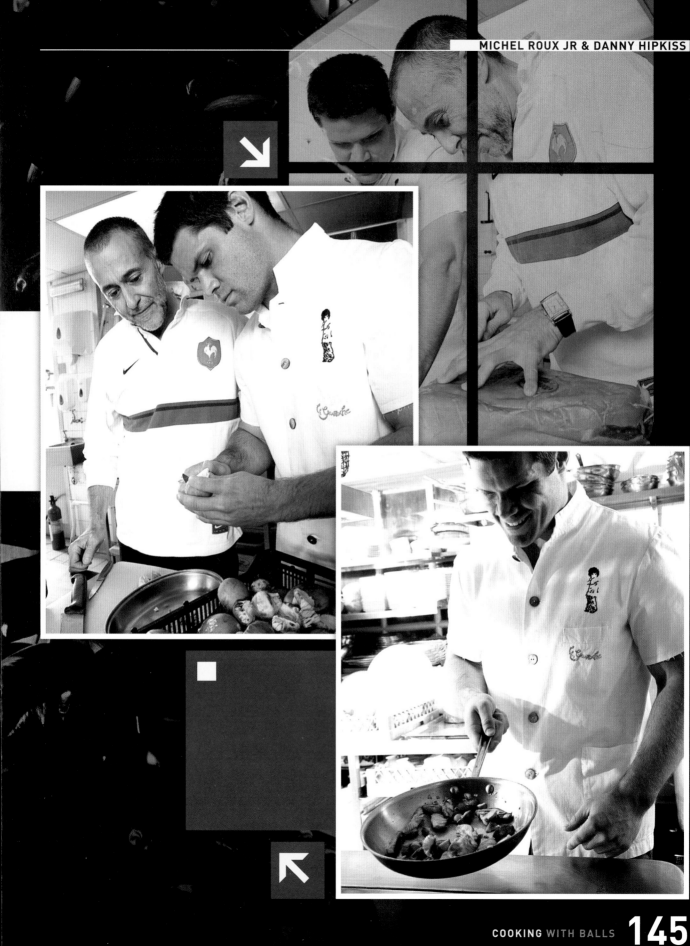

↘ BLACK BREAM
COOKED IN ITS MARINADE
BY MICHEL ROUX JR / SERVES 6

METHOD

Rinse the fish, dry with kitchen towels and remove the pin bones using a pair of tweezers.

Peel the onion, carrot and fennel. Slice the onion into thin rings. Make five cuts down the length of the carrot with a canelle knife, then slice the carrot into thin flower-shaped rounds. Slice the fennel thinly lengthwise.

Put the wine, water, vinegar, fruit juices, sugar and cumin seeds in a saucepan, bring to the boil and season with a little sea salt and pepper. Add the vegetables, stir and remove from the heat, then cover and leave to cool completely.

Lay the fish flat in an ovenproof glass or earthenware dish.

Pour on the cold marinade and the olive oil, cover and refrigerate for 6-12 hours.

TO SERVE: Preheat the oven to 190ºC. Scatter the parsley over the fish, cover with greaseproof paper and cook for 12 minutes; it should be somewhat undercooked and just warm.

SPECIAL EQUIPMENT
Tweezers, canelle knife.

PLANNING AHEAD
For the marinade allow 6-12 hours.

INGREDIENTS
- 6 x 120-150g fillets of black bream
- 1 onion
- 1 carrot
- 1 fennel bulb
- 125ml dry white wine
- 60ml water
- 1 tbsp white wine vinegar
- juice of ½ orange
- juice of ½ lemon
- 1 tsp demerara sugar
- 1 tsp cumin seeds
- sea salt and coarsely ground pepper
- 3 tbsp strong, fragrant olive oil

TO SERVE:
- small sprigs of flat-leaved parsley

↘ CHOCOLATE MOUSSE
WITH ORANGES AND WHISKY
BY MICHEL ROUX JR / SERVES 8-10

METHOD

ORANGE SEGMENTS: Douse the orange segments with Drambuie and leave to marinate in the fridge for at least 2 hours. Drain and keep the liquid to soak the genoise. Serve the oranges with the mousse.

CHOCOLATE GENOISE: Preheat the oven to 190°C. Whisk the eggs with the sugar in a double boiler, or a bowl over a pan of simmering water, until stiff, pale and tepid. Take off the heat then fold in the melted butter, sifted flour and cocoa powder.

Butter a 22cm round tin. Pour in the mixture and bake for 18 minutes or until a knife comes out clean. Take out of the tin and leave to cool on a wire rack. When cool, trim the cake and cut it in half through the middle. Place one half into a 20cm ring and pour over the reserved liquid from the orange garnish (see above), allowing any excess to drain then place the soaked genoise, still in its ring, onto a tray. Set aside. Freeze the other half for another time.

CHOCOLATE MOUSSE: To make an Italian meringue whisk the egg whites until stiff. Dissolve the sugar in the water and bring to the boil. Skim and continue to cook until it reaches 120°C. Gently pour the sugar mixture onto the whisked egg whites, while continuing to whisk – this is best done with a machine. Keep on whisking until the mixture is cool and very smooth.

In a separate bowl beat the butter, egg yolks and cocoa powder until light, then mix in the orange peel, whisky and melted chocolates. Finally, fold in the Italian meringue. Pour this onto the chocolate genoise that has been soaked in the liquid from the orange garnish. Smooth the surface and refrigerate for at least 2 hours before glazing or freeze for 1 hour. Remove the ring from the mousse and pour over the glaze (method below) to cover the mousse completely.

CHOCOLATE GLAZE: Mix the cream, glucose, oil and water in a pan and bring to the boil. Whisk in the chocolate and bring back to the boil. Leave to cool.

TO SERVE: Plate up as pictured.

SPECIAL EQUIPMENT
Thermometer, 22cm round tin, 20cm ring.

PLANNING AHEAD
Refrigerate the chocolate mousse for at least 2 hours before glazing or freeze for 1 hour.

INGREDIENTS

ORANGE SEGMENTS:
- 6 oranges, peeled and segmented
- approx 60ml of Drambuie

CHOCOLATE GENOISE:
- 4 eggs
- 125g caster sugar
- 25g butter, melted
- 125g flour, sifted
- 25g cocoa powder

CHOCOLATE MOUSSE:
- 6 egg whites
- 125ml water
- 325g caster sugar
- 250g butter
- 6 egg yolks
- 50g cocoa powder
- 1 tbsp finely chopped orange peel confit
- 50ml whisky
- 125g extra-bitter chocolate, melted
- 125g milk chocolate, melted

CHOCOLATE GLAZE:
- 250ml double cream
- 150g liquid glucose
- 1 tbsp vegetable oil
- 1 tbsp water
- 200g extra-bitter chocolate, broken up into pieces

YOU CAN ALSO DECORATE WITH ORANGE CRISPS. SLICE AN ORANGE AS THINLY AS POSSIBLE. DUST THE SLICES WITH ICING SUGAR, PLACE BETWEEN TWO SHEETS OF BAKING PARCHMENT AND PUT IN A COOL OVEN (100°C) TO DRY.
- MICHEL ROUX JR

GALTON BLACKISTON
MORSTON HALL HOTEL & RESTAURANT

↘ GRILLED WILD SEA BASS
WITH SAUTEED WILD MUSHROOMS AND CHIVE BEURRE BLANC
BY GALTON BLACKISTON / SERVES 6

INGREDIENTS

CHIVE BEURRE BLANC:
- 2 shallots, peeled and finely sliced
- 1 tbsp white wine vinegar
- 2 tbsp lemon juice
- 4 tbsp white wine
- 1 tbsp cold water
- 225g salted butter, cut into cubes

SEABASS:
- 1kg-1.4kg seabass, descaled, pin bones removed and cut into four fillets
- salt and pepper
- olive oil to brush the skin of the fish

SAUTEED WILD MUSHROOMS:
- olive (or truffle) oil for frying
- 225g wild mushrooms
- 2 tbsp Madeira (optional)
- 2 tbsp finely chopped parsley (optional)
- salt and pepper

TO SERVE:
- plenty of finely snipped chives

METHOD

CHIVE BEURRE BLANC: Place the finely sliced shallots, wine vinegar, lemon juice and white wine in a saucepan. Bring to the boil and reduce the liquid until you have about 2 tbsp. Add the cold water and reduce again until you have 1 tablespoon of liquid.

Turn the heat down and, over a low heat, slowly whisk in the butter, about 25g at a time. The sauce will emulsify (thicken and lighten in colour). Once all the butter has been added, remove the pan from the heat, then pass the sauce through a sieve into another saucepan. Set aside until needed, but do not refrigerate or the sauce will separate.

SEABASS: Preheat the grill to high.

Score the skin of the sea bass fillets, being careful not to cut too deeply into the flesh.

Season the flesh side of the fish, then arrange, skin-side up on a tray and place on the grill pan. Brush the scored skin with the oil, and place the fillets under the preheated grill.

Cook for approximately 4 minutes or until the skin has blackened and the flesh is just cooked.

SAUTEED WILD MUSHROOMS: Heat a frying pan on a high heat and when really hot add a good splash of oil and very briefly sauté the wild mushrooms adding the Madeira and parsley (if using), and check the seasoning.

TO SERVE: Gently reheat the sauce, stirring continuously and add the finely snipped chives. Serve the sea bass with the sautéed wild mushrooms and sauce.

↘ PORK BELLY

WITH PAN-FRIED LANGOUSTINE AND LUXURY MASHED POTATO

BY GALTON BLACKISTON / SERVES 8

ASK YOUR BUTCHER TO SCORE THE SKIN OF THE PORK BELLY FOR YOU

- GALTON BLACKISTON

FAVOURITE RUGBY MOMENT: ❝ SCORING THE WINNING TRY FOR ENGLAND AGAINST AUSTRALIA IN SYDNEY 2010 ❞
- BEN YOUNGS

SPECIAL EQUIPMENT

Mixer with 'K' beater.

PLANNING AHEAD

This dish needs to be started a day in advance but it's simple and delicious – make sure you get the crackling really crisp. The mashed potatoes can also be made in advance and carefully reheated.

INGREDIENTS

PORK BELLY:

- 1½kg piece of boned pork belly, skin on and trimmed, around 175g per person
- vegetable or olive oil for frying
- 2 carrots, peeled and chopped
- 4 celery sticks, chopped
- 1 onion, peeled and roughly chopped
- 3 cloves of garlic, roughly chopped
- 1 leek, sliced
- 6 ripe tomatoes, quartered
- 1 small bunch of thyme
- 1 small bunch of rosemary
- 1 bay leaf
- 1 litre (approx) chicken stock
- salt, to taste

PAN-FRIED LANGOUSTINE:

- olive oil for frying
- 8 shelled langoustine
- salt and pepper, to taste

LUXURY MASHED POTATOES:

- 900g potatoes, peeled and cut into large chunks
- 225g salted butter
- 150ml milk
- 150ml double cream
- salt and pepper

METHOD

PORK BELLY: Soak the pork belly in cold water for about an hour.

Preheat the oven to 140°C.

Remove the pork from the water, dry well and then season all over with salt. Heat a heavy-bottomed roasting tin over a high heat and when it is hot add some oil. Gently place the pork belly skin-side down in the pan, taking care because the oil may spit a little.

Cook for 5-8 minutes or until the skin has a nice colour, then turn the joint over and cook for another 5 minutes or until the meat is golden brown. Transfer the joint to a wire rack, placing it skin-side up.

Keep the roasting tin on the stove over a medium heat, and add the carrots, celery, onion, garlic and leek (you may need

to add a little more oil). Cook until well coloured, then add the tomatoes and cook until soft. Place the pork belly skin-side up on the vegetables. Add the herbs and chicken stock and bring to the boil.

Cover the roasting tin with foil and carefully place in the preheated oven. Cook for 3-3½ hours. Check the meat is done by piercing it in the middle with the tip of a sharp knife – it should slide in effortlessly. Remove the meat from the roasting tin and place onto a clean tray, place another tray on top and a weight on top of that. When cool, cover and place in the fridge, and leave overnight.

Drain the cooking liquid through a colander and then pass through a sieve lined with muslin into a heavy saucepan. Simmer until reduced by about half, skimming frequently. Season this sauce with salt if necessary, and set aside.

When ready to serve, preheat the oven to 200°C.

Remove the skin from the pork belly, taking a little of the fat beneath and leaving a good layer of fat attached to the meat. Rub some salt on both sides of the skin and place on a roasting tray and into the top of the preheated oven and cook (watching carefully) until well coloured and crisp. Set the crackling aside on kitchen paper and keep warm.

Cut the belly into portions. Heat a heavy-based pan over a high heat, add a little oil and carefully place the pieces of pork belly fat-side down into the pan to seal and colour well, then turn to seal and colour well on all sides. Remove from the

pan and place fat-side up on a trivet in a roasting tin. Transfer to the oven to cook for 6 minutes.

PAN-FRIED LANGOUSTINE: Heat a heavy-based frying pan till hot, add a splash of olive oil and fry the langoustine for about 30 seconds on each side, then season with salt and pepper.

LUXURY MASHED POTATOES: Place the potatoes into a pan of cold salted water and bring to the boil.

Place the butter, milk and cream into another saucepan.

When the potatoes are cooked, drain and return to the pan. Place the pan back on the heat to dry the potatoes to a 'floury' texture – keep shaking the pan over the heat.

Meanwhile, heat the butter, milk and cream to just below simmering point.

Pass the potatoes through a mouli or sieve into the bowl of a food mixer with a 'K' beater attachment. Turn on the machine and slowly add the hot butter, milk and cream. Continue to beat until you have a really smooth mixture (you may not need to use all the hot liquid depending on what consistency you are looking for). Season with salt and pepper.

TO SERVE: Reheat the sauce. Place some mashed potatoes into the centre of a plate and place a piece of the pork belly on top. Break off pieces of crackling and place over the pork belly. Spoon a little of the sauce over and around, and add one or two langoustines. Serve the remaining sauce in a jug.

↘ VEGETABLE SALAD
BY GALTON BLACKISTON / SERVES 8

"THE FOLLOWING VEGETABLES ARE A SUGGESTION FOR THIS SALAD DEPENDING ON WHAT IS AVAILABLE AND YOUR PERSONAL PREFERENCE. QUANTITIES WILL REALLY DEPEND ON HOW MANY PEOPLE YOU ARE SERVING. THE SALAD IS GOOD SERVED WITH SOME OF THE VEGETABLES STILL A BIT WARM."

METHOD

VEGETABLE SALAD: Place the beetroot into cold salted water, bring to the boil and cook until very soft, drain, slice thinly and place into a large bowl.

Do the same with the potatoes and the carrots, but cook these till just tender and then place into the bowl with the beetroot.

Drop the broad beans into salted boiling water and blanch for about 3 minutes, immediately refresh under cold running water and then slip off the skins and add to the bowl.

The French beans should also be dropped into salted boiling water and cooked until just tender before being refreshed under cold running water, drained thoroughly and added to the other vegetables.

Next drop the shelled peas into a pan of boiling salted water and cook for a few minutes until just tender, drain thoroughly and add to the bowl.

Slice the radishes thinly and add to the other salad ingredients.

Add enough dressing to lightly coat all the salad ingredients in the bowl and season with salt and pepper, mixing carefully with your hands. Set aside.

Preheat the grill to high, place the pancetta or bacon slices onto a tray and grill till crisp, then set aside on kitchen paper.

Place the eggs into a saucepan and add enough cold water to just cover. Bring the water up to simmering point and boil for 5 minutes.

While the eggs are boiling place the lettuce leaves into a bowl and add just enough dressing to glisten.

DRESSING: Whisk the vinegar, salt, pepper and garlic in a bowl. Continue whisking while slowly pouring in the olive oil. Set aside.

TO SERVE: Place some dressed leaves into the centre of each plate and spoon a generous serving of vegetables over the leaves. Place some crisp pancetta on top of the vegetables.

Peel the boiled eggs, remove the white of the egg and top the salad with a softly boiled egg yolk.

Drizzle over a little more dressing if desired and serve immediately.

CHEF'S TIP: An alternative way to cook the eggs would be to boil them for 5 minutes ahead of time, refresh under cold running water to stop them cooking, then peel and remove the egg whites. When ready to serve briefly plunge the yolks into boiling water to heat through and then lift out using a slotted spoon. The idea, though, is to serve a soft yolk.

INGREDIENTS

VEGETABLE SALAD:
- 2 young raw beetroot
- 500g baby new potatoes, freshly dug and scraped
- 250g new season's baby carrots, scraped
- 500g broad beans, shelled
- 500g French beans, trimmed
- 500g fresh garden peas, shelled
- 1 bunch radishes
- salt and pepper
- 8 slices of pancetta or smoked streaky bacon
- 8 pullet's egg
- 1 young oak leaf lettuce

DRESSING:
- 2 tbsp red wine vinegar
- sea salt, to taste
- black pepper, to taste
- 2 garlic cloves, peeled and finely chopped
- 175ml extra virgin olive oil

↘ STRAWBERRY SOUFFLE
WITH VANILLA ICE CREAM
BY GALTON BLACKISTON / SERVES 12

THIS STUNNING SOUFFLE IS EASY TO MAKE AND MOST OF THE WORK CAN BE DONE WELL IN ADVANCE.

SPECIAL EQUIPMENT
Ice cream machine, 12 ramekins, sugar thermometer.

PLANNING AHEAD
You can make the soufflé base mixture well in advance and store in the fridge, but bring back to room temperature before starting to prepare the dish.

INGREDIENTS

STRAWBERRY PUREE:
- 750g strawberries

STRAWBERRY SOUFFLE:
- softened butter, as needed
- caster sugar, as needed
- 500ml strawberry purée
- 40g cornflour
- water, as needed
- 70g caster sugar

MERINGUE:
- 7 egg whites
- 250g caster sugar
- icing sugar for dusting

VANILLA POD ICE CREAM:
- 2 vanilla pods
- 570ml double cream
- 275ml milk
- 10 egg yolks
- 225g caster sugar

TO SERVE:
- 300ml pouring cream

METHOD

STRAWBERRY PUREE: Place the strawberries into the food processor, purée until smooth and pass though a fine sieve.

STRAWBERRY SOUFFLE: Butter the ramekins and place them in the fridge. When they have cooled, repeat the process and sprinkle caster sugar inside the ramekins, shake to cover the sides, then return to the fridge again.

To make the soufflé base mixture place the strawberry purée into a saucepan and over a moderate heat bring to the boil.

In a small bowl mix the cornflour with enough water to make a thick cream consistency. Whisk the cornflour mixture into the hot strawberry purée and, over a gentle heat, stir continuously for 5 minutes – the mixture will thicken to a béchamel-type sauce.

Meanwhile place the caster sugar and 3 tablespoons water into another saucepan and, over a low heat, allow the sugar to dissolve. Turn up the heat and bring to the boil. Continue to boil till the sugar mixture reaches 116°C (soft ball stage) – use a sugar thermometer if you have one.

Pour the hot sugar mixture into the hot strawberry purée and continue to cook. Stir for a further 5 minutes, pass through a sieve into a large bowl and allow to cool.

MERINGUE: Preheat the oven to 200°C.

Whisk the egg whites in a food mixer at high speed till they form soft peaks. Still whisking, slowly add the caster sugar. Then, using a slotted metal spoon,

vigorously beat one-third of the egg whites into the soufflé base mixture before carefully folding in the remainder.

Fill the ramekins with the mixture, levelling it off with a palette knife. Then run your thumb around the edge of each ramekin (this is important as it helps the soufflés to rise straight up). Place on a baking tray and cook on the top shelf of the oven for 8-10 minutes, by which time the soufflés will have risen dramatically.

Dust with icing sugar.

VANILLA POD ICE CREAM: Cut the vanilla pods in half lengthways using a sharp knife and scrape the vanilla seeds into a saucepan. Add the cream, milk and the vanilla pods and, stirring frequently, bring slowly to the boil. Remove from the heat and leave to infuse.

Meanwhile, place the egg yolks and sugar in a large bowl and whisk well with a hand-held electric whisk. Remove the vanilla pods and, while continuing to whisk the egg yolks and sugar, add the infused cream and milk to create a light custard.

Pass the custard through a sieve, add back to the saucepan and stir continuously over a low heat until the custard thickens sufficiently to coat the back of a spoon. Be cautious as you do this, as even heating the mixture a fraction too much will cause it to curdle. If, however, it does curdle you can usually retrieve it by whizzing it up on the highest speed setting in a blender. The consistency will be thinner, but usable.

Finally, pass the custard through a sieve and allow to cool completely before churning to a soft consistency in an ice cream machine. Serve immediately, or freeze in an air-tight container.

TO SERVE: At the table, make a hole in the centre of each soufflé and pour in some purée to serve. Add a scoop of vanilla pod ice cream.

GEORDAN MURPHY
LEICESTER TIGERS & IRELAND

SAT BAINS
RESTAURANT SAT BAINS

↘ ROE DEER,
CELERIAC, CHOCOLATE AND WATERCRESS
BY SAT BAINS / SERVES 5

PLANNING AHEAD
Allow 2 hours for cooking the roast onions.

INGREDIENTS

VENISON BURGER:
- 100g loin of venison, minced
- 50g diced shallots
- ½ tsp chopped thyme
- ½ tsp chopped pine nuts

ROAST ONIONS:
- 1 sliced Spanish onions
- butter, as needed
- sunflower oil, as needed

CARAMELISED CELERIAC PUREE:
- 25g shallots
- butter, as needed
- sunflower oil, as needed
- 125g diced celeriac
- white chicken stock, as needed

PICKLED CELERIAC:
- 25g white wine vinegar
- 25g sugar
- 50g shaved celeriac around 1mm thick

BEETROOT SAUCE:
- 50g butter
- 50g beetroot juice
- 25g damson vinegar

VENISON STEAKS:
- 5 x 175g venison steaks
- sunflower oil, as needed
- salt and cracked black pepper, to taste

TO SERVE:
- 1 fresh pear, cut into quarters and dusted with Szechuan pepper
- handful of watercress
- 100% chocolate, as needed

METHOD

VENISON BURGER: Mix all the ingredients together. Shape into burgers of approximately 25g each and set on a tray in the fridge to rest.

ROAST ONIONS: Sweat the onions in a little butter and oil for 2 hours on a very low heat until completely caramelised.

CARAMELISED CELERIAC PUREE: Sweat off the shallots in a little butter and oil for 2 minutes, add the celeriac and sauté for a further 2 minutes. Reduce the heat and gently cook the mix for around 1 hour until lightly caramelised. Deglaze with the stock and blitz to a fine purée.

PICKLED CELERIAC: Heat the vinegar with the sugar, cool and pour over the celeriac. Leave to stand until ready to use.

BEETROOT SAUCE: Heat the butter until it turns nut brown, add the beetroot juice and the vinegar. Leave to stand as a split dressing, taking care not to emulsify.

VENISON STEAKS: Preheat the oven to 160ºC. Heat the oil in a pan over a hot heat. Season the steaks with salt and pepper and sear both sides for 3 minutes. Then cook in the oven for 4 minutes then remove and leave to rest on a mesh rack in a warm place for 10 minutes.

TO SERVE: Cook the burger to your liking, place the onions on top and keep warm.

Place the celeriac purée on the plate followed by the venison steak. pear, and the burger.

Add a few shavings of pickled celeriac and drizzle the split sauce over and around the venison, top with watercress and finish by shaving 100% chocolate over the dish.

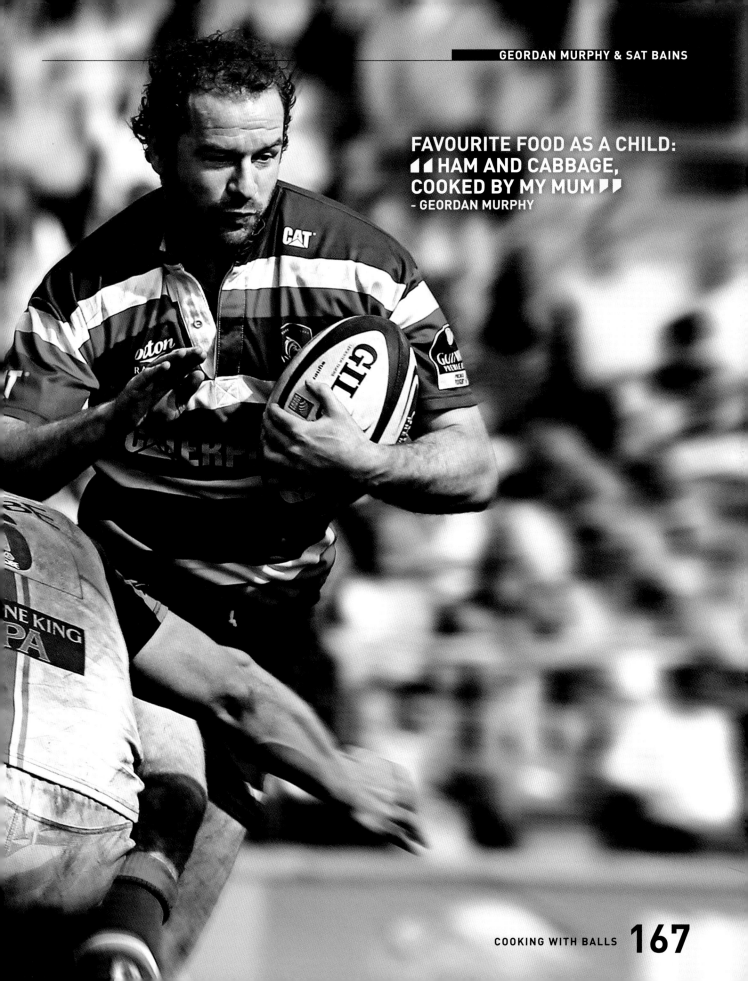

FAVOURITE FOOD AS A CHILD:
❝HAM AND CABBAGE,
COOKED BY MY MUM❞
- GEORDAN MURPHY

↘ SCALLOP
WITH PORK, APPLE AND CHORIZO
BY SAT BAINS / SERVES 10

SPECIAL EQUIPMENT
Pressure cooker, squeezy bottle.

PLANNING AHEAD
You will need to immerse the pork belly in salted water and leave for 6 hours.
The picked apple mixture needs to be left to stand overnight in the fridge until ready to use.

INGREDIENTS

CHORIZO JAM:
- 1 shallot, diced
- 50g chorizo
- 250ml apple juice
- 100g fresh apple, diced
- 50g sugar

PORK BELLY:
- 2kg pork belly
- salt, to taste

BLACK PUDDING BEIGNET:
- 200g black pudding
- 50g sultanas poached in apple juice
- 75g diced Granny Smith apples
- plain flour, as needed
- salt and pepper, to taste
- 2 beaten eggs
- 150g breadcrumbs

PICKLED APPLE:
- 2 Granny Smith apples, diced
- 100g apple vinegar
- 50g sugar, left to macerate overnight

APPLE PUREE:
- 100g Granny Smith apples, diced
- 100g Bramley apples, diced
- 100g apple juice
- 50g sugar

TO SERVE:
- sunflower oil, as needed
- 10 scallops
- lemon juice, to taste
- salt, to taste
- 10 slices of ham (shonka or bellotta)

METHOD

CHORIZO JAM: Sweat the shallot with the chorizo over a low heat before adding the rest of the ingredients. Continue to cook for approximately 10 minutes until the mixture has reached a firm but jellied consistency. Set aside to cool and reserve in an airtight jar.

PORK BELLY: Immerse the pork belly in salted water and leave for 6 hours. Wash thoroughly, removing all of the salt. Place in a pressure cooker and cook on full pressure for 45 minutes. When cooked place between two trays, weight the top and press for a minimum of 2 hours.

BLACK PUDDING BEIGNET: Blitz the black pudding to a purée and fold in the sultanas and diced apples. Shape the mixture into 10 balls and roll in seasoned flour, followed by beaten egg and then breadcrumbs. Set aside in the fridge until ready to use.

PICKLED APPLE: Mix all ingredients together and leave to stand overnight in the fridge until ready to use.

APPLE PUREE: Steam the apples for 10 minutes. Add the apple juice and sugar and blitz to a fine purée. Reserve in a squeezy bottle.

TO SERVE: Slice the pork belly and fry in a little sunflower oil, season and keep warm.

Warm the chorizo jam.

Roast the scallops and season with lemon juice and salt.

Place the apple purée on the plate, followed by the scallop and belly pork, top with the jam and the sliced ham.

Place the cubes of pickled apple around the plate and finish with the black pudding beignet.

LAST SUPPER:
❝STEAK AND CHIPS. KEENS STEAKHOUSE IN NEW YORK PREPARES THE BEST STEAK❞
- SAT BAINS

↘ WALDORF SALAD
1893 - 2010
BY SAT BAINS / SERVES 10

PLANNING AHEAD

You need to allow 6 hours to macerate the grapes in the wine.
Allow 6 hours for the celery panna cotta to set in the fridge.

INGREDIENTS

CELERY PANNA COTTA:
- 250g milk
- 250g double cream
- 1 head of celery, chopped
- 50g celery cress
- 2½ gelatine leaves

SULTANA PUREE:
- 200g sultanas
- fresh apple juice

POACHED SULTANAS:
- 200g sultanas
- fresh apple juice

GRAPES:
- 20 peeled grapes
- 1 litre Gewürztraminer wine

WALNUTS:
- 5 walnuts (one will cater for 2 portions)
- sunflower oil, as needed

TO SERVE:
- celery cress, as needed
- Granny Smith, freshly diced, as needed

METHOD

CELERY PANNA COTTA: Mix the milk with the cream and bring up to 80°C, add the celery and infuse for 30 minutes. Allow to cool and blitz the liquid with the celery cress. Pass through a fine muslin. Weigh out 500g of this juice. Add the gelatine while the liquid is still hot and stir to dissolve. Place in moulds and set in the fridge for 6 hours.

SULTANA PUREE: Cover the sultanas in the apple juice and bring to the boil. Simmer for 4 minutes and blitz to a purée. If the mix is too thick, loosen with a little more apple juice. Leave to stand.

POACHED SULTANAS: Cover the sultanas with the apple juice and leave to hydrate over a low heat until plump and juicy.

GRAPES: Cover the grapes in the wine and leave to macerate for 6 hours.

WALNUTS: Peel the walnuts and fry in fresh sunflower oil at 160°C until golden brown. These will be grated over the dish at the end.

TO SERVE: Place a panna cotta in the middle of a plate. Drizzle sultana purée around the side and scatter five poached sultanas and three grapes to decorate. Cover with celery cress and sprinkle with grated walnuts and the diced Granny Smith apple.

↘ CHOCOLATE FONDANT,
PEANUT BUTTER ICE CREAM AND CUMIN CARAMEL
BY SAT BAINS / SERVES 10

SPECIAL EQUIPMENT
Ice cream machine, thermometer.

PLANNING AHEAD
Leave the peanut butter ice cream mixture to stand in the fridge for 12 hours before pouring churning in an ice cream machine.

INGREDIENTS

CHOCOLATE FONDANT:
- 225g 70% chocolate
- 225g salted butter
- 10 eggs
- 225g sugar

PEANUT BUTTER ICE CREAM:
- 250g milk
- 250g double cream
- 100g egg yolks
- 40g sugar
- 150g salted peanuts

CUMIN CARAMEL:
- 100g sugar
- 150g double cream, warmed
- 2g ground cinnamon

TO SERVE:
- chopped salted peanuts
- coriander cress

METHOD

CHOCOLATE FONDANT: Melt the chocolate with the butter. Whisk the eggs with the sugar for 10 minutes, add the chocolate mixture and whisk further to emulsify. Place in a piping bag and pipe into oven-proof serving bowls to a depth of 2.5cm. Reserve in the fridge.

PEANUT BUTTER ICE CREAM: Mix the milk, cream, egg yolks and sugar together and heat to an approximate temperature of 86°C. Add the salted peanuts and blitz to a fine purée, strain and leave to stand in the fridge for 12 hours before churning in an ice cream machine to the correct consistency.

CUMIN CARAMEL: Caramelise the sugar by heating in a flat-bottomed pan until the crystals have dissolved and turned a golden brown. Add the cream followed by the spices and leave to infuse for 20 minutes, stirring occasionally. Strain and decant into a squeezy bottle, ensuring that the caramel stays at room temperature.

TO SERVE: Pre-heat the oven to 180°C then bake the fondant for 8 minutes. Remove and leave to rest for 2 minutes. Place a pile of chopped salted peanuts in the centre of the cooked fondant and squeeze some of the caramel over the top. Garnish with the ice cream and a little coriander cress.

BEN FODEN
NORTHAMPTON SAINTS & ENGLAND

↘ PAN ROAST FILLET OF TURBOT,
SMOKED EEL CANNELLONI, ALMONDS AND BUTTERMILK
BY PHIL THOMPSON / SERVES 4

"THIS DISH IS ON MY A LA CARTE MENU AT THE AUBERGE DU LAC AT THE MOMENT. I LOVE TURBOT (THE KING OF FISH) AND THE SMOKINESS OF THE EEL IN THE BACKGROUND SETS OFF THIS DISH."

METHOD

EEL CANNELLONI: Cut the crusts off the sliced bread and roll out with a rolling pin, then brush with the melted butter, Mix the eel, raisins, and parsley and almonds together. Place onto the slices of bread and roll into a tube, then place in the fridge – this will help the butter to set and stay together.

Just before serving gently roll the eel cannelloni in a hot frying pan until crispy.

CAULIFLOWER PUREE: Chop the cauliflower into small pieces, cover with the milk and simmer for 20 minutes. When soft, blend and season to taste.

TURBOT: In a frying pan on a medium heat, pour in the olive oil and gently place the turbot fillets into the pan. Cook for 2 minutes on either side until golden brown.

Gently warm the buttermilk, making sure not to allow it to boil.

TO SERVE: Spoon the cauliflower purée onto the bottom of the plate, then add the broad beans, put the fish on top and gently place the eel cannelloni behind. Sprinkle with the samphire and, with a hand blender, whip the buttermilk to make a froth and spoon over the top.

SPECIAL EQUIPMENT
Hand blender.

PLANNING AHEAD
You can make the cannelloni and the cauliflower purée the day before.

INGREDIENTS

EEL CANNELLONI:
- 4 slices brown bread
- 100g butter, melted
- 50g smoked eel, diced
- 30g golden raisins
- 1 tbsp parsley, chopped
- 20g almonds, toasted

CAULIFLOWER PUREE:
- 200g cauliflower
- 150ml milk
- salt and pepper, to taste

TURBOT:
- 2 tbsp olive oil
- 4 turbot fillets
- 250ml buttermilk

TO SERVE:
- 200g broad beans, blanched
- 100g samphire, sautéed

AT THE AUBERGE WE GARNISH THIS DISH WITH SOME GARLIC MILK JELLIES AND FRESH ALMONDS
- PHIL THOMPSON

↘ SHELLFISH TAGLIATELLE
WITH COURGETTE AND RAZOR CLAM
BY PHIL THOMPSON / SERVES 4

"BEN SAID HE LIKED ITALIAN FOOD SO BEING FROM THAT PART OF ITALY CALLED 'ESSEX' I CHOSE A SIMPLE DISH WHICH INCLUDES SOME OF MY FAVOURITE INGREDIENTS."

PLANNING AHEAD
Make the garlic butter the day before. You can also pre-cook and refresh the pasta.

INGREDIENTS

TAGLIATELLE:
- 10ml olive oil
- 2 shallots
- 2 garlic cloves, peeled and finely chopped
- 1kg razor clams
- 1kg clams or cockles
- 200ml white wine
- 2 courgettes, cut into thin spaghetti-type strips
- 100ml double cream
- 200g brown shrimps
- 2 tbsp parsley, finely chopped
- 500g tagliatelle, pre-cooked
- black pepper, to taste
- 30g butter, softened

TO SERVE:
- chive flowers
- parmesan
- lemon juice
- fresh bread

METHOD

TAGLIATELLE: Pour the olive oil into a hot deep saucepan, add the shallot and a clove of chopped garlic and stir, making sure not to burn, quickly add the razor clams, cockles or clams, still in the shell, to the pan.

Pour over the wine and cover with a lid, keeping the heat on full. The steam from the wine will help cook the shellfish and the shells will open – this should only take a minute. Remove the lid and carefully take out the razor clams, putting them to one side.

To the pan, add the strips of courgette and stir, then add the cream, shrimps and parsley and bring to the boil. Add the pre-cooked tagliatelle, a good twist of black pepper, mix and take off the heat.

Remove the soft bottom part of the razor clam and discard. Slice the body of the clam into rings and place back into the shell. Mix the remaining clove of garlic with the soft butter, spoon over the top and grill for 1 minute.

TO SERVE: Separate the tagliatelle into four bowls, making sure everyone has equal amounts of shellfish. Spoon over the shellfish juices and lemon juice, sprinkle with the chive flowers and shavings of parmesan. Finally, place the grilled razor clam on top and serve with the bread.

TRY TO BUY FRESH SHELLFISH IN ORDER TO ENHANCE THE FLAVOURS AND DON'T OVERCOOK THEM OR THEY WILL TURN RUBBERY
- PHIL THOMPSON

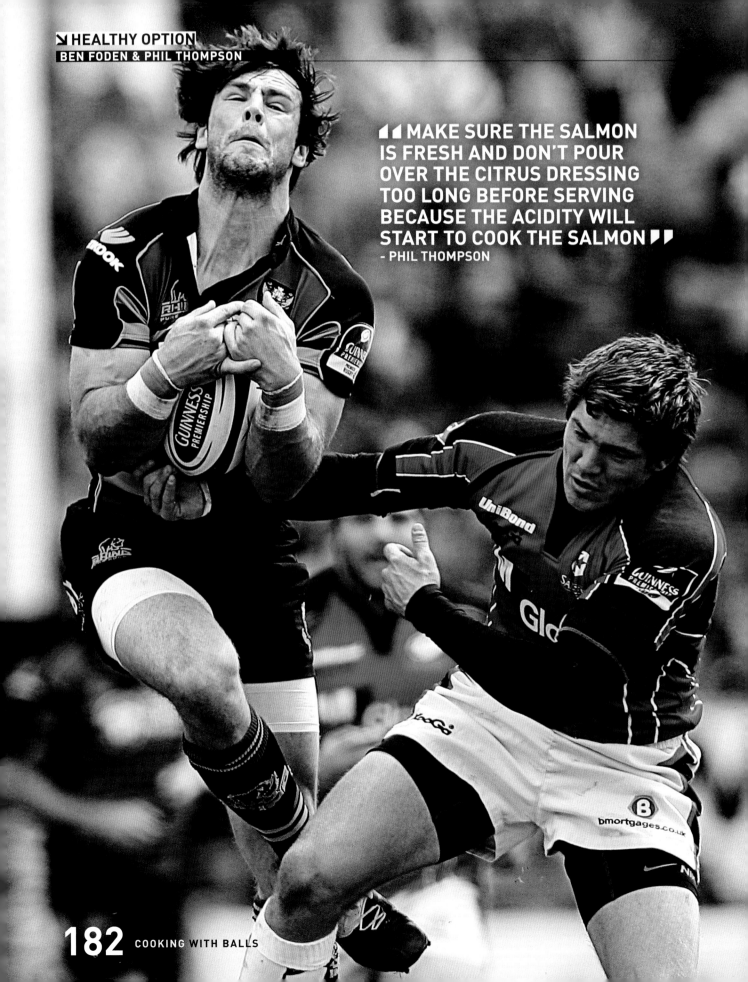

❝❝ MAKE SURE THE SALMON
IS FRESH AND DON'T POUR
OVER THE CITRUS DRESSING
TOO LONG BEFORE SERVING
BECAUSE THE ACIDITY WILL
START TO COOK THE SALMON ❞❞
- PHIL THOMPSON

⬂CITRUS MARINATED ORGANIC SALMON WITH BASIL

BY PHIL THOMPSON / SERVES 4

"THIS IS A LIGHT SUMMERY DISH WITH FRESH CLEAN FLAVOURS AND THE BASIL ADDS A TOUCH OF SWEETNESS, A FANTASTIC START TO ANY MEAL. IT WILL GET THE TASTE BUDS GOING IN NO TIME AT ALL!"

METHOD

Remove the skin from the salmon and, with a sharp knife, slice the fillet across into thin slivers.

With a knife peel all of the citrus fruit, making sure you take off all of the bitter white pith. Over a bowl, gently cut out the segments of the grapefruit, orange and lime, carefully catching the juices – you'll need these for the dressing. Slice the radishes into thin discs.

For the dressing, mix the citrus juice, olive oil and mustard together, and season to taste.

TO SERVE: Lay five or six slices of salmon onto the plate, just overlapping slightly. Place the mixed segments of fruit over and around, spoon over the dressing and garnish with the sliced radishes and basil.

INGREDIENTS

- 400g-500g fresh salmon fillet
- 1 pink grapefruit
- 2 orange
- 1 lime
- 1 bunch radishes
- 100ml citrus juice (from the above fruits)
- 10ml olive oil
- 10g whole grain mustard
- salt and pepper, to taste

TO SERVE:
- basil leaves

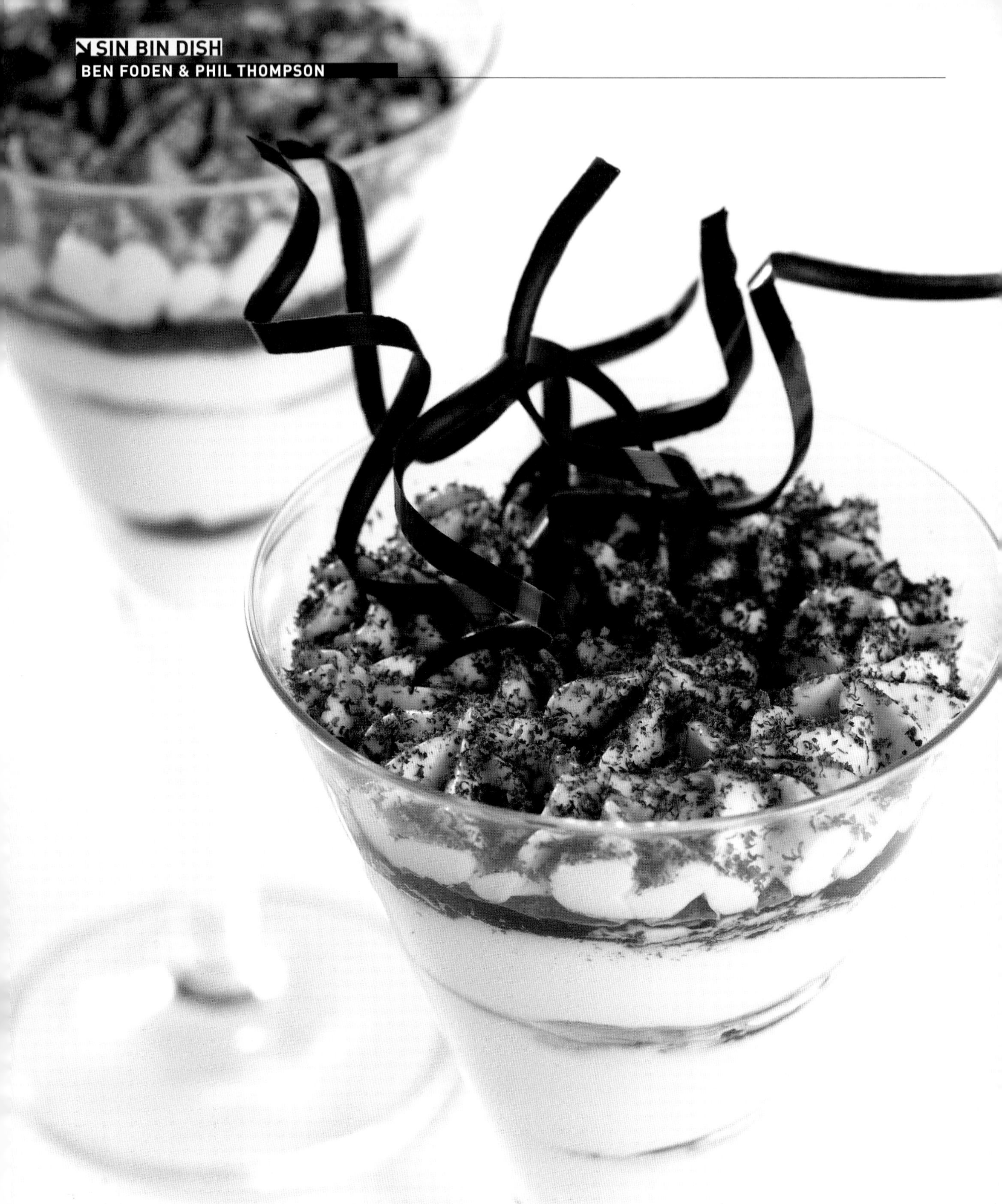

↘ TIRAMISU
WITH CHOCOLATE SPONGE AND PISTACHIO BISCOTTI
BY PHIL THOMPSON / SERVES 4

"A LIGHT BUT INDULGENT DESSERT THAT CAN BE MADE BOOZY OR ADAPTED TO YOUR OWN INDIVIDUAL FLAVOURS. HERE I'VE ADDED A CHOCOLATE SPONGE SOAKED IN COFFEE BUT YOU COULD USE CHOCOLATE LIQUOR FOR EXTRA NAUGHTINESS!"

METHOD

PISTACHIO BISCOTTI: Preheat the oven to 180°C.

In a food processor, chop the pistachios, lemon zest and juice with the amaretto.

In a separate bowl mix together the flour, sugar, baking powder and egg till it begins to form a dough. Add the nut mix and bring together quickly – the mix will be very sticky.

On a heavily floured surface, roll the mix into a sausage shape about 4cm wide and cook on a baking tray in the oven for 25 minutes. Once cooked, slice while warm and place back in the oven for a further 2 minutes on each side.

CHOCOLATE SPONGE: Preheat the oven to 180°C.

In a bowl over a pan of hot water melt the chocolate. Once melted whisk the egg whites and sugar to a stiff meringue. Remove the chocolate from the heat and whisk in the butter and egg yolk. Whisk in half the meringue until smooth, then fold in the remainder. Pipe into a tray lined with greaseproof paper and cook in the oven for 15 minutes. Allow to cool before cutting then soak the pieces in the espresso coffee.

TIRAMISU: Whisk the eggs till they are light and fluffy. Boil the sugar with water, pour onto the eggs and whisk until cool. Fold in the alcohol followed by the mascarpone, but don't overmix as it will cause it to spilt.

TO SERVE: Layer the tiramisu mix with the coffee-soaked sponge into a glass and finished with shavings of chocolate and biscotti on the side.

SPECIAL EQUIPMENT
Food processor.

PLANNING AHEAD
The chocolate sponge and biscotti can be made the day before or even be kept in the freezer for up to 2 months.

INGREDIENTS

PISTACHIO BISCOTTI:
- 100g pistachios
- 1 lemon, zest and juice
- 20ml amaretto
- 100g plain flour
- 100g caster sugar
- ½ tsp baking powder
- 1 egg

CHOCOLATE SPONGE:
- 100g dark, 70% chocolate
- 3 egg whites
- 40g caster sugar
- 25g butter
- 1 egg yolk
- 250ml espresso

TIRAMISU:
- 2 eggs
- 100g caster sugar
- 20ml water
- 25ml chocolate liquor
- 40ml Marsala
- 700g mascarpone

TO SERVE:
- chocolate shavings

FOR A LITTLE EXTRA KICK SOAK THE SPONGE IN TIA MARIA
- PHIL THOMPSON

PIERRE KOFFMANN

KOFFMANN'S

↘ PIEDS DE COCHON AUX MORILLES
PIG'S TROTTERS WITH MOREL MUSHROOMS
PIERRE KOFFMANN / SERVES 4

INGREDIENTS
- 4 pig's trotters (back legs which have been boned)
- 100g carrots, cubed
- 100g onions, cubed
- 150ml white wine
- 1 tbsp port
- 120ml veal stock
- 225g calf sweetbreads, blanched and chopped
- 65g butter
- 20 dried morel mushrooms, soaked in water
- 1 small onion, chopped
- 1 breast of chicken, cubed
- 1 egg white
- 200ml double cream
- salt and pepper, to taste

TO SERVE:
- butter, as needed
- salad leaves, as needed

METHOD
Preheat the oven to 160ºC.

Braise the trotters with the carrots, onions, wine, port and veal stock in the oven for 3 hours.

Fry the sweetbreads in 65g butter for 5 minutes, then add the morels and onions and cook for another 5 minutes. Leave to cool.

Purée the chicken breast with the egg white and cream, and season. Combine with the sweetbread mixture to make the stuffing.

Remove the trotters from the oven and increase the temperature to 220°C, keeping the liquid but discarding the vegetables. Put the trotters wide open on tin foil and allow to cool. Stuff them with the chicken preparation and roll in foil. Chill for at least 2 hours. Remove the foil and cook with very little water in a casserole dish in the oven for 15 minutes at 220ºC.

TO SERVE: When cooked, remove the trotters. Add the stock saved from earlier, reduce by half and add a knob of butter. Pour over the trotters and serve with salad leaves.

↘ COTE DE BOEUF
BY PIERRE KOFFMANN / SERVES 4

SPECIAL EQUIPMENT
Fryer, muslin-lined sieve.

INGREDIENTS

COTE DE BOEUF:
- 2 x 800g côte de boeuf
- salt and pepper
- 2 tbsp vegetable oil

CHUNKY CHIPS:
- 6 large chipping potatoes
- 2 litres vegetable oil
- salt and pepper

BEARNAISE SAUCE:
- 240g unsalted butter
- 2 tbsp white wine vinegar
- 4 tbsp tarragon, finely chopped
- 30g shallots, finely chopped
- 10 peppercorns, crushed
- 4 egg yolks
- 1 tbsp cold water
- 2 tbsp finely chopped chervil (optional)
- lemon juice, as needed
- freshly ground salt and black pepper

TO SERVE:
- watercress, as needed

METHOD

COTE DE BOEUF: Preheat the oven to 180ºC.

Season the meat well on all sides with salt and pepper. Heat the oil in a large oven-proof pan until very hot and seal the meat well on all sides. Place in the oven for 20 minutes (rare) or 25 minutes (medium), but check by feeling the firmness of the meat. Leave to rest for 10 minutes.

CHUNKY CHIPS: Peel the potatoes and cut into the size you prefer, then place the cut chips in ice-cold water and leave for 1 hour.

Heat the oil in the fryer to 160ºC. Drain the potatoes and pat dry. Place them in the fryer in batches and cook until tender, drain on kitchen paper and place in the fridge until you are ready to serve.

When you are ready to serve the chips heat the oil to 190ºC and fry until crisp and golden.

Drain and sprinkle with salt and pepper.

BEARNAISE SAUCE: First clarify the butter by placing it in a small saucepan over a low heat. When the milky sediment rises to the top, either skim off the sediment with a spoon or pour the butter through a small muslin-lined sieve set over a bowl.

Put the vinegar, 2 tablespoons of the tarragon, the shallots and crushed peppercorns in a small, heavy-based saucepan. Simmer gently until reduced by half. Remove from the heat and allow to cool.

Add the egg yolks and cold water to the vinegar mixture. Set the pan over a low heat and whisk continuously for about 10 minutes until the sauce emulsifies. Do not allow it to reach boiling point. Remove the pan from the heat. Whisk in the clarified butter a little at a time. Season to taste, then push the sauce through a fine sieve. Stir in the remaining tablespoons of tarragon, the chervil (if using) and lemon juice to taste. Season and serve immediately.

TO SERVE: Cut the côte de boeuf in thin slices cut across the grain. Serve with béarnaise sauce and fries. Garnish with watercress.

FAVOURITE FOOD:
"TRADITIONAL ENGLISH FOOD
– MEAT, POTATOES, SAUSAGES,
BACON, FISH AND CHIPS – NOT
A VERY SOPHISTICATED PALATE!"
- MARTIN JOHNSON

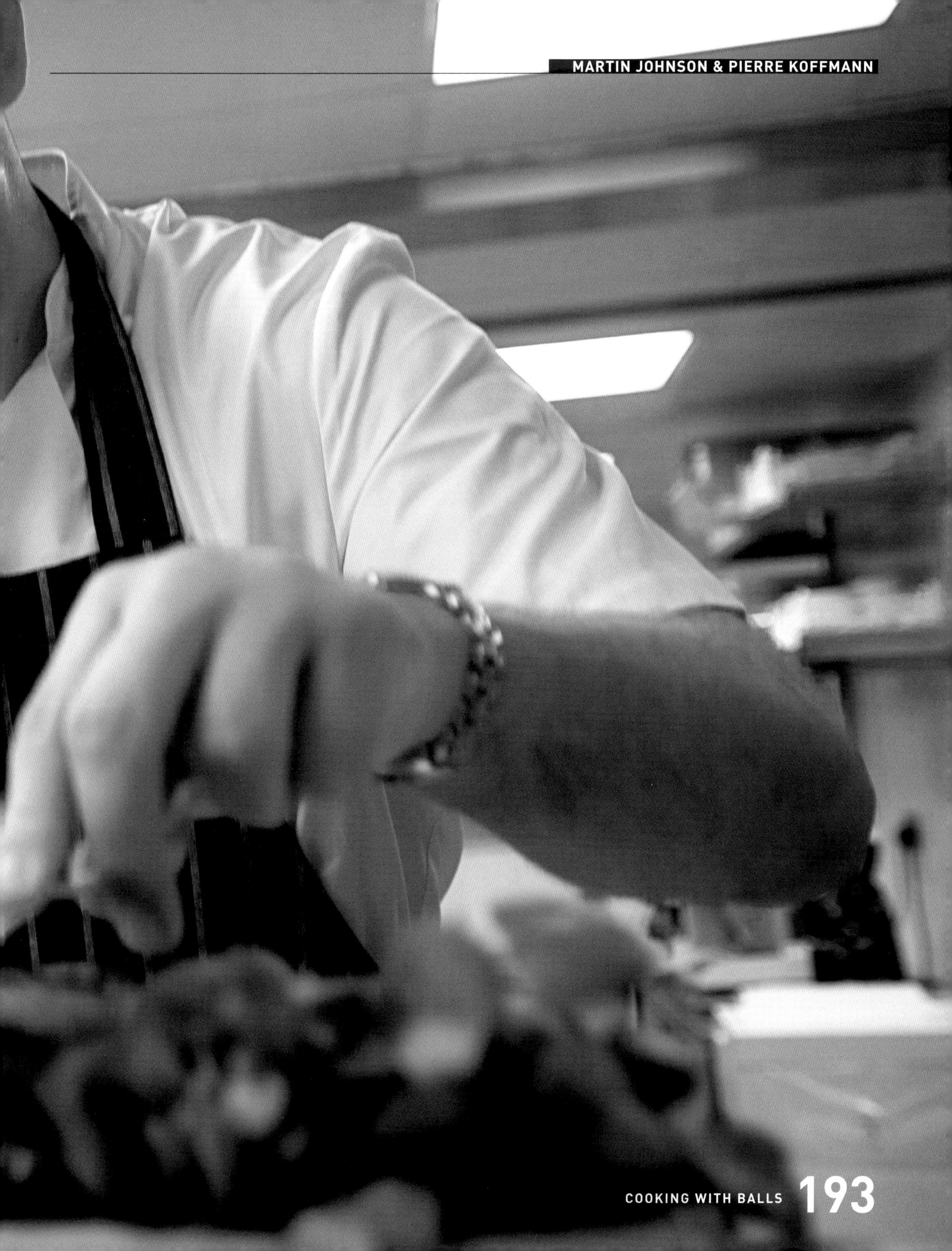

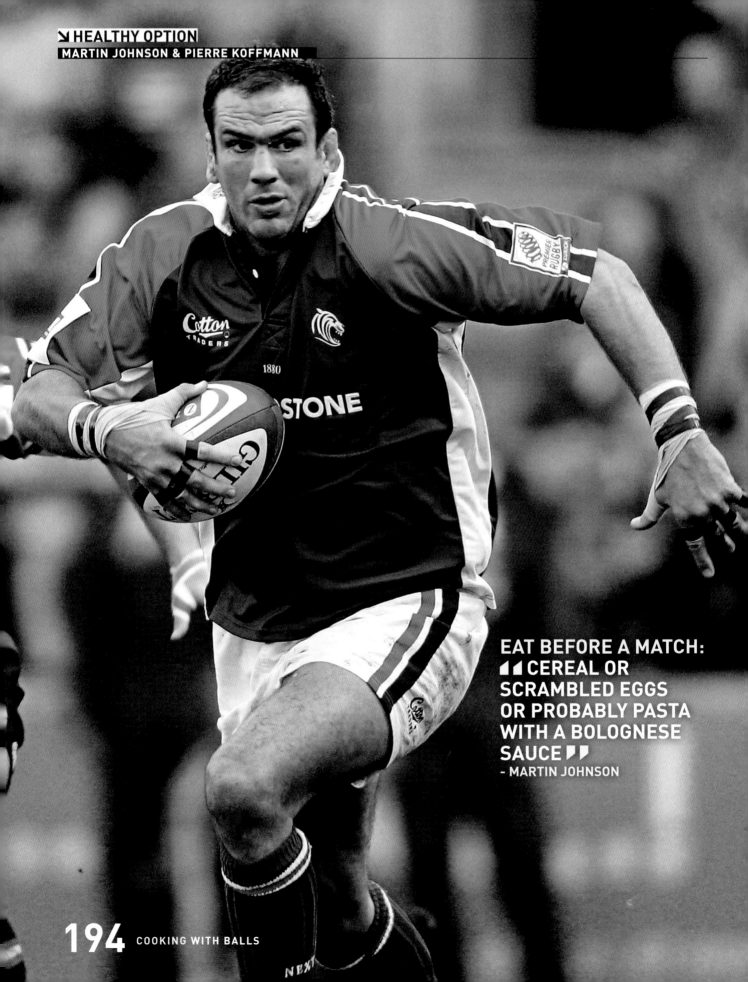

EAT BEFORE A MATCH:
❝CEREAL OR
SCRAMBLED EGGS
OR PROBABLY PASTA
WITH A BOLOGNESE
SAUCE❞
- MARTIN JOHNSON

↘ LEEK TERRINE
WITH SMOKED EEL
BY PIERRE KOFFMANN / SERVES 8

METHOD

TERRINE: Wash the leeks thoroughly, ensuring all soil is removed. Tie in bunches of four, making sure they are all the same size so they cook evenly. Place in a large shallow pan and just cover with water, then cook gently until tender. Season with salt and sugar to taste. Remove from the pan and drain in a colander.

Line a small terrine with two layers of cling film and, while the leeks are still warm, layer, alternating between green and white until all the leeks are used. Fold over the cling film, place another terrine on top and place weights inside to press the terrine. After 15 minutes turn upside down and repeat to draw out any excess water. Refrigerate overnight. Unmould the terrine with a sharp knife.

VINAIGRETTE: Place all the ingredients in a jar and, with the lid on, shake to emulsify, check the seasoning and add more if required.

TO SERVE: Slice the terrine into eight and serve with pieces of smoked eel and a drizzle of the vinaigrette.

SPECIAL EQUIPMENT
20cm small loaf tin or terrine.

PLANNING AHEAD
The terrine must be refrigerated overnight.

INGREDIENTS

TERRINE:
- 8 small new season leeks, trimmed to fit the length of the terrine
- salt and sugar, to taste

VINAIGRETTE:
- 2 tbsp white wine vinegar
- salt and pepper, to taste
- 2 tsp Dijon mustard
- 6 tbsp vegetable oil

TO SERVE:
- 500g smoked eel

THIS DISH ALSO WORKS WELL WITH LANGOUSTINE OR BLUE CHEESE AND WALNUTS AS A REPLACEMENT TO THE EEL
- PIERRE KOFFMANN

↘ PISTACHIO SOUFFLE
BY PIERRE KOFFMANN / SERVES 4

SPECIAL EQUIPMENT
4 x souffle dishes.

INGREDIENTS
- 500ml milk
- ½ vanilla pod
- 120g egg yolks
- 100g caster sugar
- 50g plain flour
- 25g butter, softened
- 25g dark chocolate, grated
- 4 egg whites
- 1 tbsp caster sugar
- 40g pistachio paste

TO SERVE:
- icing sugar, as needed

METHOD

Preheat the oven to 240°C.

Boil together the milk and vanilla pod. Simultaneously whisk together the egg yolks and 100g caster sugar, whisk until the mixture slightly thickens and turns light in colour.

Sieve the flour and add into the mixture, then whisk until smooth. Add half of the milk to the base and whisk until there are no lumps. Sieve through a fine strainer, remove the vanilla pod, return the mixture back to the pan and add the remaining milk. Using a whisk, stir the mixture. When it comes to the boil, bring the temperature down to a simmer. Continue to stir and cook out for 8-10 minutes.

Pour this pistachio paste onto a shallow tray and cool.

Generously butter four individual soufflé dishes. Put the grated chocolate inside and rotate the moulds so that the chocolate completely covers the inside, sticking to the softened butter.

Beat the egg whites until firm, add the tablespoon of caster sugar and whisk until stiff. Add a small quantity of the whites to the pistachio paste to soften it, then fold in the rest of the egg whites and pour into the soufflé dishes.

Bake in the oven for 15 minutes or until well risen.

TO SERVE: Dust the top with icing sugar and serve with ice cream of your choice.

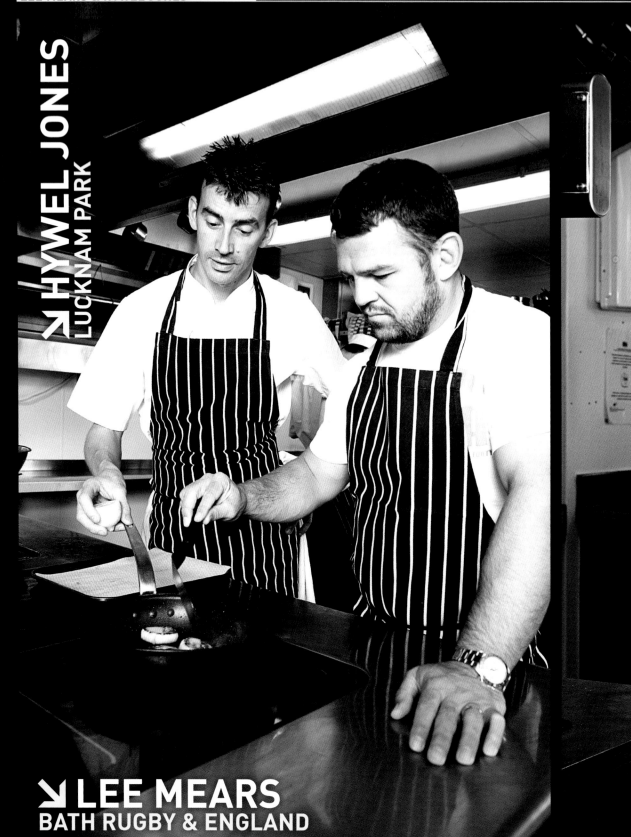

HYWEL JONES
LUCKNAM PARK

↘ LEE MEARS
BATH RUGBY & ENGLAND

↘ BRAISED BELLY OF CAMERON NAUGHTON'S FREE-RANGE PORK,
CARAMELISED APPLES, ORGANIC WEST COUNTRY CIDER SAUCE
BY HYWEL JONES / SERVES 4

METHOD

PORK BELLY: Preheat the oven to 130ºC.

Trim any excess fat from the pork belly. Season with salt and pepper and roll into a cylinder, then gently tie with butcher's string to retain the shape.

In a hot pan add a little oil and then brown the meat on all sides.

Remove the meat from the pan and set aside, then add the root vegetables and garlic, and cook until golden brown. Remove any excess fat from the pan, add the honey and cook until lightly caramelised. Add the vinegar and cider, and reduce to a syrupy consistency. Pour in the stock, bring to the boil and add the seared pork back into the pan together with the spices.

Cover and cook in the oven for 4 hours at 130ºC or until the meat is tender. Once the meat is tender, remove from the stock and allow to cool slightly, then cut the string. Roll in cling film and refrigerate. Pass the leftover sauce through a fine sieve and reduce a little to concentrate its flavour.

CARAMELISED APPLES: Cook the apple rings in the sugar and butter until lightly caramelised just before serving.

TO SERVE: Cut the pork into four even medallions. Pan fry until golden brown and the heat through in the oven at 180ºC, ensure hot in the middle. Place two apple rings on each pork medallion. Season the foie gras slices and cook in a very hot non-stick pan until tender (this will only take around 20 seconds so be careful not to overcook the foie gras). Place on the top of the caramelised apples. Cook all the vegetable accompaniments separately and arrange in serving bowls. Place the pork in the centre and spoon over the sauce.

SPECIAL EQUIPMENT
Butcher's string.

PLANNING AHEAD
Trim the pork belly the night before and cure with rock salt and pepper. The vegetables can be cooked in advance.

INGREDIENTS

PORK BELLY:
- 1kg pork belly, skinned and boned
- salt and pepper, to taste
- rapeseed oil, as needed
- 250g root vegetables, chopped
- 2 garlic cloves
- 1 tbsp honey
- 50ml balsamic vinegar
- 500ml organic cider
- 1 litre brown meat stock (ideally chicken)
- 2 star anise
- 10g coriander seeds

CARAMELISED APPLES:
- 8 Granny Smith apple rings, cut to around 0.5cm thick
- 20g demerara sugar
- 10g butter

TO SERVE:
- salt and pepper
- 4 x 15g slices of foie gras
- 8 baby leeks
- 12 baby onions
- 100g baby spinach

YOUR BUTCHER WILL BE HAPPY TO TRIM, ROLL AND TIE YOUR PORK BELLY FOR YOU. ALTERNATIVELY, YOU COULD BRAISE IT FLAT AND CUT IT INTO SQUARES
- HYWEL JONES

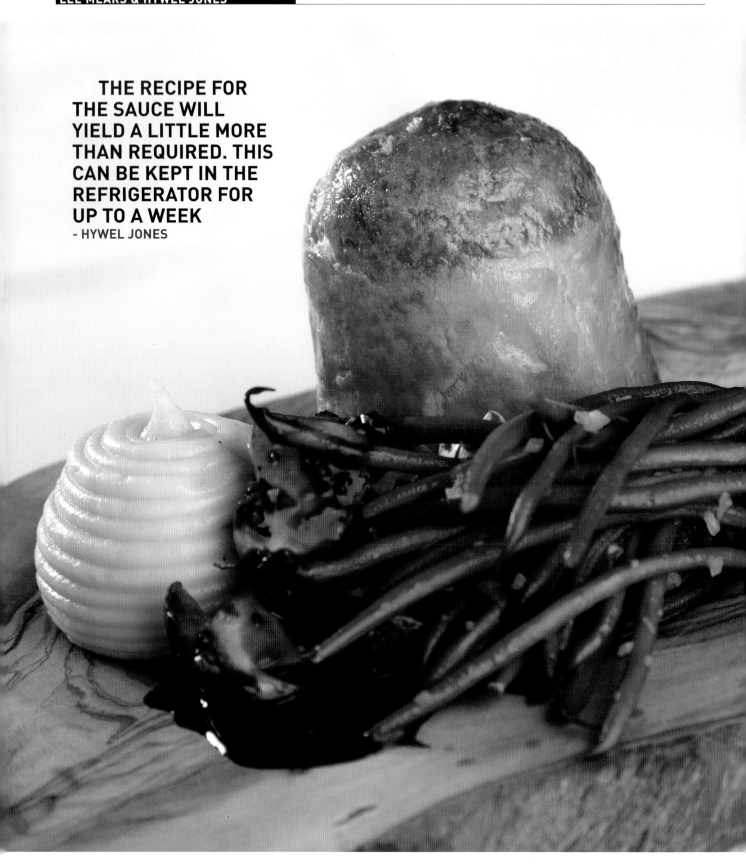

THE RECIPE FOR
THE SAUCE WILL
YIELD A LITTLE MORE
THAN REQUIRED. THIS
CAN BE KEPT IN THE
REFRIGERATOR FOR
UP TO A WEEK
- HYWEL JONES

↘ INDIVIDUAL BEEF WELLINGTONS,
EURIDGE FARM BOBBY BEANS, WILD MUSHROOMS, TRUFFLE SAUCE
BY HYWEL JONES / SERVES 4

SPECIAL EQUIPMENT
Temperature probe.

PLANNING AHEAD
The mushroom duxelles, crêpes and truffle sauce may be made a day in advance.

INGREDIENTS

TRUFFLE SAUCE:
- 100g beef trimmings
- olive oil, as needed
- 4 shallots, roughly chopped
- 250ml red wine
- 250ml ruby port
- 750ml beef stock
- 2 garlic cloves, crushed
- 1 sprig thyme
- 1 bay leaf
- truffle oil, as needed
- unsalted butter, as needed
- salt and pepper, to taste

MUSHROOM DUXELLES:
- 150g firm button mushrooms
- 2 large shallots, finely chopped
- 1 small garlic clove, crushed
- butter, as needed
- 50ml double cream
- 2 sprigs of tarragon
- salt and pepper, to taste

BEEF WELLINGTONS:
- 4 x 140g fillet steaks
- salt and pepper
- olive oil, as needed
- 8 x 20cm paper-thin crêpes
- 250g puff pastry
- 1 egg, beaten

TO SERVE:
- 4 servings creamed potatoes
- 200g Euridge Farm bobby beans or fine green beans
- 100g wild mushrooms

METHOD

TRUFFLE SAUCE: Fry off the meat trimmings in a splash of oil until browned. Remove from the pan, then add the shallots and cook gently until golden brown. Pour in the wine and port and reduce to 150ml. Add the beef stock and bring to a simmer. Return the meat trimmings to the pan along with the garlic and herbs, and simmer gently for 1 hour. Remove any fat or impurities during cooking with a ladle. Pass the sauce through a fine sieve, return to the pan over a medium heat and reduce to a syrupy consistency. Whisk in the truffle oil and butter, check the seasoning and set aside.

MUSHROOM DUXELLES: Wash and dry the mushrooms. Chop them as finely as possible by hand. Cook the shallots and garlic in the butter until soft. Add the mushrooms and cook until dry (the mushrooms will release moisture when initially added). Add the cream and cook for a few seconds until it binds the mushrooms and shallots together. Remove from the heat. Pick and chop the tarragon and add to the mushroom mix. Check and adjust the seasoning, then set aside.

BEEF WELLINGTONS: Season the fillet steaks and brown very quickly in a little hot vege oil (you are only sealing the beef and not cooking it). Remove and refrigerate until cold. Top with the mushroom duxelles and shape into a neat dome. Carefully wrap each fillet steak in the crêpes, trimming any excess crêpe away. Roll out the puff pastry to roughly 3-5mm in thickness. Cut out 4 x 20cm discs. Carefully wrap each steak in the pastry with the mushroom end being the top and the pastry joining at the other end. Allow to set in the refrigerator and then glaze with the beaten egg, twice. You may make a pattern on the pastry if you wish.

TO SERVE: Place the Wellingtons in an oven preheated to 180°C. For medium-cooked steaks you should cook for roughly 20 minutes. However, it may be necessary to either increase/decrease the temperature to achieve a golden pastry. To ensure the beef is cooked inside insert a small temperature probe into the core. For a medium steak you need a reading of around 60°C.

Cook the vegetables as desired and arrange onto four serving plates. Place the Wellingtons next to the garnishes and drizzle the sauce around.

EAT BEFORE A MATCH:
**"SANDWICHES!
I LOVE SANDWICHES!"**
- LEE MEARS

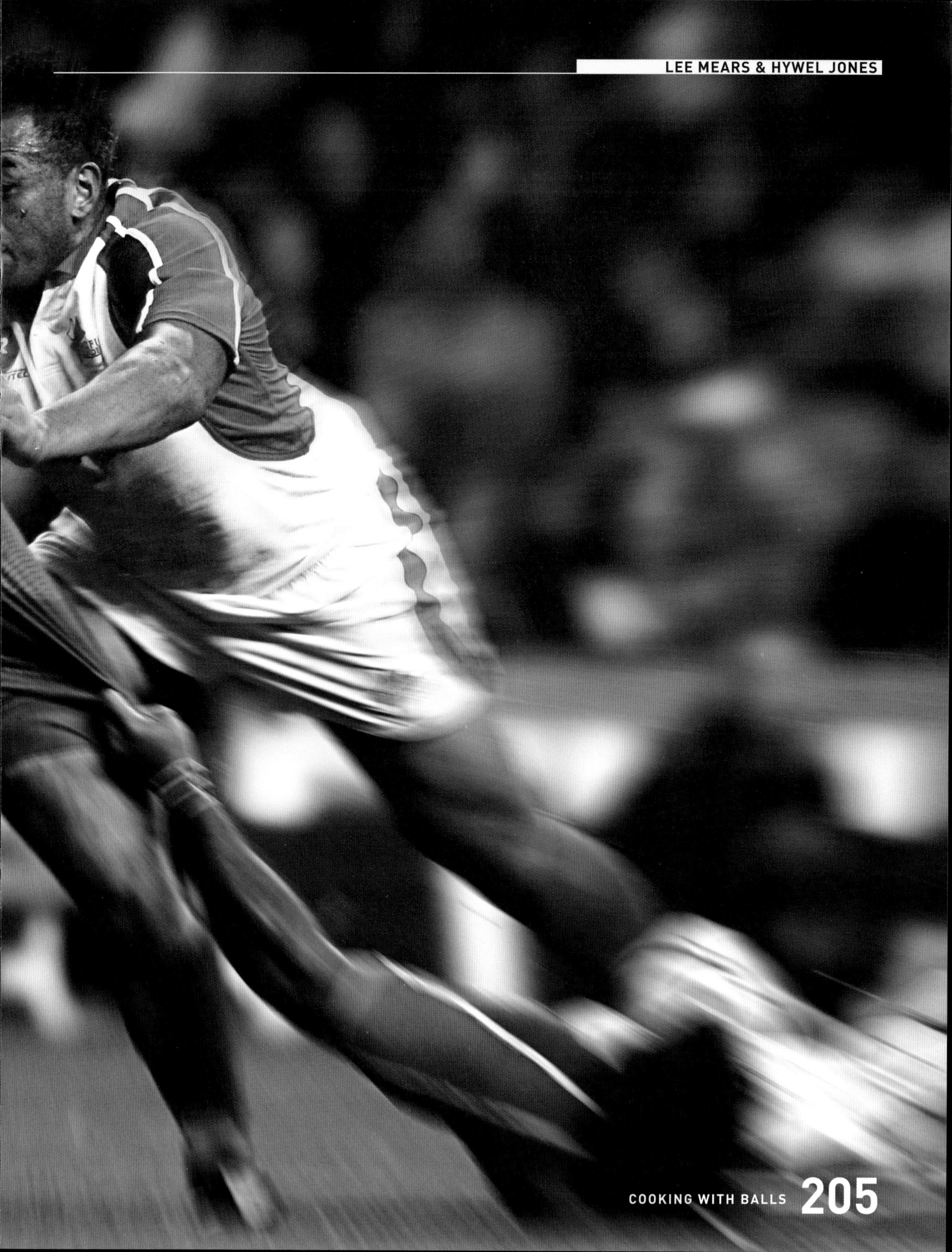

↘ SEARED FILLET OF CORNISH MACKEREL,

SWEET POTATO AND LIME PICKLE, YOGHURT AND CUCUMBER

BY HWYEL JONES / SERVES 4

SPECIAL EQUIPMENT

Pestle and mortar.

INGREDIENTS

SWEET POTATO AND LIME PICKLE:

- 1 x 2.5cm piece of tamarind
- 1 chilli, deseeded
- 1 x 2.5cm piece of ginger
- 6 garlic cloves
- 2 tbsp cumin seeds
- 1 cardamom
- 1 tbsp coriander seeds
- 1 tbsp fennel seeds
- 1 tbsp caraway seeds
- 1 star anise
- 1 cinnamon stick
- ¼ tsp nutmeg
- salt and pepper, to taste
- 2 sweet potatoes, cut into 5mm x 5mm squares
- 3 limes, cut into segments
- 150ml extra-virgin olive oil

CUCUMBER:

- 1 cucumber, peeled, deseeded and finely sliced
- 10g salt
- 150g natural yoghurt

MACKEREL:

- 2 large Cornish mackerel, filleted and pin boned
- oil, as needed

TO SERVE:

- mustard cress, as needed
- coriander leaves, as needed

METHOD

SWEET POTATO AND LIME PICKLE: Blend the tamarind, chilli, ginger and garlic together with a pestle and mortar. Toast the cumin, cardamom, coriander, fennel, caraway, star anise, cinnamon and nutmeg. Mix all together and season with salt.

Mix the spice mix, sweet potatoes and lime together. Bind with some extra-virgin olive oil and adjust the seasoning.

CUCUMBER: In another mixing bowl salt the cucumber slices. Wash after 10 minutes so they are tender, dry and then mix with the yoghurt.

MACKEREL: Preheat the oven to 180ºC.

Clean the mackerel fillets in cold water and pat dry on a clean kitchen towel. With the aid of a sharp knife score the mackerel fillet on the skin to allow even cooking.

Heat a non-stick pan large enough to hold the mackerel fillets – if you don't have a large pan then cook the fillets in two batches. Add some oil and then place in the mackerel, skin-side down, and sear gently until the skin is golden brown. Then place in the oven for approximately 2 minutes until the flesh is cooked.

Take the mackerel filets out of the pan and drain on the kitchen towel.

TO SERVE: On the serving plate, spoon out about three tablespoons of sweet potato and lime pickle, and same amount of the cucumbers in yoghurt adjacent to it. Place the mackerel filet on top and garnish with some mustard cress and coriander leaves.

↘ CROUSTILLANT OF PINEAPPLE,
RUM AND RAISIN PARFAIT, COCONUT SORBET
BY HYWEL JONES / SERVES 4

METHOD

CROUSTILLANT: Preheat the oven to 210ºC.

Cut the small pineapple into four lengthways. Remove the core and trim the edges to create a neat cylinder, so they are about 2.5cm in diameter. Dust with icing sugar

Melt 25g butter in a non-stick pan and fry the pineapple until well caramelised. Retain the juices from the pan. Chill the pineapple pieces in the fridge overnight.

Roll the pineapple in the spring roll pastry, ensuring at least two layers all around. Melt the remaining butter and brush over the pastry, then dust with icing sugar. Cook in the oven for around 8 minutes until golden brown and crispy.

PARFAIT: Whisk the yolks and sugar in a bowl over steaming water until pale and fluffy. Allow to cool.

Whisk the cream until it forms soft peaks and fold into the egg mix. Mix in the raisins, spoon onto a lined 1cm thick tray and freeze until set.

COCONUT SORBET: Mix the coconut milk, water and sugar and lemon together then freeze in an ice cream machine.

TO SERVE: Cut the croustillant on the angle and trim off the excess pastry so that it stands up. Cut the parfait into 50cm discs, and plate up with the coconut sorbet and mint sprigs as pictured.

SPECIAL EQUIPMENT
Ice cream machine.

PLANNING AHEAD
Soak the raisins in a good rum overnight. Chill the caramelised pineapple in the fridge overnight.

INGREDIENTS

CROUSTILLANT:
- 1 small peeled pineapple
- icing sugar, as needed
- 50g butter
- 4 sheets of spring roll or filo pastry

PARFAIT:
- 2 egg yolks
- 20g sugar
- 180ml double cream
- 30g raisins soaked in a good rum

COCONUT SORBET:
- 100ml coconut milk (unsweetened)
- 35ml water
- 60g sugar
- 1 lemon, juiced

TO SERVE:
- sprig of mint
- pineapple disc

↘ **ALAN MURCHISON**
L'ORTOLAN RESTAURANT / LA BECASSE / PARIS HOUSE

IF YOU FIND THAT THE TARRAGON IS A LITTLE OVERPOWERING, BEFORE DRYING, BLANCH IT IN BOILING SALTED WATER FOR 30 SECONDS AND REFRESH, THIS LEAVES YOU WITH A MUCH MILDER FLAVOUR
- ALAN MURCHISON

↘ COQ AU VIN, BRAISED CORN-FED CHICKEN
IN RED WINE AND TARRAGON, POMME PURÉE, ROAST SHALLOTS AND CEPE FRICASSEE
BY ALAN MURCHISON / SERVES 4

"A CLASSIC DISH THAT IS HARD TO BEAT. IT IS VERY IMPORTANT TO MAKE SURE THAT THE CHICKEN YOU BUY IS OF THE BEST QUALITY, PREFERABLY CORN-FED. I SUGGEST USING A TRADITIONAL FREE-RANGE CHICKEN FROM LOUÉ IN SOUTH-WEST FRANCE."

PLANNING AHEAD

Marinate the chicken for 24 hours in the refrigerator before cooking. The confit tomato and confit shallots also need to be made in advance.

INGREDIENTS

CHICKEN:
- 1 x 1.5kg corn-fed Loué chicken
- 750ml red wine
- 2 heads garlic
- 2 sprigs of thyme
- 2 bay leaves
- 600ml brown chicken stock
- 600ml white chicken stock
- 150g unsalted butter

WHITE CHICKEN STOCK:
- 1½kg chicken wings
- 1½ litres water
- 1 onion
- 2 sticks celery
- 1 leek
- 1 bay leaf
- 1 sprig thyme
- 2 garlic cloves

BROWN CHICKEN STOCK:
- 1½kg chicken wings
- 1½ litres white chicken stock
- 1 onion, diced
- 2 celery sticks, diced
- ½ leek, diced
- 150g unsalted butter
- 1 bay leaf
- 1 sprig thyme
- 2 garlic cloves

CONFIT TOMATO:
- 1kg vine-ripe cherry tomatoes
- 100ml extra virgin olive oil
- salt and pepper, to taste

POMME PUREE:
- 250g coarse sea salt
- 2 large potatoes (Desiree)
- 50g butter
- salt and pepper, to taste

DRIED TARRAGON:
- dash of olive oil
- 12 large sprigs of tarragon

TO SERVE:
- 12 shallots, roasted
- olive oil, as needed
- 200g bouchon cèpes
- 100g unsalted butter
- 5g garlic, chopped

METHOD

CHICKEN: Portion the chicken by removing the legs and splitting the drumsticks from the thighs. Split the crown into four even pieces. Marinate the chicken in the red wine, garlic, thyme and bay leaves for 24 hours in the refrigerator.

Preheat the oven to 150ºC. Strain the red wine, garlic and herbs and add to the chicken stocks. Dry the chicken thoroughly on kitchen paper. Caramelise the chicken in the butter – it should be golden brown all over.

Place the chicken in a casserole dish and cover with the red wine and chicken stock mixture. Bring to the boil and skim. Place the casserole dish in the oven and cook for 1 hour. Remove from the oven and allow to cool for 30 minutes, then strain off the stock into a pan and reduce quickly by two-thirds. Check the seasoning and pour over the cooked chicken.

WHITE CHICKEN STOCK: Place 1kg of the chicken wings in the water and bring up to the boil. Skim and simmer for 45 minutes. Pass through a colander and add the remaining chicken wings and vegetables.

Bring back to the boil and simmer for 30 minutes, skimming every 10 minutes.

Pass through a fine sieve and reduce by half.

BROWN CHICKEN STOCK: Place the chicken wings in the oven at 200°C for 30 minutes and roast until golden brown, turning every 10 minutes. Place 1kg of the roasted bones in the stock and bring up to

the boil. Skim and simmer for 45 minutes. Caramelise the vegetables in the butter then pour into a colander to remove the excess fat.

Add to the stock with the bay, thyme and garlic and simmer for 30 minutes. Pass through a colander and add the remaining chicken wings. Bring back to the boil and simmer for 30 minutes, skimming every 10 minutes. Pass through a fine sieve and reduce by half.

CONFIT TOMATO: In small batches, blanch the tomatoes in boiling salted water for 10 seconds and refresh in iced water. Peel off the skins and arrange the tomatoes evenly on a non-stick tray. Sprinkle with the olive oil, salt and pepper and put into a very low oven at 60-70ºC overnight or until the tomatoes have reduced in volume by 50 per cent. Allow to cool, then place in a sealed container in the refrigerator.

POMME PUREE: Preheat the oven to 180ºC. Cover a small baking tray with the salt and place the potatoes on it, making sure there is an even layer under each potato. Bake the potatoes for about 1½ hours until soft – the skin should not be too dark. Remove the potatoes from the tray and cut them in half. Scoop out the cooked potato and pass through a fine sieve. Place the dry mash in a pan and beat in the butter over a low heat. Season to taste.

DRIED TARRAGON: Take a large plate and cover it tightly with cling film. Brush lightly with olive oil then carefully place the herb sprigs onto the cling film. Microwave on full power for 60-80 seconds until the herbs start to dry out. Remove from the microwave and place above the stove in a hot dry place for 1 hour.

TO SERVE: Cover the shallots in oil and confit at 80ºC for around 4 hours or until tender, then roast in the oven at 180ºC for around 10 minutes or until golden. Plate up as pictured.

↘ MOROCCAN LAMB,
HARISSA-SPICED COUSCOUS, CONFIT CHERRY TOMATOES AND ROASTING JUICES
BY ALAN MURCHISON / SERVES 4

PLANNING AHEAD

This recipe makes enough to marinate 20 lamb rumps but is not easily made in smaller batches, so portion it into bags and freeze for later. The lamb must be left to marinate for 48 hours in the refrigerator. Lamb jus can be made at least 24 hours in advance. The confit tomato needs to be cooked overnight.

INGREDIENTS

MORROCCAN MARINADE:
- 5g coriander seeds, roasted
- 4g cumin seeds, roasted
- 1 large pinch saffron
- 5g black peppercorns
- 4g juniper berries
- 25g orange zest
- 15g lemon zest
- 8g rosemary
- 50g garlic
- 15g coriander stalks
- 150ml olive oil

LAMB JUS:
- 1kg lamb bones, coarsely chopped
- 750ml dry white wine
- 2 large onions, finely chopped
- 6 garlic cloves
- 150g unsalted butter
- 10 very ripe vine tomatoes, chopped
- 1 litre white chicken stock
- 1 litre brown chicken stock
- 6 sprigs rosemary
- 2 ripe vine tomatoes, chopped
- 1 clove garlic, crushed
- 2 sprigs rosemary
- 1 sprig thyme
- salt and pepper

LAMB:
- 2 x 240g lamb rumps
- 75ml olive oil

CHICKPEA SALSA:
- 240g cooked chickpeas, peeled
- 5g red chillis, finely diced
- 4 very fine slivers garlic
- 1g coriander leaf, finely sliced
- 25ml lemon juice
- 25ml olive oil
- 2g sugar
- salt and pepper, to taste

HARISSA-SPICED COUSCOUS:
- 7 red peppers
- 15 red chillis, deseeded
- 1g saffron
- 7g salt
- 160g tomato purée
- 4g cayenne pepper
- 7g ground coriander
- 120ml tomato juice
- 120ml white chicken stock
- 160g couscous
- 15g courgettes, diced
- 15ml olive oil
- 40g harissa
- 10g chopped coriander
- salt and pepper, to taste

MOUTABAL:
- 4 large aubergines
- 1 garlic clove, crushed
- 10g tahini
- 35g crème fraîche
- 25ml lemon juice
- salt and pepper, to taste

DRIED CORIANDER:
- 12 large sprigs coriander
- olive oil, as needed

CONFIT TOMATO:
- 1kg ripe cherry vine tomatoes
- 100ml extra virgin olive oil
- salt and pepper, to taste

METHOD

MORROCCAN MARINADE: Put all the ingredients into a food processor and blitz to a smooth paste, scraping the sides of the bowl as you go. To marinate the lamb rump, rub in the paste and allow to marinate in the refrigerator for 48 hours.

LAMB JUS: In a large roasting tray, roast the lamb bones in the oven at 200°C with no added fat for 30-40 minutes, turning every 10 minutes to ensure they are golden brown. Pour into a colander to strain off any excess fat. Reserve 200g of the lamb bones to refresh the sauce later. Deglaze the roasting tray with 200ml of the white wine; set the juices aside.

Sauté the onions and six garlic cloves in the butter until golden brown. Add the very ripe vine tomatoes and cook until the mixture has reduced by half, then add the remaining white wine and reduce by half. Add the lamb bones, chicken stocks and 6 sprigs of rosemary to the tomato mixture and bring to the boil.

Simmer for 50 minutes, skimming every 10 minutes. Pass through a coarse sieve and reduce by one-third very quickly.

Add the reserved lamb bones, fresh ripe vine tomatoes, crushed garlic clove and the remaining two sprigs of rosemary and thyme. Bring to the boil, skim and simmer for 10 minutes. Pass through a fine sieve and season to taste.

LAMB: Preheat the oven to 190°C.

Scrape off any excess marinade then caramelise the lamb evenly in the olive oil in a non-stick pan, ensuring that it does not catch and burn – this will take 4-5 minutes. Then put the lamb in the oven for 8-9 minutes or until the lamb is medium rare, turning twice. (Lamb is not a meat that eats well when cooked rare.) Rest for a further 10 minutes.

CHICKPEA SALSA: Mix all the ingredients together and season to taste.

HARISSA-SPICED COUSCOUS: Cut the peppers into quarters, discarding the stalk and seeds. Lay the quarters skin-side up on a baking tray and lightly brush with oil. Place under a hot grill until the skin has lightly blackened but not burnt. Cover with cling film and leave in a warm place for 1 hour.

Peel the skin from the red pepper flesh and place the cheeks with the chillis, saffron, salt, tomato purée, cayenne and coriander into a food processor. Blitz to a smooth paste.

Bring the tomato juice and chicken stock to the boil and season to taste. Place the couscous in a large bowl and pour on the boiling stock, then immediately cover the bowl with cling film and leave to steam for 2 minutes. Stir the couscous with a fork to separate the individual grains, then re-cover and leave for a further 4 minutes. Stir again.

YOU COULD USE ALMOST ANY CUT OF IAMB FOR THIS DISH. FILLET, LOIN, SHOULDER OR LEG COULD ALL BE RUBBED WITH THE MARINADE AND COOKED ACCORDINGLY

- ALAN MURCHISON

In a hot frying pan, quickly fry the courgettes in the oil. Transfer to a tray to cool. Mix the courgettes through the couscous along with the harissa and the coriander. Season to taste.

MOUTABAL: Peel the green fir from the outside of the aubergine stalk and score a line all the way round each of the aubergines lengthways. Place under a hot grill until they start to char and take on a smoky smell.

Allow the aubergines to cool then cut in half and scrape out the flesh, trying not to take the fibres from the skin with it. Place the flesh in a food processor along with all the other ingredients and blitz until smooth. Season to taste.

DRIED CORIANDER: Take a large plate and cover it tightly with cling film. Brush lightly with olive oil then carefully place the herb sprigs onto the cling film. Microwave on full power for 60-80 seconds until the herbs start to dry out. Remove from the microwave and place above the stove in a hot dry place for 1 hour.

CONFIT TOMATO: In small batches, blanch the tomatoes in boiling salted water for 10 seconds and refresh in iced water. Peel off the skins and arrange the tomatoes evenly on a non-stick tray. Sprinkle with the olive oil, salt and pepper and put into a very low oven at 60-70ºC overnight or until the tomatoes have reduced in volume by 50 per cent.

Allow to cool, then place in a sealed container in the refrigerator.

TO SERVE: This dish is served ambient – the lamb will be hot, but the garnish should be at room temperature. Remove the couscous and salsa from the refrigerator 30 minutes in advance of serving and plate up as pictured.

FAVOURITE FOOD
AS A CHILD:
"CHICKEN DIPPERS,
BEANS AND CHIPS"
- TOM CROFT

↘ FILLET OF BREAM, PAK CHOI, WILD MUSHROOMS,
VIETNAMESE-STYLE BROTH WITH CITRONELLA AND CRISP SHALLOTS
BY ALAN MURCHISON / SERVES 4

"BREAM CONTAINS OMEGA-3 AND IS ALSO A GOOD SOURCE OF PROTEIN. THE RICH PHYTONUTRIENT CONTENT OF PAK CHOI INCREASES ANTIOXIDANT LEVELS IN THE BODY, PROTECTING OUR CELLS FROM FREE-RADICAL DAMAGE. THIS IS ONE OF THE EASIEST DISHES TO PREPARE AND SERVE, AND IT IS ALSO ONE OF THE HEALTHIEST. THE IDEA FOR THE DISH CAME WHILE I WAS TRAVELLING WITH MY FAMILY IN VIETNAM."

INGREDIENTS

WHITE CHICKEN STOCK:
- 1.5kg chicken wings
- 1.5 litres water
- 1 onion
- 2 sticks celery
- 1 leek
- 1 bay leaf
- 1 sprig of thyme
- 2 cloves garlic

BROTH:
- 2 x 500g gilt-head bream, scaled, filleted and pin-boned
- 750ml white chicken stock
- 55ml light soy sauce
- 50ml Thai fish sauce
- 100g fresh ginger
- 10 sticks fresh lemon grass
- 1 bunch fresh coriander
- 1 red chilli
- 1 lime

CRISPY SHALLOTS:
- 2 large banana shallots
- 20g cornflour
- salt and pepper, to taste

TO SERVE:
- 2 heads pak choi, cut in half
- batons of red chilli
- 400g mixed mushrooms (enoki, shiitake, oyster)
- salt and pepper
- 1 bunch spring onions, finely sliced
- coriander cress

METHOD

WHITE CHICKEN STOCK: Place 1kg of the chicken wings in the water and bring up to the boil. Skim and simmer for 45 minutes. Pass through a colander and add the remaining ingredients. Bring back to the boil and simmer for 30 minutes, skimming every 10 minutes. Pass through a fine sieve and reduce by half.

BROTH: Make the broth by bringing all except the bream to the boil. Simmer for 5 minutes, then remove from the heat and allow to infuse for 1 hour. Strain through a sieve.

CRISPY SHALLOTS: Peel and slice the shallots into very fine rings. Separate the rings and place on greaseproof paper. Allow to dry in a very low oven at 80°C for 24-48 hours.

When ready to cook, dust in cornflour and deep fry at 170°C for 2-3 minutes, until golden brown. Season to taste.

TO SERVE: To finish the dish, bring the broth to the boil and poach the pak choi for 3 minutes. Add the fish fillets, chilli and mushrooms, and simmer for 3 minutes. Correct the seasoning and serve, finishing at the last minute with the crispy shallots, spring onions and coriander cress.

CHEF'S TIP: A welcome addition could be some cooked chicken pieces. Chicken stock can be replaced with fish stock for our non-meat-eating friends!

A BEAUTIFUL SUMMER DESSERT
MADE EVEN BETTER IF YOU CAN
PICK THE RASPBERRIES YOURSELF.
IF YOU CAN FIND THEM, GOLDEN
RASPBERRIES ARE A LOVELY
ADDITION TO THE DISH.
- ALAN MURCHISON

↘WHITE CHOCOLATE RICE PUDDING
WITH RASPBERRY JAM JELLY
BY ALAN MURCHISON / SERVES 4

SPECIAL EQUIPMENT

Ice cream machine, 6cm acetate ribbon, digital thermometer, paint brush, 4 x napkin rings.

PLANNING AHEAD

Make the chocolate cylinders as far in advance as possible.

INGREDIENTS

WHITE CHOCOLATE CYLINDERS:
- 400g Valrhona white chocolate

WHITE CHOCOLATE RICE PUDDING:
- 125ml milk
- 125ml whipping cream
- seeds from ½ a vanilla pod
- 25g short grain rice
- 50g white chocolate

STREUSEL CRUMBLE:
- 45g demerara sugar
- 45g caster sugar
- 75g cold diced butter
- seeds from ½ a vanilla pod
- ½ tsp salt
- 175g plain flour

RASPBERRY JAM JELLY:
- 1½ leaves of gelatine (8.5g)
- 110g raspberry jam
- 100ml apple juice

RASPBERRY SORBET:
- 225ml water
- 225g caster sugar
- 500g raspberry purée
- 20ml lemon juice

CHANTILLY CREAM:
- 50g double cream
- 50g whipping cream
- 15g caster sugar
- seeds from ½ a vanilla pod

TO SERVE:
- freeze-dried raspberries, as needed
- melted white chocolate, as needed
- fresh raspberries, as needed

METHOD

WHITE CHOCOLATE CYLINDERS: Cut eight strips of acetate ribbon long enough so they form a cylinder inside the napkin rings – there needs to be at least a 1cm overlap.

Chop the white chocolate and place in a small plastic bowl. Three-quarters fill a small pan with water straight from the kettle and place the bowl on top but do not let the water touch the bottom. Very gently bring the temperature of the chocolate up to 33ºC, stirring every couple of minutes – it might be necessary to replenish the water half-way through. It is very important to do this slowly, take your time and make sure the chocolate never goes above 33ºC.

With a palette knife spread an even layer of chocolate over a strip of acetate. Pick it up by the corners and tease it into the napkin ring with the chocolate on the inside. The aim is to have an unbroken layer of chocolate on the inside of the acetate. It is fine to repair the odd patch once the chocolate has set a bit by dabbing a little melted chocolate onto the affected area with your finger.

WHITE CHOCOLATE RICE PUDDING:
Half fill a medium-sized pan with water and bring to a simmer. Place all the ingredients except the chocolate into a metal bowl that sits on top of the pan without touching the water. Cook over this bain marie, stirring every couple of minutes, until the rice is soft. Remove the bowl from the heat and allow it to cool for 5 minutes. Beat in the white chocolate then chill in the fridge. Once the rice pudding is cold, transfer it into a piping bag and reserve in the fridge.

STREUSEL CRUMBLE: Preheat your oven to 150ºC.

Mix all the ingredients together and spread onto a shallow roasting tray lined with greaseproof paper. Bake for 10 minutes then stir the mix with a wooden spoon to form lumps. Bake for 5 minutes, then stir again. Bake the mix for a final 5 minutes then allow to cool. Try to make the lumps as evenly sized as possible so that they bake evenly.

RASPBERRY JAM JELLY: Soak the gelatine in a large quantity of cold water until it is fully dissolved.

Warm the jam and apple juice in a small pan until it is hot and liquid. Remove the pan from the heat and whisk in the soaked gelatine, squeezing any excess water from

it when you remove it from the water. Pass the jelly through a sieve into a small bowl and allow it to set in the fridge. When set cut the jelly into nugget shapes around the size of half a raspberry.

RASPBERRY SORBET: Bring the sugar and water to the boil in a small pan and whisk until the sugar is fully dissolved. Pour the sugar syrup into the raspberry purée then add the lemon juice and mix well. Chill the mix in the fridge. Once the mix is cold, churn it in an ice cream machine following the manufacturer's guidelines. Transfer to a container and reserve in the freezer.

CHANTILLY CREAM: Whip all the ingredients together until the mixture forms soft peaks. Reserve in the fridge.

TO SERVE: Sprinkle a little of the streusel in the bottom of the cylinders then one-third fill with rice pudding, then a couple of raspberries, then three-quarters fill with rice pudding and finally top with the chantilly cream. Reserve the cylinders with their acetate still on in the fridge until ready to serve.

With a paint brush stripe a bit of melted white chocolate onto a plate. Arrange the fresh raspberries, freeze-dried raspberries, streusel and nuggets of jelly onto the stripe, leaving room for the sorbet and the cylinder.

Take the cylinders from the fridge and very gently remove the acetate from the outside of the chocolate, being extra careful with the last centimetre where the chocolate has doubled up.

Finally place the cylinder on the plate and finish with a scoop of sorbet.

CHEF'S TIP: If you can't find Valrhona chocolate, buy the most expensive you can afford, you really get what you are paying for with chocolate. Make the cylinders at least a week in advance to avoid disappointment as they are a fiddly job and require a little practice, so take your time and be prepared for a few failures. If the chocolate is setting in your bowl, gently warm it in the same way as before. Store the cylinders somewhere cool and out of the sun.

NICK EASTER
HARLEQUINS & ENGLAND

↘ ABERDEEN ANGUS BEEF FILLET,
CARROT, NAVET, TREVISO AND CAPERS
BY MARCUS WAREING / SERVES 4

"THIS DISH ENCOMPASSES THE RICH FLAVOUR OF THE ABERDEEN ANGUS FILLET, WHICH IS PERFECTLY COMPLEMENTED BY THE SWEET CARROT PUREE AND THE TANGY SALTINESS OF THE CAPERS. ENSURE YOU REST YOUR MEAT FOR AT LEAST 5 MINUTES AFTER COOKING TO ENSURE THE JUICES ARE RETAINED."

METHOD

BEEF SAUCE: Heat a saucepan over a high heat with the vegetable oil. Season the beef and fry until dark golden. Remove and set aside. Add the onion, carrot, celery and garlic to the pan with another tablespoon of oil. Brown then add the tomato purée, peppercorns and red wine. Simmer gently until a syrup consistency forms, then add the remaining ingredients (excluding the capers). Simmer for 30 minutes, skimming regularly to remove any fat. Strain then adjust the seasoning if necessary. To finish the sauce add the capers.

CARROT PUREE: Bring a medium-sized pan of water to the boil with the salt added. Add the carrots and cook until soft; strain (reserving the liquid) then place straight into a blender. Allow to blend for 3 minutes while reducing the cooking liquor and add this as and when needed to make a smooth purée. Pass through a fine sieve then set aside. When ready to serve heat in a small pan.

SHALLOTS AND NAVETS: Preheat the oven to 160°C. Leaving the skins on, wrap the shallots well in foil and place in the oven for 15 minutes until soft. Allow to cool then peel the skin off and cut in half. Heat a chargrill for a good 15 minutes until smoking then season the shallots and grill until well charred.

Cut the navets in half and, just prior to serving, brown the flat side in a pan with a little oil until golden.

BEEF FILLET: To cook the beef fillet heat a large frying pan over a moderate heat with the vegetable oil. Season the beef then place carefully in the pan and brown all over. Add the butter and when foaming spoon over the beef while regularly turning it. Remove from the pan and allow to rest for 5 minutes before carving and serving.

TO SERVE: Place a spoonful of the warmed carrot purée on each plate, add the beef, then garnish with the navets, the treviso leaves and a spoonful of the sauce, heating the sauce and pouring over as you serve the dishes.

SPECIAL EQUIPMENT
Blender.

INGREDIENTS

BEEF SAUCE:
- 1 tbsp vegetable oil
- 80g beef trim or rump steak, diced
- 1 onion, peeled and diced
- 1 carrot, peeled and diced
- 1 stalk celery, diced
- 2 cloves garlic
- 1 tbsp tomato purée
- 4 black peppercorns
- 200ml red wine
- 1 bay leaf
- 300ml beef or chicken stock
- ½ tsp table salt
- ½ tsp beef extract
- ½ bunch tarragon
- 75g capers, chopped

CARROT PUREE:
- 1 tsp table salt
- 4 carrots, peeled and finely diced

SHALLOTS AND NAVETS:
- 2 banana shallots
- 8 baby navets; blanched, scraped to remove the skin then halved

BEEF FILLET:
- 2 tbsp vegetable oil
- 1 tsp table salt
- 4 x 150g pieces of Aberdeen Angus beef fillet
- 25g unsalted butter

TO SERVE:
- 8 leaves of treviso

EAT BEFORE A MATCH:
❝SPAGHETTI BOLOGNESE❞
- NICK EASTER

↘ CUSTARD TART,
FRESH RASPBERRY CREME, VANILLA ICE CREAM
BY MARCUS WAREING / SERVES 8

"THIS WAS THE DISH I COOKED FOR THE QUEEN'S 80TH BIRTHDAY CELEBRATION. DUE TO ITS WIDESPREAD PRESS, AND AMAZING TEXTURE AND TASTE, WE ARE UNABLE TO TAKE IT OFF THE MENU! WHEN MAKING IT BE PATIENT – GOOD THINGS TAKE TIME AND THIS NEEDS TO BE COOKED SLOWLY TO ENSURE THE SILKY TEXTURE IS ACHIEVED."

PLANNING AHEAD
Mix the pastry and refrigerate for 2 hours before rolling out.

INGREDIENTS

PASTRY:
- 225g flour, plus extra for dusting
- pinch of salt
- 1 lemon, zest only
- 150g butter
- 75g caster sugar
- 1 free-range egg yolk
- 1 free-range egg

CUSTARD FILLING:
- 500ml whipping cream
- 9 free-range egg yolks
- 75g caster sugar
- 2 nutmegs

RASPBERRY CREME:
- 200ml double cream
- 100g crème fraîche
- 1 vanilla pod, seeds scraped only
- 1 tsp icing sugar
- 1 punnet raspberries, blitzed to a purée then passed through a fine sieve

TO SERVE:
- ½ punnet raspberries, sliced horizontally
- few sprigs of baby basil
- freeze dried raspberries, crumbled
- your favourite vanilla ice cream

METHOD

PASTRY: Preheat the oven to 170ºC.

For the pastry, rub together the flour, salt, lemon zest and butter until the mixture resembles breadcrumbs. Add the sugar, then beat together the egg yolk and whole egg and slowly add these, mixing until the pastry forms a ball. Wrap tightly in cling film and refrigerate for 2 hours.

Roll out the pastry on a lightly floured surface to 2mm in thickness. Use to line an 18cm flan ring placed on a baking sheet. Line with greaseproof paper and fill with baking beans, then bake blind for about 10 minutes or until the pastry is starting to turn golden brown. Remove the paper and beans, and allow to cool.

Turn the oven down to 130ºC.

CUSTARD FILLING: For the filling, bring the cream to the boil. Whisk the yolks and sugar together then add the cream and mix well. Pass the mixture through a fine sieve into a jug.

Place the pastry case in the oven then pour the custard mix right to the brim. Grate the nutmeg liberally over the top and bake for 30-40 minutes or until the custard appears set, but not too firm. Remove from the oven and cool to room temperature before serving.

RASPBERRY CREME: Whisk the cream, crème fraîche, vanilla seeds and sugar together until stiff. Fold in the raspberry purée.

TO SERVE: Take a spoonful of the raspberry crème and dollop on each plate; smear with a small palette knife. Slice the custard tart and place a piece in the centre, garnish with the raspberries, basil and a scoop of ice cream.

↘ HEIRLOOM TOMATOES,
BLACK OLIVE CARAMEL, BURRATA
BY MARCUS WAREING / SERVES 4

"WITH RIPE, SWEET AND JUICY HEIRLOOM TOMATOES THIS DISH IS TRANSFORMED FROM THE ORDINARY TO THE SUBLIME. ENSURE YOU CHOOSE TOMATOES THAT ARE NOT TOO FIRM AND HAVE AN AROMA ALSO!"

INGREDIENTS

BLACK OLIVE CARAMEL:
- 100g sugar
- 50g dried black olives, blitzed into a smooth purée

TOMATOES:
- 4 tbsp olive oil
- 1 tsp Chardonnay vinegar
- selection of 4 heirloom tomatoes, sliced and cut into wedges (at room temperature not fridge cold to ensure maximum flavour)
- Maldon sea salt
- freshly milled black pepper

TO SERVE:
- 1 ball (250g) Burrata, cut into 8 pieces
- baby basil cress

METHOD

BLACK OLIVE CARAMEL: Make the caramel first; caramelise the sugar in a saucepan over a moderate heat. When a pale golden carefully whisk in the olive purée until smooth. Add a touch of water if necessary to create a paste. Pass through a sieve and allow to cool (if it sets up too much just reheat and add a little more water).

TOMATOES: Mix the olive oil and vinegar together and spread liberally over the cut tomatoes, then sprinkle with the salt and pepper.

TO SERVE: You can make one large platter or individual plates; drizzle the caramel on the plates then add the tomatoes and two pieces of Burrata. Garnish with the basil and serve immediately.

↘ICED LIME MOUSSE
WITH SWEET AND SOUR PINEAPPLE, LIQUORICE
BY MARCUS WAREING / SERVES 8

"THIS IS SUCH A REFRESHING, YET INTENSELY SATISFYING, PUDDING WHICH IS THE PERFECT END TO A SUMMER'S MEAL. WE USE A SOFT LIQUORICE FROM NEW ZEALAND WHICH ADDS A COMPLEX RICHNESS TO THE DISH."

INGREDIENTS

MERINGUE:
- 2 medium free-range egg whites
- 60g caster sugar
- 60g icing sugar
- zest of 1 lime

MARINATED PINEAPPLE:
- ½ supersweet pineapple
- 50g demerara sugar
- 3 star anise
- 4 black peppercorns
- juice of 1 lime

MOUSSE IGLOOS

LIME CREAM:
- juice and zest of 2 limes
- 150g double cream, lightly whipped

GLOSSY MERINGUE:
- 100g caster or granulated sugar
- 50ml water
- 2 egg whites

SABAYON:
- 100g caster or granulated sugar
- 50ml water
- 2 medium free-range egg yolks
- 1 medium free-range egg

TO SERVE:
- ½ log soft liquorice, cut in half lengthways then into crescents

METHOD

MERINGUE: Preheat the oven to 70°C.

Whisk the egg whites until very stiff then add the caster sugar and continue whisking until glossy and smooth. Add the icing sugar and mix until combined. Spread onto a sheet of greaseproof paper, zest the lime over the top then place in the oven for 1-2 hours or until crispy and dry.

MARINATED PINEAPPLE: For the pineapple, slice the skin off carefully then cut into thirds. Using a large ring cutter (or a circle shape and a knife) cut three perfect circles out of the flesh. Place the pineapple trim with the remaining ingredients into a pan, cover with cold water and simmer gently for 20 minutes. Slice the pineapple into thin slices and place in a shallow tray. When the syrup is ready strain onto the sliced pineapple and place in the fridge to cool.

MOUSSE IGLOOS

LIME CREAM: Gently fold the lime zest and juice into the whipped cream.

GLOSSY MERINGUE: Place 100g of sugar in a pan with 50ml of water and bring to a rapid boil for 3 minutes, meanwhile slowly whisk the egg whites. Whisk the hot syrup into the stiff whites to create a glossy meringue. Set aside.

SABAYON: Place the whole egg and egg yolks in a mixing bowl and whisk until thick and fluffy. As with the meringue, add the hot syrup (formed from the other 100g sugar and 50ml water) and whisk until the bowl is cool to touch, creating a sabayon.

TO COMBINE: Carefully fold the glossy meringue into the lime cream then add the sabayon. Spoon or pipe into dome moulds and place in the freezer until firm.

TO SERVE: Place a couple of slices of pineapple on each plate. Soak the liquorice crescents in a little warm water then arrange on the plates. Break up the meringue into small pieces. Warm the igloo moulds in your hand then scoop out the dome parfait and place on a frozen tray. Freeze for 5 minutes then remove and cover with the meringue pieces (do these one at a time with the finished igloos going back in the freezer until all are done). Place the igloo on the pineapple and serve immediately.

FRANCESCO MAZZEI
L'ANIMA

↓ JAMES HASKELL
STADE FRANCAIS & ENGLAND

↘ SICILIAN RABBIT
BY FRANCESCO MAZZEI / SERVES 4

"THE INSPIRATION BEHIND THIS RECIPE CAME FROM ONE OF MY TRIPS BETWEEN ISCHIA ISLAND AND SICILY AND MY MOTHER'S FAMILY RECIPE. IT TOOK ME SIX YEARS TO DEVELOP THIS RECIPE TO GET THE PERFECT BALANCE BETWEEN SWEET AND SOUR 'AGRO DOLCE' USING NUTS, SULTANAS, CALABRIAN TROPEA ONIONS, OLIVES AND FENNEL TO ENRICH THE DISH."

METHOD

RABBIT: Divide the rabbit into approximately 16 pieces and dust with flour. Brown the pieces in a pan in the oil then set aside.

Cut the celery, fennel, onions, tomatoes, shallots, garlic and carrots into small pieces (mirepoix) and add them to the pan with the fennel seeds and sweat in the oil for a few minutes.

Add the vinegar, sugar and tomato paste and simmer until reduced. Add the rabbit pieces and stock and gently simmer for 20 minutes. When the rabbit is cooked add the olives, sultanas, marjoram and thyme.

TO SERVE: Serve the rabbit with crushed pistachios, pine nuts and a drop of extra virgin olive oil on top, season to taste.

KEEP AN EYE ON THE RABBIT AS A OVER COOKING CAN RESULT IN A VERY HARD MEAT
- FRANCESCO MAZZEI

PLANNING AHEAD
Debone the rabbit and make a stock the day before.

INGREDIENTS

RABBIT:
- 1 x 1.3kg whole rabbit
- plain flour, as needed
- 15g olive oil
- 70g celery
- 70g fennel
- 70g onions
- 10g sun-dried tomatoes
- 50g shallots
- 10g garlic
- 80g chantenay carrots
- 5g fennel seeds
- ½ litre red wine vinegar
- 20g muscovado sugar
- 20g tomato paste
- 1.3 litres rabbit stock
- 70g taggiasca (Ligurian) olives
- 20g sultanas
- 5g marjoram, chopped
- 1 sprig thyme

TO SERVE:
- 5g pistachios
- extra-virgin olive oil, as needed
- 5g pine nuts, toasted
- 10g fine salt
- 10g black pepper

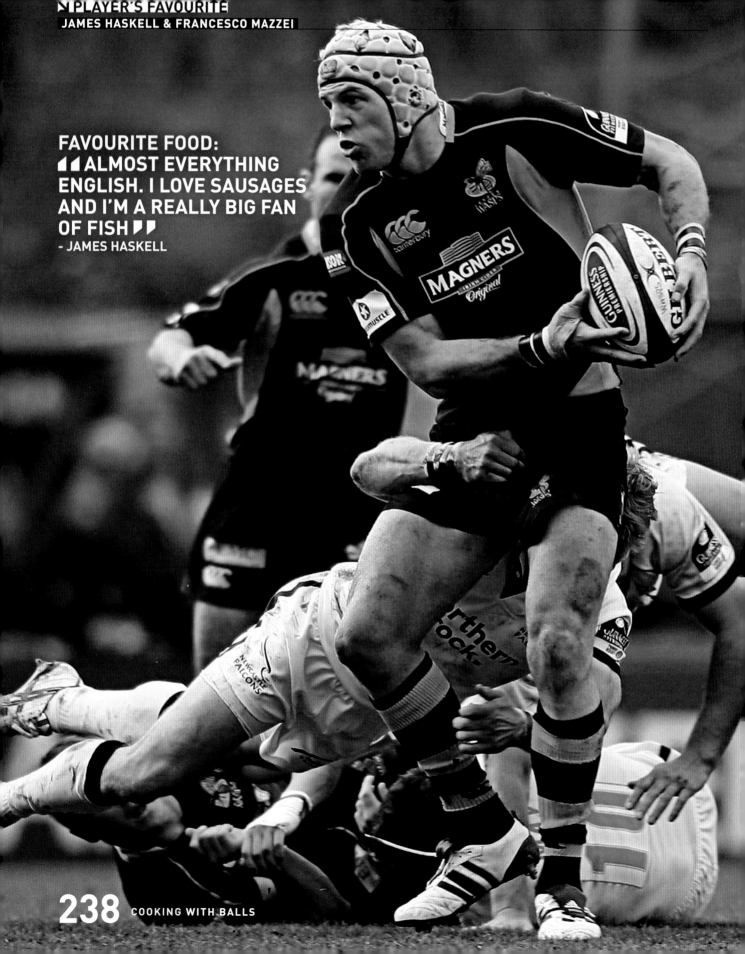

FAVOURITE FOOD:
❝**ALMOST EVERYTHING ENGLISH. I LOVE SAUSAGES AND I'M A REALLY BIG FAN OF FISH**❞
- JAMES HASKELL

↘ SPAGHETTI LOBSTER
BY FRANCESCO MAZZEI / SERVES 4

PLANNING AHEAD

Make the lobster stock and tomato sauce in advance.

INGREDIENTS

LOBSTER:
- extra virgin olive oil, as needed
- 2 garlic cloves
- 10g thyme
- 10g red chillis
- 10g spring onions
- 2 x 600g Scottish lobster
- 20ml brandy
- 2 star anise
- 100g fresh cherry tomatoes, halved

TOMATO SAUCE:
- 1 garlic clove, crushed
- basil, as desired
- 20g onions, chopped
- 200g fresh san marzano tomatoes

LOBSTER STOCK:
- 400g lobster carcasses
- 1 onion
- 1 celery
- carrot
- 1 star anise
- 1 glass of dry white wine
- 25ml cooking brandy
- 1 tsp tomato paste

PASTA:
- 360g dried linguine
- 80ml extra virgin olive oil
- salt and pepper
- 10g flat parsley, chopped
- 10g basil, chopped

TO SERVE:
- basil tips

METHOD

LOBSTER: Shallow fry in the olive oil the garlic, thyme and chillis in a pan and then add the spring onions. Cut the lobsters in half lengthwise while they are still alive. Add to the hot pan and pour over the brandy. Add the star anise, tomatoes, tomato sauce and some lobster stock. Cover with a lid and let it cook for approximately 5-8 minutes.

TOMATO SAUCE: Sweat the garlic in a pan, when golden add basil and onion straight away, add tomatoes and cook for 5 minutes, pass through Moulin and keep to one side.

LOBSTER STOCK: Roast the lobster carcasses and vegetables in the oven at 185ºC for 25 minutes. Then add to a pot, add brandy and let evaporate completely, then do the same with white wine. Then add star anise and tomato paste, cover with lid and simmer for approximately 1½ hours. Remove any foam on top.

PASTA: In the meantime boil the pasta. When it is al dente mix together with the sauce (remove the lobster halves and keep on the side). Finish the pasta with some olive oil, salt, pepper, parsley and basil.

TO SERVE: Serve on a plate with the lobster half and basil tips to garnish.

CHEF'S TIP: Be careful not to overcook the lobster. If you have garlic oil, add 1 teaspoon right at the end before serving to give it more flavour.

FAVOURITE FOOD AS A CHILD:
❝ SUNDAYS WERE ALWAYS A BIG CELEBRATION WITH LUNCHES USING THE BEST INGREDIENTS FROM OUR GARDEN – EVERYTHING WAS HOME-MADE INCLUDING THE BREAD, THE PASTA AND EVEN THE ICE CREAMS. ❞
- FRANCESCO MAZZEI

↘ OVEN ROASTED PEACH
WITH LAVENDER
BY FRANCESCO MAZZEI / SERVES 4

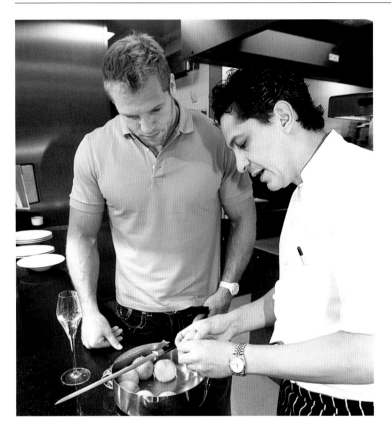

INGREDIENTS
- 4 peaches
- 100g demerara sugar
- 50g honey
- 200ml Prosecco
- 200ml Moscato di Saracena
- 4 twigs lavender or rosemary flowers
- ½ small cinnamon stick
- 1 star anise

TO SERVE:
- sprigs of lavender

"PEACH IS VERY LOW IN SUGAR AND HAS NO FAT. WARMTH BRINGS OUT THE GORGEOUS AROMAS AND COLOURS OF PEACHES AND ROASTING THEM IS THE SIMPLEST TREATMENT OF A SPECTACULAR SUMMER FRUIT."

METHOD

Preheat the oven to 190ºC.

Cut the peaches in half, remove the stone and place in a pan with the cut side down. Add the remaining ingredients and cook in the oven for 15 minutes until soft.

Take the peaches out of the liquid and let them cool down. In the meantime, on a medium heat, reduce the liquid by half to make a sauce.

TO SERVE: Decorate the peaches with a lavender sprig and serve with the sauce.

> YOU NEED TO MAKE SURE THAT THE PEACH IS NOT TOO SOFT AND NOT TOO HARD – IT HAS TO BE PERFECT TO GET THE FULL FLAVOURS AND RIGHT TEXTURE OF THE FRUIT
> - FRANCESCO MAZZEI

↘ BLACK SCOTCH BEEF TAGLIATA
WITH MARROW BONE, OVINSARDO AND MAGLIOCCO SAUCE
BY FRANCESCO MAZZEI / SERVES 4

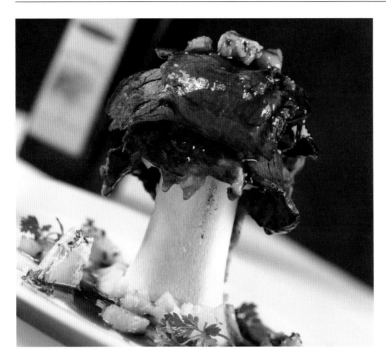

"A TYPICAL CLASSIC ITALIAN DISH THAT I HAVE AMENDED MAINLY IN THE PRESENTATION BY STUFFING THE MARROW BONE WITH POTATO MASH AND DRAPING THE SLICED BEEF OVER THE MARROW."

METHOD

Remove the marrow from the bones and place in the fridge in water. Leave to soak overnight.

Clean the sirloins and marinate with the olive oil and thyme.

Melt half of the bone marrow in a pan until it is liquefied and place aside. Cut the other half in pieces and fry to use as a garnish.

In a frying pan, briskly sear the steaks on one side until well browned, then turn once and cook briefly for a medium-rare result. Set aside to rest. Slice just before serving.

Boil the potatoes in salted water. When cooked pass through the moulis and mix with the chives, salt and the melted marrow.

In the meantime take the clean marrow bone from the fridge and place in the oven until it is hot 185ºC, then fill with the mashed potatoes. Put the marrow bones in the oven until hot for approximately 10 minutes.

TO SERVE: Let the Magliocco wine, shallots and thyme simmer until reduced to a syrupy sauce (approximately two tablespoons of sauce), then mix with the veal jus.

Dress the marrow bones in the middle of a round plate, place the sliced meat on top and finish with pieces of Ovinsardo cheese and magliocco sauce.

SPECIAL EQUIPMENT
Moulis.

PLANNING AHEAD
Clean the marrow bones the day before and soak in water overnight in the fridge.

INGREDIENTS
- 600g marrow bones
- 800g beef sirloin
- 80g extra virgin olive oil
- 20g thyme
- 800g potatoes
- 20g chives, chopped
- 12g salt

TO SERVE:
- 40g Ovinsardo cheese
- 750ml Magliocco wine
- 2 shallots, finely chopped
- bunch of thyme
- 80ml veal jus

MAKE SURE THAT THE BEEF IS AT LEAST 4 WEEKS AGED
- FRANCESCO MAZZEI

↙ **JOE WORSLEY**
LONDON WASPS & ENGLAND

↘ LOBSTER MIMOSA
BY JONAS KARLSSON / SERVES 4

METHOD

LOBSTER: Bring the vegetable trimmings, wine, water, salt, peppercorns and parsley to the boil and then simmer for up to 5 minutes. Remove from the heat, then add the lemon slices and keep covered for 10-15 minutes to infuse.

Pass the cooking stock through a sieve and bring to the boil again in a pan. Kill the lobsters by inserting a knife in the middle of the head about 2cm above the eyes. Add the lobsters into the boiling stock and bring to a simmer once again. Simmer for 8-10 minutes. Remove the lobsters from the pan, leave to cool down on a tray until cool enough to handle. Using scissors, remove the shell from the tail and claws.

MIMOSA SALAD: For the mimosa salad, mix all of the ingredients and then bind with the mayonnaise. Check and correct the seasoning to taste.

TO SERVE: When the lobster is still warm serve with the mimosa salad and mixed salad dressed with vinaigrette.

INGREDIENTS

LOBSTER:
- 4 x 550-600g live lobsters
- 500g of any vegetable trimmings e.g onion, carrot, leek, fennel, celery
- 200ml dry white wine
- 2 litres water
- 100g fine sea salt
- 20 pink peppercorns
- few leaves or parsley stalks
- 2-3 slices of lemon

MIMOSA SALAD:
- 1 globe artichoke, cooked and diced
- 150g new potatoes, peeled, cooked and diced
- 1 tbsp dill, chopped
- 1 tbsp chives, chopped
- 1 large hard boiled egg, peeled and chopped
- 1 Granny Smith apple, peeled, cored and chopped
- 60-80g mayonnaise
- seasoning, to taste

MIXED SALAD:
- mixed salad leaves like mache, oak leaf, mizuna and frisée, as needed
- French vinaigrette, as needed

IF HOSTING A DINNER PARTY YOU CAN PRESENT THE DISH STARTER SIZE IN MARTINI GLASSES TO CREATE A WOW FACTOR WITH YOUR GUESTS – THIS RECIPE WILL MAKE 8 STARTER PORTIONS
- JONAS KARLSSON

↘ RUGBY PLAYER'S ROAST

BY JONAS KARLSSON / SERVES 2

INGREDIENTS

CHATEAUBRIAND:
- 1 x 550g chateaubriand
- salt and finely ground pepper
- vegetable oil, as needed
- 2 tbsp salted butter

YORKSHIRE PUDDINGS:
- 90g plain flour
- 3 eggs
- 230ml full fat milk
- salt and pepper, to taste
- beef drippings or vegetable oil, as needed

VEGETABLES:
- 2 large potatoes (Maris Piper)
- 2 tbsp duck fat
- 1 bunch of baby carrots
- salt, pepper and sugar, to taste
- ½ tbsp butter

GRAVY:
- 100ml red wine
- 500ml beef stock
- 2-3 tbsp whipping cream
- 1 tbsp redcurrant jelly
- salt and pepper, to taste

TO SERVE:
- 1 small bunch of parsley or watercress

METHOD

CHATEAUBRIAND: Preheat the oven to 160ºC.

Season the meat, then heat up a cast-iron pan with the vegetable oil and butter, and sear the meat all around. Transfer the pan into the hot oven and cook for 8-12 minutes. Leave to rest.

YORKSHIRE PUDDINGS: Preheat the oven to 220ºC. Sieve the flour and put in a bowl together with the eggs and mix gently to incorporate the eggs into the flour. Pour in the milk and beat until smooth, season with a pinch of salt and fine pepper from the mill. Heat up pudding moulds (around 10cm in diameter) in the oven and pour in a little dripping or oil.

Half fill the moulds with the mixture and bake in the oven for 5-6 minutes until they rise. Then turn down the heat to 190ºC and finish until desired crispiness.

VEGETABLES: Preheat the oven to 180ºC.

Peel and cut the potatoes into four, then bring them up to the boil in a pan of salted water, drain and leave to dry.

Heat the duck fat in a frying pan and then colour the potatoes until golden, transfer to a roasting tray and finish in the oven until cooked through.

Peel the carrots and bring to the boil with a little water, seasoning, butter and a touch of sugar. Simmer until tender.

GRAVY: Using the roasting pan juices from the meat, drain the fat away then pour in the red wine and reduce until down to one-third. Add the stock and reduce again to one-third. Add the cream and jelly and bring to the boil. Check the seasoning then pass through a strainer if needed.

TO SERVE: Plate the meat and vegetables up as pictured and garnish with a little parsley or watercress.

EAT AFTER A MATCH:
❝ ANYTHING NOT ALLOWED IN
THE WEEK (I CALL IT THE DIRTY
MEAL) – IT'S DELICIOUS ❞
- JOE WORSLEY

⬔ POACHED ORGANIC SALMON,
PICKLED CUCUMBER, HERB SALAD, SOFT-BOILED EGG VINAIGRETTE
BY JONAS KARLSSON / SERVES 4

SPECIAL EQUIPMENT
Thermometer.

PLANNING AHEAD
Prepare the cucumber the night before.

INGREDIENTS

PICKLED CUCUMBER:
- 200ml water
- 1 tbsp fine sea salt
- 1½ tbsp sugar
- 100ml distilled vinegar
- 1 tbsp dill, chopped
- 1 cucumber

SALMON:
- 1-2 handfuls of vegetable trimmings like onion, carrot, leek, fennel and celery
- 2 tbsp salt
- 1 litre water
- 4 x 160g portions of organic salmon

EGG VINAIGRETTE:
- 2 soft-boiled eggs, cooked for around 4-5 minutes
- 1-2 tbsp French vinaigrette
- 1 tbsp chives, chopped
- salt and pepper

HERB SALAD:
- mixed herbs including dill, chervil, flat-leaf parsley and tarragon
- rapeseed oil, as needed
- fine sea salt, to taste

METHOD

PICKLED CUCUMBER: Bring the water, salt, sugar and vinegar to the boil just enough to dissolve the salt and sugar. Remove from the heat and allow to cool. Add the dill.

Peel the cucumber then slice into long ribbons using a vegetable peeler or mandolin. Add the cucumber to the marinade and leave for at least for 4 hours or overnight. Drain the cucumber before serving.

SALMON: Bring the vegetables, salt and water to the boil for 5 minutes then remove from the heat until the stock reaches half boil, around 55ºC. Drop the salmon portions into the poaching liquid and leave to cook slowly at this temperature for about 12-15 minutes.

EGG VINAIGRETTE: Mash the soft-boiled eggs with a fork then mix with the French vinaigrette and chives. Taste and season accordingly.

HERB SALAD: Dress the herbs with a little rapeseed oil and add a touch of salt.

TO SERVE: Serve the poached salmon on top of the drained pickled cucumber with the herb salad on the side and drizzle with the egg vinaigrette.

↘ WHOLE ROASTED FOIE GRAS,
BRAISED PUY LENTILS, FRIED QUAIL EGG, CABERNET SAUVIGNON DRESSING
BY JONAS KARLSSON / SERVES 4

INGREDIENTS

DRESSING:
- 50g shallots, diced
- olive oil, as needed
- 50ml medium-bodied red wine
- 50ml Cabernet Sauvignon vinegar
- 200ml beef stock
- seasoning, to taste

PUY LENTILS:
- 200g puy lentils
- 1 litre chicken stock
- 1 whole garlic clove
- 1 large bay leaf
- 1 carrot
- 200g celeriac
- 100g unsalted butter, diced
- 200g baby spinach
- salt and finely ground pepper, to taste

FOIE GRAS:
- 1 x 600g whole foie gras around (local butcher can usually pre-order)
- salt and finely ground pepper
- butter, as needed
- 10 sprigs of thyme

QUAIL EGGS:
- 4 quail eggs
- butter, as needed
- salt and pepper, to taste

METHOD

DRESSING: Sweat the shallots in a little olive oil then deglaze with the wine (reduce until syrup like), then add the vinegar and simmer until a syrupy consistency again. Add the beef stock and again simmer to reduce to a quarter of the original amount. Season to taste and keep warm.

PUY LENTILS: Rinse the lentils then bring to the boil with the chicken stock, garlic clove and bay leaf, reduce to a simmer, adding the whole carrot and celeriac. Simmer for about 25 minutes or until the lentils are tender, but not mushy. When cooked drain off one-third of the stock, keeping a small amount.

Discard the bay leaf and garlic clove. Grate the carrot and celeriac and then mix through the lentils. Add the butter little by little and keep warm. Just before serving add seasoning and the baby spinach to wilt.

FOIE GRAS: Preheat the oven to 160°C. Season the foie gras. In a cast-iron pan melt a knob of butter then at medium heat sear the foie gras, adding the thyme, turning until brown. Finish in the oven for around 8 minutes or until tender to the touch.

QUAIL EGGS: Fry the quail eggs gently in butter with a little seasoning.

TO SERVE: Slice the foie gras into four large pieces, spoon a quarter of the lentil garnish onto a plate and add a slice foie gras on top. Top with a fried quail egg and drizzle the dressing around the plate.

ANDRE GARRETT
GALVIN AT WINDOWS

WHEN BLENDING THE PUREE,
USE A BLENDER WITH A TIGHT-
FITTING LID AND START ON LOW
SPEED THEN MOVE UP TO HIGH

- ANDRE GARRETT

↘ SOUTH COAST JOHN DORY,
ORANGE GLAZED ENDIVE, CAULIFLOWER PUREE, CURRY OIL, PINE NUTS AND GOLDEN RAISINS
BY ANDRE GARRETT / SERVES 4

"ONE OF MY FAVORITE FISH DISHES, THE BLEND OF CAULIFLOWER AND CURRY WITH THE RAISINS IS A GREAT CONTRAST TO THE JOHN DORY."

SPECIAL EQUIPMENT
Cheesecloth.

PLANNING AHEAD
Soak the golden raisins in hot water overnight, toast the pine nuts and keep until needed. The cauliflower purée can be made in advance and will keep in the fridge for 1-2 days.

INGREDIENTS

CAULIFLOWER PUREE:
- 1 large white cauliflower
- 30g butter
- salt, to taste
- 200ml milk
- 200ml single cream or crème fraîche

ORANGE GLAZED ENDIVE:
- 2 lemons
- 2 oranges
- 2 large Belgian endive or chicory
- 50g icing sugar
- olive oil, for cooking

CURRY OIL, JOHN DORY, PINE NUTS AND GOLDEN RAISINS:
- 50g Cochin curry powder
- 200ml corn oil
- juice of ½ lemon
- 2 x 600g-800g John Dory, filleted by the fishmonger
- 20g soaked golden raisins
- 10g salted capers
- 20g toasted pine nuts

METHOD

CAULIFLOWER PUREE: Cut the cauliflower into small florets and discard the stalks. Heat the butter in a large pan until foamy, then add the cauliflower, season with a little salt and sweat gently over a low heat for 2 minutes, turn up the heat to high and add the milk, cover with a lid and cook very quickly until the cauliflower is tender, about 5-6 minutes.

Drain in a colander then transfer the cooked cauliflower to a blender, discard any left-over milk, cover the blender and blend on medium speed.

Bring the single cream to the boil and add into the cauliflower while still blending to make a thick yet smooth purée. Pass through a fine strainer and check for seasoning. This can be done in advance and will keep in the fridge for 1-2 days.

ORANGE GLAZED ENDIVE: Zest both lemons and oranges, juice and keep aside. Trim any dirty leaves from the endives, wash and dry on kitchen paper. Heat a large frying pan on a medium heat, cut both endives in two lengthways and dip the cut side in the sugar.

Add a splash of olive oil to the pan, add the endive sugar-side down and allow to caramelise. When coloured turn over and colour on the other side, then add the juices and zests, and a little more sugar. Allow to simmer and reduce for 10-12 minutes to cook through and glaze – the endive should be soft and glazed with the sticky caramel coating – then set aside.

CURRY OIL, JOHN DORY, PINE NUTS AND GOLDEN RAISINS: Heat the curry powder in a dry pan over a medium heat to toast and cook the curry, keep moving and smelling as you cook and the flavour and aroma will develop in a warm, sweet curry fragrance. Pour in the oil and mix, bring to around 60ºC and take off the heat. Leave to settle and cool. When cool, pass though a cheesecloth to leave behind any sediment.

Marinate the John Dory fillets in the curry mixture for 20 minutes before serving. When ready to serve reheat the cauliflower purée in a pan. Reheat the endive in the pan, warm the raisins, capers and pine nuts add in the lemon juice some of the oil to make a dressing.

Heat a large frying pan over a high heat and place in the John Dory skin-side down, using the curry oil as the cooking medium – do not move while the skin is crisping – and fry for 3 minutes, turn and cook for a further 2-3 minutes until the fish is firm and opaque then take out and drain.

TO SERVE: Swipe some purée onto warmed serving plates, top with the endive and arrange the fish across, dress with the warmed dressing and serve.

FAVOURITE FOOD AS A CHILD:
❝ FISH FINGER SANDWICHES
AND MY MUM'S CAKES. SHE MAKES
A FANTASTIC FRUIT CAKE AND
I WAS ALWAYS AROUND HER APRON
STRINGS HELPING HER COOK ❞
- ANDRE GARRETT

↘ SEAFOOD LASAGNE
BY ANDRE GARRETT / SERVES 4

METHOD

PASTA: Mix the eggs and egg yolk, a splash of oil and salt together. With the flour on your work surface make a well in the centre and slowly add some egg mixture. With your fingers start to mix the outside into the liquid to mix and slowly repeat this until a smooth dough is reached – do not work too much. Wrap in cling film and place in the fridge for at least 12 hours to rest.

The next day take the dough out of the fridge 1 hour before needed. Set up your pasta machine, break your dough into a small enough size to roll to a thin sheet – make sure you stretch and fold the pasta so as to make a strong elastic dough.

Bring a large pan of water to the boil with a little oil. Cut the pasta with the ring to make four discs per person. Blanch your pasta in the water for 1 minute and take out into iced water. Keep with a little oil in the fridge until needed.

FISH MOUSSE: Chill the bowl of your blender in the fridge beforehand, then blend the salmon and egg white until a fine paste. Take the mixture from the blender and place in a large bowl over ice. Gradually incorporate the cream and beat with a spatula until smooth, season with a little salt, pepper and a pinch of cayenne, then keep in a piping bag.

SHELLFISH: Clean the scallop meat and slice in half. Cook the washed clams in a very hot pan with a splash of water and white wine until opened and cooked, then remove from the shells.

Peel the prawns, wash the octopus well and cook in simmering salted water for 30 minutes. Cool in the water, take out while still warm and cut into small slices. Set all seafood aside until ready to serve.

LASAGNE: Take your metal rings for the lasagne and grease the inside with a little oil. Make up the lasagnes with a pasta sheet first, pipe over some mousse and repeat this until you reach the top of the ring. Use four sheets of pasta per lasagne, then wrap each one tightly in cling film and place into a hot steamer for 10 minutes. Take out and rest for a further 5 minutes.

TO SERVE: Heat a little olive oil in a large frying pan and sauté all the seafood carefully until they take on a little colour, then drain. Place the lasagne back in the steamer for 2 minutes. Take out and remove the cling film, place in the centre of your serving bowl and dress around your shellfish with the seafood liquid. Any juice that remains can be mixed with a dash more olive oil and used as an extra dressing.

SPECIAL EQUIPMENT
Blender, pasta machine, stove-top steamer, small metal rings 3-5cm.

PLANNING AHEAD
Make the pasta at least 12 hours in advance. Wash the clams the day before use. The lasagne can be made up and kept in the fridge well in advance and cooked later when needed.

INGREDIENTS

PASTA:
- 4 whole eggs
- 1 egg yolk
- olive oil, as needed
- salt, as needed
- 500g 00 pasta flour

FISH MOUSSE:
- 100g salmon fillet
- 20g egg whites
- 100g double cream
- salt, pepper and cayenne, to taste

SHELLFISH:
- 4 large scallops
- 20 clams, washed
- white wine, to taste
- 4 king prawns
- ½ small octopus

ASK YOUR FISHMONGER TO SELECT THE BEST SHELLFISH AND THE FRESHEST. YOU CAN ALSO BUY PRE-COOKED OCTOPUS FROM GOOD FISHMONGERS
- ANDRE GARRETT

↘ SALAD OF HEIRLOOM TOMATOES,
YELLOW CARROTS, WATERMELON AND FRESH GOAT'S CURD
BY ANDRE GARRETT / SERVES 4

"THIS IS A VERY FRESH EASY SALAD TO PREPARE THAT HAS INTERESTING TASTE AND TEXTURE COMBINATIONS."

SPECIAL EQUIPMENT
Japanese mandolin, piping bag.

PLANNING AHEAD
All ingredients can be prepared well in advance and dressed at the last moment.

INGREDIENTS
- 1kg assorted shape and colour heirloom tomatoes
- 200ml rice wine vinegar
- 100ml good floral olive oil (Arbequina)
- salt and pepper, to taste
- 4 large beetroots
- 50g honey
- black pepper, as needed
- coriander seed, as needed
- 200ml red wine
- 4 large yellow carrots
- ½ watermelon

TO SERVE:
- 200g fresh goat's curd (or a mild soft goat's cheese)
- small selection hand-picked salad or chard leaves, washed

METHOD

Cut the tomatoes into various shapes and arrange in a dish. Mix the rice wine vinegar and the olive oil together, season with a little salt and pepper and pour over the tomatoes to marinate – leave in the fridge for a minimum of 1 hour.

Peel the beetroot and slice very thinly on the mandolin, being carful not to cut your fingers (use the guard). Caramelise the honey over a medium heat in a large pan, take off and add the spices, movig the pan to allow the spices to move around and aromatise. Add the wine and bring back to the boil on the heat, reduce by half, then pour over the beetroot and leave to cool.

Peel and slice the carrots on the mandolin, blanch the slices in boiling salted water for 1 minute, then refresh immediately in iced water to stop them over cooking.

Cut the watermelon into large 3cm dice; take out as many seeds as you can.

TO SERVE: Soften the goat's curd by mixing in a bowl and add to a piping bag, take half the carrot slices and lay on a clean surface, pipe a small bean-sized amount of the curd onto each carrot, then roll the carrots up into small rolls like cannelloni.

Drain the beetroot slices on some kitchen paper and place onto your serving plates. Arrange the melon, carrot and tomatoes in an attractive way, dress the top with a small amount of hand-picked leaves and finish by drizzling around some beetroot reduction and olive oil.

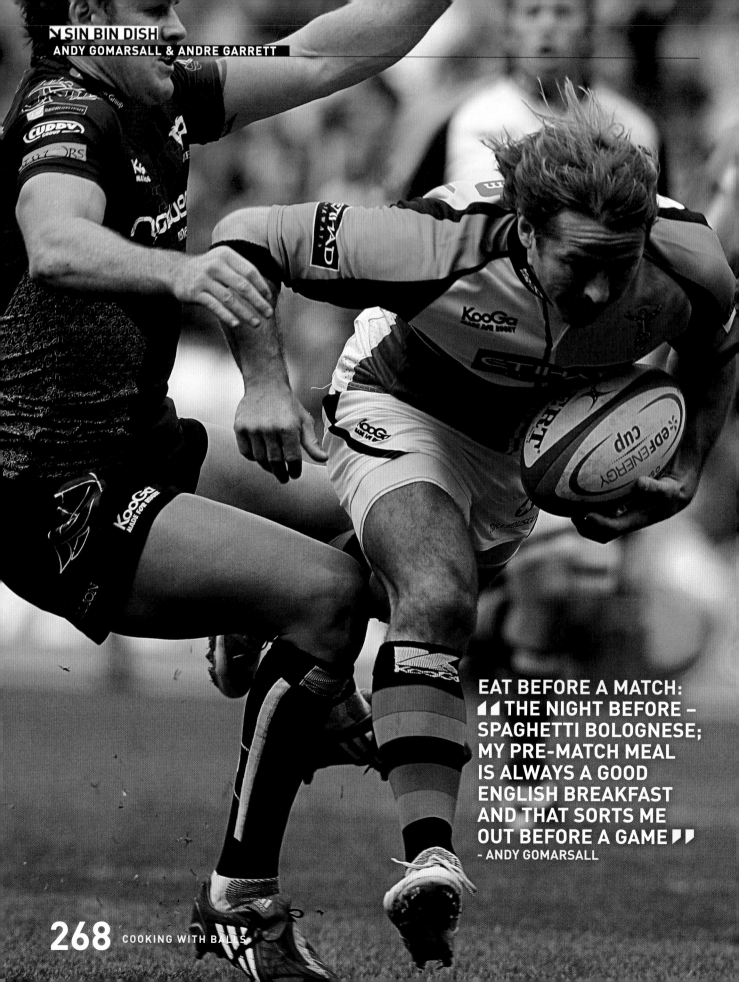

EAT BEFORE A MATCH:
❝ THE NIGHT BEFORE –
SPAGHETTI BOLOGNESE;
MY PRE-MATCH MEAL
IS ALWAYS A GOOD
ENGLISH BREAKFAST
AND THAT SORTS ME
OUT BEFORE A GAME ❞
- ANDY GOMARSALL

↘ DARK CHOCOLATE PALET
WITH MANGO SORBET
BY ANDRE GARRETT / SERVES 8

"THIS IS THE ULTIMATE CHOCOLATE GANACHE DESSERT – SOFT, DARK CHOCOLATE, CRISPY BASE AND COOL MANGO SORBET."

SPECIAL EQUIPMENT
Ice cream machine, small metal ring moulds, blow torch, piping bag.

PLANNING AHEAD
The sorbet should be made in advance depending on the ice cream machine manufacturer's instructions. The palet also needs 4 hours to set.

INGREDIENTS

SORBET:
- 200g frozen mango purée
- 50g sugar
- 100g water
- 10g glucose

DARK CHOCOLATE PALET:
- 350g 72% Valrhona chocolate
- 250g whipping cream
- 30g trimoline (inverted sugar syrup)
- 60g cold unsalted butter

BASE:
- 4-5 crushed digestive biscuits
- 20-30g melted white chocolate

HAZLENUT CREAM:
- 250ml whipped double cream
- 30g hazlenuts, chopped

TO SERVE:
- melted white chocolate, as needed

METHOD

SORBET: Defrost the purée, boil the sugar, water and glucose together, pour onto the mango purée, then pass through a sieve and churn in an ice cream machine, following the manufacturer's instructions.

DARK CHOCOLATE PALET: Gently melt the chocolate over a bain marie. Warm the cream and trimoline gently over a low heat. When the chocolate is melted fold the cream into the chocolate and emulsify the two together (both chocolate and cream must be only just warm or the mix will split). Fold the cold butter into this until there is a smooth chocolate mix to go into the moulds.

BASE: Mix the biscuits and chocolate together. Press the mix into the moulds in a very thin layer with a spoon; pour in the chocolate palet mix to reach the top of the mould, set aside in a cool place (but not the fridge) for 4 hours to set.

HAZLENUT CREAM: Mix both ingredients together and reserve.

TO SERVE: Dress the plates with a swipe of melted chocolate using a small brush. With a blow torch, heat the metal rings very gently so the palet will come free. Being careful, with a palette knife lift the ring with the chocolate inside then release the palet and it should slide out onto your plate. If it is still stuck repeat with the blow torch on a low heat to loosen some more. Form the sorbet into quenelles and add to the other end of the chocolate swipe, finally add the hazlenut cream to a piping bag and squeeze out the cream at the other end of the swipe.

MARK JORDAN
THE ATLANTIC HOTEL

↘ **BEN KAY**
LEICESTER TIGERS & ENGLAND

"THE MACARONI CAN BE MADE
SEVERAL DAYS IN ADVANCE AND
LEFT TO DRY UNTIL REQUIRED
– IT WILL KEEP WELL FOR
SEVERAL DAYS IN THIS FORM.
ALSO, THE LOBSTER CAN BE
PREPARED WELL IN ADVANCE."
- MARK JORDAN

↘ POACHED JERSEY LOBSTER SURPRISE
WITH CRAB AND SWEETCORN KERNEL MACARONI
BY MARK JORDAN / SERVES 2

"I LIKE THE SURPRISE ELEMENT OF THIS DISH BECAUSE THE MAIN PART OF THE DISH IS HIDDEN UNDER THE TOP PLATE AND IT IS ONLY WHEN YOU HAVE EATEN THE LOBSTER ON TOP THAT THE PLATE IS REMOVED TO REVEAL THE CRAB MACARONI UNDERNEATH."

METHOD

MACARONI: Pour the flour onto a work unit and make a well in the centre. Place into the well the egg yolks and the cracked whole eggs. Using your fingers in a circular motion gently start incorporating the flour until you end up with a dough. Knead the dough with your hands until it become smooth and lump free. Wrap the dough in cling film and place into a fridge for a couple of hours.

Cut the dough into smaller pieces and, using a rolling pin, roll the dough out lengthways until it will fit through the largest setting on the pasta machine, which is around the number 9. Gradually pass the dough through the machine coming down a size every two passes. If the pasta becomes a little sticky, just add a sprinkle of flour to each layer. I like to take the thickness of my pasta down to around number 4 on the machine.

Once all the pasta is in sheets cut them into 5cm size squares, roll the pasta around a pen and, sealing it with a little water, twist the pen out and leave the macaroni to dry.

FISH CREAM SAUCE: Place a saucepan on to a low heat and add a drop of oil. Add the vanilla, garlic, shallots, thyme, star anise and the white wine and gently heat and reduce until the wine is like syrup consistency.

At this point add the fish stock and again reduce by half, pour in the double cream and allow to boil for 10 minutes. Add the lemon juice to the sauce and check the seasoning with the salt. Pass the sauce through a fine sieve and place into the fridge until required.

TO SERVE: Place the macaroni into a pan of boiling salted water for around 5 minutes. While the pasta is cooking, heat up the fish cream sauce, add the sweetcorn and the crab meat, sprinkle in some of the chives and keep warm. Remove the macaroni from the water and add to the crab and sweetcorn mix.

In a hot pan wilt the spinach with a little butter and seasoning. Remove from the pan and place a bed of spinach in the centre of each plate. Take a nice thick slice of the poached lobster and sit on top of the spinach. In two separate bowls split the macaroni between the two and place on top of these the plates with the lobster on. Garnish with a little cress, cover with a see-through cloth and serve straightaway.

SPECIAL EQUIPMENT
Pasta machine.

PLANNING AHEAD
Poach the lobster for 8 minutes and then shell.

INGREDIENTS

MACARONI:
- 300g plain flour
- 6 egg yolks
- 3 large eggs

FISH CREAM SAUCE:
- oil, as needed
- 1 vanilla pod
- 1 garlic clove
- 2 shallots sliced
- 1 sprig fresh thyme
- 1 star anise
- 175ml white wine
- 570ml fish stock
- 570ml double cream
- lemon juice, to taste
- salt, to taste

LOBSTER:
- 1 lobster, cooked and shelled
- 100g sweetcorn
- 125g fresh white crab meat
- 30g freshly chopped chives
- baby spinach, as needed
- butter, as needed
- salt and pepper, to taste
- baby basil cress, as needed

↘ PAN ROAST FILLETS OF SOLE
WITH CRAB CRUSHED JERSEY ROYALS AND SAUCE GRENOBLE
BY MARK JORDAN / SERVES 2

"I LOVE THIS DISH AS IT'S VERY DIFFERENT TO EAT SOLE WHICH HAS BEEN PREPARED LIKE THIS. IT'S FULL OF FLAVOUR, IS SIMPLE TO PREPARE AND HAS VERY FEW INGREDIENTS."

METHOD

FISH BUBBLES: Place the shallots, garlic, mushrooms and thyme into a saucepan and gently fry with a little vegetable oil, add the white wine and reduce by half. Add the fish stock and vanilla pod to the wine mix and reduce by two-thirds. Add the double cream and gently simmer for about 10 minutes, then add the seasoning and finish with the lemon juice. This sauce can be frozen if required.

LEMON SOLE AND JERSEY ROYALS: Lay all the fillets of sole onto a chopping board and, one-by-one, lay the fillets on top of each other almost like building a wall. Skewer together with six cocktail sticks. Trim off the edges and cut in half equally so you end up with two nice portions. Place in the fridge to rest.

While resting, place the Jersey Royals into a pot of boiling salted water to cook for about 10 minutes.

Remove the sole from the fridge and place a sauté pan on a medium heat, add a little vegetable oil and place the sole fillets in the hot pan. Sauté on one side until they are golden brown. At this point turn them over and do the same again – this will take about 10 minutes. Once the sole is coloured on both sides, add a good knob of butter to the pan and baste over the sole, season with salt and add a good squeeze of lemon juice. Leave in the pan to finish cooking.

Drain the water off the potatoes and lightly crush with the back of a fork. Add the crab and a little knob of butter, and a squeeze of lemon juice. Check the seasoning.

TO SERVE: Place two spoons of the potatoes into a ring on a plate add a few baby spinach leaves. Remove the ring and then remove cocktail sticks from the sole and place on top of the spinach. Add the capers and gherkins to the pan with the butter the sole was cooked in and mix well. Spoon over the sole. Finally foam with a hand blender the fish sauce and place a spoonful of foam on top of each sole fillet. Garnish with the baby cress, season to taste and serve straight away.

SPECIAL EQUIPMENT
Sauté pan, cocktail sticks.

INGREDIENTS

FISH BUBBLES:
- 2 shallots, sliced
- 1 clove garlic
- 3 mushrooms, sliced
- 1 sprig of thyme
- vegetable oil, as needed
- 115ml white wine
- 575ml fish stock
- ½ vanilla pod
- 275ml double cream
- salt, to taste
- lemon juice, to taste

LEMON SOLE AND JERSEY ROYALS:
- 2 lemon sole, skinned and filleted
- 100g Jersey Royals
- vegetable oil, as needed
- 250g butter
- salt, to taste
- juice of ½ lemon
- 100g fresh white crab meat

TO SERVE:
- baby spinach, as needed
- 100g capers, chopped
- 100g gherkins, chopped
- salt and pepper , to taste
- mixed baby cress, as needed

THIS DISH CAN BE ALL PREPARED THE DAY BEFORE, IF REQUIRED, AND SIMPLY PUT TOGETHER WHEN NEEDED ON THE DAY
- MARK JORDAN

THE TAGLIATELLI CAN BE MADE SEVERAL DAYS IN ADVANCE AND LEFT TO DRY OVER A BROOMSTICK UNTIL REQUIRED – IT WILL KEEP WELL FOR SEVERAL DAYS IN THIS STATE
- MARK JORDAN

↘ TAGLIATELLI OF WILD MUSHROOMS
AND JERSEY ASPARAGUS WITH POACHED FREE-RANGE HEN'S EGG AND SHAVED PARMESAN CHEESE
BY MARK JORDAN / SERVES 2

"THIS IS A GREAT DISH BECAUSE YOU GET TO MAKE YOUR OWN PASTA WHICH IS FUN AND ALSO IT'S A GREAT DISH TO EAT AS A SNACK OR MAIN MEAL. THE COMBINATION OF THE PASTA WITH THE WILD MUSHROOMS AND A GENTLY POACHED HEN'S EGG IS A PERFECT MARRIAGE."

SPECIAL EQUIPMENT
Pasta machine.

PLANNING AHEAD
Make the pasta dough 2 hours in advance.

INGREDIENTS
- 300g strong plain flour
- 6 egg yolks
- 3 large eggs
- vegetable oil
- 300g fresh mixed wild mushrooms
- 100g fresh asparagus
- baby spinach
- 100ml double cream
- 2 free-range eggs
- white wine vinegar, to taste

TO SERVE:
- shaved parmesan cheese
- baby cress
- truffle oil (optional)
- fresh black pepper and rock salt

METHOD

Pour the flour onto a work unit and make a well in the centre. Place into the well the egg yolks and the 3 cracked whole eggs. Using your fingers in a circular motion gently start incorporating the flour until you end up with a dough. Knead the dough with your hands until it become smooth and lump free. Wrap the dough in cling film and place into a fridge for a couple of hours.

Cut the dough into smaller pieces and, using a rolling pin, roll the dough out lengthways until it will fit through the largest setting on the pasta machine which is around the number 9. Gradually pass the dough through the machine coming down a size every two passes. If the pasta becomes a little sticky, just add a sprinkle of flour to each layer. Take the thickness of the pasta down to around number 4 on the machine.

Once all the pasta is in sheets, start putting the sheets through the tagliatelli cutter on the machine. This is the one with large cutters. Once all the pasta is through and into tagliatelli hang it over a broomstick to dry a little.

Place a sauté pan onto the heat and add a little vegetable oil. Start by lightly sautéing the wild mushrooms for a minute or two, add the asparagus and the spinach and stir together. Now add the double cream and leave the mixture over a low heat while you cook the pasta.

Place the pasta into a pan of boiling water with a little vegetable oil and cook for around two minutes.

Strain the pasta and add to the cream and wild mushroom mixture, stirring it all in well so that all the pasta is coated with the sauce.

Crack the 2 free-range eggs one at a time into a ladle and then gently slide the eggs into a pan of rapidly boiling water with a splash of white wine vinegar. Keep the boiling water moving with a spoon for around 3 minutes so the eggs stay nice and round.

TO SERVE: While the eggs are poaching split the tagliatelli mix between two bowls.

Remove the eggs from the water and place one egg on top of each bowl of pasta. Shave some fresh parmesan cheese all over the pasta and sprinkle with the baby cress, add a dash of truffle oil if you would like and serve straightaway with the pepper and salt.

CHEF'S TIP: I like my pasta with a little texture, but if you prefer softer pasta leave it in for an extra minute or so.

↘ RASPBERRY NOUGATINE
WITH FRESH JERSEY PISTACHIO CREAM
AND RASPBERRY SORBET
BY MARK JORDAN / SERVES 2

"THIS DISH JUST SHOUTS OUT SUMMER TIME TO ME – THE FRESHEST OF THE SUMMER RASPBERRIES AND THE RICHEST JERSEY CREAM, AND IT IS SO REFRESHING WITH THE RASPBERRY SORBET. PURE HEAVEN."

SPECIAL EQUIPMENT
Silpat mat, ice cream machine.

PLANNING AHEAD
Churn the sorbet the night before.

INGREDIENTS

SORBET:
- 250ml stock syrup
- 250ml raspberry coulis

NOUGATINE:
- 500g caster sugar

PISTACHIO CREAM:
- 250ml double cream
- 1 tsp pistachio paste

TO SERVE:
- 1 punnet of raspberries
- fresh mint

METHOD

SORBET: Place the stock syrup and raspberry coulis together into a saucepan and bring to a quick boil. Remove from the pan and leave to cool. Once the liquid is cool, place into an ice cream machine and churn until the sorbet starts to set. Remove from the machine and place in a freezer to set completely overnight.

NOUGATINE: Put the caster sugar into a heavy-bottomed saucepan and place over a very low heat. Gently melt the sugar to a golden caramel. This will take about 20 minutes. Once all the sugar has melted, pour onto the silpat mat, taking care as the sugar is very, very hot.

Leave the sugar to set and go cold. Once cold, crack with a rolling pin, then place into a food blender and whiz until the caramel looks like a fine powder. With a sieve, sprinkle the sugar powder over the silpat mat again nice and evenly, about 1-2mm thick. Place this into an oven and watch as the sugar turns back into a liquid within seconds. Take it out of the oven again and, using a metal cutter, cut out six round discs. Once cold place the discs into an air-tight container until required.

PISTACHIO CREAM: Add the pistachio paste to the double cream and whip to form soft peaks. Place the cream into a piping bag and place into a fridge.

TO SERVE: Place one disc of the nougatine in the centre of two plates. Onto that pipe a small ball of the pistachio cream and arrange five or six raspberries around the cream. Once you have done both plates place another disc of sugar on top, repeating the process for both plates so that you are forming layers. Place another disc on the top as the final layer.

Remove the raspberry sorbet from the fridge and, using an ice cream baller, make two neatly shaped balls of sorbet and place onto the raspberry plates. Garnish with the picked mint and serve straightaway.

CHEF'S TIP: The stock syrup and raspberry coulis can both be bought in the supermarket.

If the sugar discs break you can simply place the sugar back into the food processor again, whiz back to a powder and start again.

↘ MATT LOVELL
ENGLAND RUGBY NUTRITIONIST

⬐ MATT LOVELL
ENGLAND RUGBY NUTRITIONIST
INTRODUCTION

FOR ENGLAND NUTRITIONIST MATT LOVELL HIS LOVE OF RUGBY ISN'T JUST ABOUT THE GAME BUT THE SCIENCE THAT DRIVES THE PLAYERS THEMSELVES.

Together with personal training company Perform and Function Matt's ultimate goal is to bring maximum health, wellness and performance to all those following the programmes – as well of course as keeping the players happy!

Food and exercise go hand in hand in helping to make the body strong and healthy. In this section of the book Matt has donated some of his favourite recipes perfect for those watching their weight or looking for meals to aid in muscle recovery and muscle growth.

Easy-to-follow dishes with calorie and fat content ensure that healthy meals need never be dull. Choose from a selection of starters, mains and desserts to help keep your lifestyle balanced.

A LITTLE ABOUT MATT...

After finishing a degree in political philosophy at Bristol Matt re-trained as a personal trainer with the YMCA. He worked for 5 years in the city for his company Excel Personal Training and is a grade 1 Master Personal Trainer. This led to an interest and passion in nutrition which resulted in 3 years study and graduation at the Institute for Optimum Nutrition.

During his running of a personal training company in the City of London Matt gained wide experience in body composition change and physical preparation for general and elite level sports.

Further grounding and experience was gained while practising clinical nutrition alongside doctors and dietitians on Harley Street, leading to specialist areas in performance-based nutrition and diet applications for elite athletes, female hormonal health and body composition management.

In 2002 Matt started working with the England Rugby Team and was part of Clive Woodward's team that lifted the World Cup in 2003. He continues in the same role working with the England team and was a member of the team who against all the odds reached the final of the 2007 Rugby World Cup. Matt is the Sports Nutritionist for London Wasps, London Irish, Saracens and Leicester Rugby Clubs.

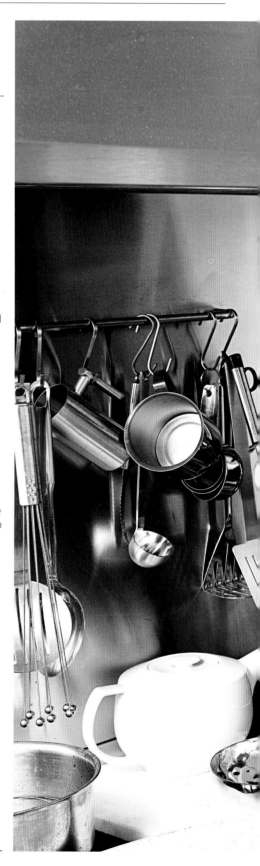

EASY-TO-FOLLOW DISHES WITH CALORIE AND FAT CONTENT ENSURE THAT HEALTHY MEALS NEED NEVER BE DULL
- MATT LOVELL

↘ CRAB SALAD
BY MATT LOVELL / SERVES 1

"A GEM OF A SALAD – CRUSTACEANS LIKE CRAB PROVIDE A USEFUL SOURCE OF ZINC, THE MINERAL REQUIRED FOR OPTIMUM TESTOSTERONE PRODUCTION, WITH AN 85G SERVING CONTAINING 6.5MG. OTHER INGREDIENTS INCLUDE BLOOD-THINNING CHILLI AND GARLIC ALONG WITH ONIONS AND ROCKET."

FAT: 1.2G, SATURATES 0.6G

KCAL: 250

PLANNING AHEAD
You can make the relish ahead of time if you wish to.

INGREDIENTS
- 20g pine nuts
- 200g fresh crab meat (or tinned if fresh is not available)
- ½ red onion, finely chopped
- 1 garlic clove, finely chopped
- 2 large chillis, finely chopped
- 30g rocket
- 20g watercress
- 10 cherry tomatoes

DRESSING:
- 1 tbsp red wine vinegar
- 1 tbsp tamari sauce
- 1 tbsp olive oil

TO SERVE:
- coriander (optional)

FRESH CRAB IS ALWAYS BETTER BUT INCREASES THE PREPARATION TIME SIGNIFICANTLY
- MATT LOVELL

METHOD
Lightly brown the pine nuts in a pan, taking care not to burn them.

Mix the crab with the onion, garlic and chilli.

DRESSING: Mix all the ingredients together. Add to the crab mix and leave to infuse if desired for how 20 minutes.

TO SERVE: Mix the remaining salad ingredients together and then dress with the crab mixture. Add the coriander if desired.

↘ TOM YUM SOUP

MATT LOVELL / SERVES 1

"SOUP MADE FROM GOOD STOCK IS A NATURAL HEALER. THE STOCK CONTAINS HIGH LEVELS OF PROTEINS AND COMPONENTS THE BODY USES TO REBUILD TISSUE, JOINTS AND BODY DAMAGE. FOR A RUGBY PLAYER HOME-MADE STOCK IS AN ESSENTIAL PART OF THEIR WEEKLY DIET. ADDING TOM YUM SPICES INCREASES THE IMMUNE BOOSTING PROPERTIES OF THIS SIMPLE STARTER. THIS IS ALSO VIRTUALLY ZERO CARB AND ZERO FAT."

FAT: 2G SATURATES 0.5G

KCAL: 300

PLANNING AHEAD
Make the stock in advance.

INGREDIENTS
- ½ litre chicken stock
- 1 tbsp of tom yum soup paste
- 200g raw jumbo prawns, ready peeled

TO SERVE:
- fresh coriander

THIS IS A GREAT SOUP TO HAVE THE MOMENT YOU FEEL A LITTLE RUN DOWN. IT IS ALSO GREAT AS PART OF YOUR POST-GAME RECOVERY ROUTINE.

TOM YUM SOUP PASTE CAN BE BOUGHT FROM YOUR SUPERMARKET.
- MATT LOVELL

METHOD
Heat the stock on a low heat until heated through and then stir in the tom yum paste. Add the prawns and cook for 5 minutes on a high heat.

TO SERVE: Ladle into a bowl and add the coriander to garnish.

↘ TUNA AND CHILLI FRITTATA
BY MATT LOVELL / SERVES 1

"OMEGA EGGS ARE A DECENT WAY TO INCREASE YOUR OMEGA-3 FATTY ACID INTAKE. NORMAL EGGS ARE ALSO A VERY NUTRIENT DENSE FOOD. EGGS ARE STILL THOUGHT TO INCREASE CHOLESTEROL, WHICH IS NOT IN FACT THE CASE WHEN THEY ARE EATEN ON AVERAGE TWO PER DAY. THE SATURATED FAT CONTENT OF EGGS IS LOW. THIS OMELETTE COMES IN WITH A HIGH-PROTEIN AND LOW-CARB CONTENT, MAKING IT A PERFECT FILLING SNACK OR MEAL."

FAT: 14.7G, SATURATES 3.6G

KCAL: 350

SPECIAL EQUIPMENT
Omelette pan.

INGREDIENTS
- 1 large chilli, chopped
- 1 garlic clove, chopped
- coconut oil, as needed
- 1 tin of albacore tuna, drained
- 3 omega eggs

METHOD

Fry the chilli and garlic in the coconut oil with the tuna.

Beat the eggs with a fork in a bowl until the yolks are well mixed with the whites. Add the eggs to the tuna mixture and cook slowly over a medium heat, taking care not to burn the eggs.

OTHER INGREDIENTS CAN BE ADDED TO INCREASE THE PORTION SIZE, SUCH AS ONIONS AND PEPPERS
- MATT LOVELL

↘ CORONATION CHICKEN

BY MATT LOVELL / SERVES 4

"THE ENGLISH CLASSIC – AND A PERSONAL FAVOURITE OF MINE. THIS MAKES A PERFECT HIGH PROTEIN AND HIGH CARB RECOVERY MEAL. IT'S A PERFECT COMBINATION OF SPICES, SAUCE AND INGREDIENTS FROM AROUND THE GLOBE."

THIS IS ACTUALLY A VERY LOW-FAT DISH IF YOU USE LOW-FAT MAYONNAISE – THE BEAUTY IS IN THE ABILITY YOU HAVE TO TWEAK THE INGREDIENTS, ADDING MORE CURRY, GARLIC AND ALSO APRICOT JAM

- MATT LOVELL

FAT: 4G, SATURATES 2G

KCAL: 352

INGREDIENTS
- 1 whole organic chicken
- 1 bay leaf
- 15 peppercorns
- 1 stalk celery
- 1 small onion
- 1 tbsp olive oil
- 2 tsp curry powder
- 1 tbsp red wine
- lemon juice
- 1 tsp tomato purée
- 2 tsp apricot jam
- 120g low-fat mayonnaise

TO SERVE:
- 400g wild and basmati rice
- 200g peas
- almond flakes, as needed

METHOD

Poach the chicken for 1 hour 15 minutes in filtered water with the bay leaf, peppercorns and celery.

While this is poaching fry the onion in the olive oil until soft, then add the curry powder and stir through. Add the wine, apricot jam, lemon juice and tomato purée and continue stirring. Set the sauce aside and leave to cool.

Once the chicken is cooked allow the water to cool – this will allow the chicken to absorb some of the water and moisten it up a bit. Shred the chicken.

Stir the mayonnaise into the curry sauce and add the shredded chicken.

TO SERVE: Boil enough rice for each person and add the peas 3 minutes before the rice is done, straining the mixture. Serve on a plate in the shape of a ring and put the chicken mixed with the sauce in the middle. Adding almond flakes finishes the dish off nicely.

↘ PORK AND PRUNES

BY MATT LOVELL / SERVES 2

"THIS IS A CLASSIC DISH WHICH YOU CAN EAT WITH FRIENDS FOR A CLASSY DINNER PARTY OR WITH SOME SIMPLE TWEAKS IT MAKES A GREAT RECOVERY MEAL WHEN SERVED WITH RICE. PRUNES SCORE VERY HIGH ON THE ORAC SCALE, MEANING YOU GET LOTS OF PROTECTION FROM EATING THEM. THEY ALSO HELP KEEP YOU REGULAR! PORK LOIN OFFERS QUALITY LOW-FAT PROTEIN TO REBUILD ACHING MUSCLES."

FAT 7G, SATURATES 3G

KCAL: 400

PLANNING AHEAD

Soak the prunes in the wine the night before and store in the fridge.

INGREDIENTS

- 24 giant prunes
- ½ bottle of medium dry white wine
- 500-700g of pork loin
- Celtic sea salt and pepper
- spelt flour, as needed
- 60g of coconut oil
- 1 tbsp redcurrant jelly
- 250g double cream or Greek yoghurt

METHOD

Place the soaked prunes in the oven at 160°C for 2 minutes, making sure the liquid doesn't boil away.

Cut the pork loin into mini medallions, coat with flour, and season with salt and pepper. Fry the pork in the coconut oil till golden brown on both sides, set aside and leave the meat juices in the pan.

Drain the prune juice into the meat juices and add the prunes to the pork.

In a pan simmer the meat juices and prune juice, stirring in the redcurrant jelly.

Finally stir in the cream or Greek yoghurt, taking care not to curdle the sauce.

Pour over the pork while still hot and serve.

⅃ COMPLEX SALMON SALAD

BY MATT LOVELL / SERVES 1

"THE COMPLEX SALAD IS THE CORNER-STONE TO A HEALTHY DIET AND MAINTAINING LOW BODY FATS. YOU NEED AT LEAST 10 INGREDIENTS AND A CREATIVE MIND AROUND DRESSINGS. COMPLEX SALADS CAN BE CREATED FROM SCRATCH IN 10 MINUTES, MAKING THEM CONVENIENT AS WELL AS HEALTHY AND VERSATILE."

FAT: 10G, SATURATES 2G

KCAL: 350 APPROX

INGREDIENTS

SALAD:
- 1 fillet of wild Alaskan salmon
- coconut oil, as needed
- 1 garlic clove
- ½ lemon juice, freshly squeezed
- 100g broccoli
- olives, as preferred
- celery, as preferred
- 1 large sprig of dill
- 1 dsp capers
- 1pack bistro-style salad – lamb's lettuce and beetroot
- 30g broad beans
- 1 large sprig of parsley

DRESSING TO SERVE:
- olive oil
- honey
- garlic
- 2 tbsp cider vinegar

KEEP A CAREFUL EYE WHEN COOKING THE SALMON AND LOOK INSIDE TO CHECK IF IT IS COOKED.

THE DRESSING CAN BE MADE WITH MORE VINEGAR AND LESS OIL TO LOWER THE FAT CONTENT.
- MATT LOVELL

METHOD

SALAD: Pan fry the salmon in the coconut oil and cook for 3-4 minutes each side.

Chop the remaining ingredients as desired.

DRESSING TO SERVE: Mix all the ingredients together in a bowl and pour over the salad ingredients. Toss the salad in the mixture.

↘ SYLLABUB
BY MATT LOVELL / SERVES 6

"THIS IS A RECOVERY DISH BUT IT'S ONE FOR AN 'OFF' DAY – IT'S BASICALLY AN ADVANCED MUSCLE- GAINING FORMULA – EGG WHITES, SUGAR, CREAM AND ALCOHOL MAKE A HIGH-CALORIE HIGH-INSULIN RAISING DISH WHICH IS DELICIOUS. YOU CAN TAKE THE CALORIES DOWN USING SWEETENER AND CREME FRAICHE INSTEAD OF NORMAL CREAM – BUT IT DOES CHANGE THE NATURE OF THE DISH. ADDITIONAL GINGER AND SPICES SUCH AS CINNAMON CAN BE ADDED TO ENHANCE THE FLAVOUR AND MEDICINAL PROPERTIES OF THIS DISH."

FAT: 14.7G, SATURATES 12G

KCAL: 252

SPECIAL EQUIPMENT
Blender.

INGREDIENTS
- 1 lemon rind, thinly sliced
- 4 tbsp lemon juice
- 4 egg whites
- 125ml white wine or sherry
- 2 tbsp brandy
- 75g caster sugar or sweetener
- 250ml cream or crème fraîche, lightly whipped

TO SERVE:
- grated nutmeg

METHOD

Beat the egg whites until slightly stiff and combine the ingredients, finally stir in the sugar. Use a blender to increase the thickness of the mixture without allowing it to become too thick.

⬊ BLUEBERRIES AND YOGHURT
BY MATT LOVELL / SERVES 1

"POWER-PACKED BERRIES SCORE HIGHLY ON THE ORAC SCALE (THE AMOUNT SOMETHING PROTECTS CELLS AGAINST DAMAGE) – AND THE TOTAL 0% GREEK YOGHURT IS HIGH IN PROTEIN AND CONTAINS ZERO FAT. IT'S AN EXCELLENT RECOVERY MEAL AND IS ALSO LOW ENOUGH IN ENERGY TO MAKE A PERFECT END TO A MEAL. ALL GOOD."

FAT: 0G

KCAL: 220

INGREDIENTS
- 250g 0% Greek yoghurt
- 60g blueberries

WASH THE BLUEBERRIES IF BOUGHT FROM A SUPERMARKET. IDEALLY GROW YOUR OWN – A COUPLE OF BLUEBERRY PLANTS IN POTS CAN SEE YOU RIGHT FOR EIGHT LARGE BOWLS OF BERRIES
- MATT LOVELL

METHOD

Combine the yoghurt and blueberries together and serve.

↘ PISTACHIO CAKE
BY MATT LOVELL / SERVES 10

"I LOVE THIS DISH – AND I'VE TWEAKED THE RECIPE FROM THE RIVER CAFÉ COOK BOOK! WHEN YOU USE COCONUT OIL AND SWEETENER INSTEAD OF THE BUTTER AND SUGAR IT STARTS TO LOOK LIKE A LOW-CARB POWER HOUSE OF A CAKE! PISTACHIOS ARE A GOOD SOURCE OF COPPER, PHOSPHORUS, POTASSIUM, MAGNESIUM AND B6. THE NUTS DELIVER 30 VITAMINS, MINERALS AND PHYTONUTRIENTS, SO THEY HAVE A CONSIDERABLE POWER-PACKED PUNCH FROM A NUTRITIONAL STANDPOINT."

FAT: 5.7G, SATURATES 0.9G

KCAL: 225.7

INGREDIENTS

CAKE:
- 200g pistachios
- 50g spelt flour
- 2 tbsp coconut oil
- 1 lemon
- 1 vanilla bean
- 200g sweetener
- 4 eggs

TO SERVE:
- low-fat crème fraîche

METHOD

CAKE: Preheat the oven to 160ºC.

Blend the pistachios into the flour then combine all the remaining ingredients and mix together thoroughly.

Grease a 20cm cake tin with coconut oil or use baking paper. Bake until golden brown and cooked through – the centre shouldn't be too moist for around 30-40 minutes.

TO SERVE: Serve with a dollop of low-fat crème fraîche.

⬊ GLOSSARY

AL DENTE:
Meaning 'to the tooth'; a slight resistance in the centre after cooking.

AROMATISE:
To fill or impregnate with an aroma or scent; 'leave the herbs in to aromatise the meat'.

BAIN MARIE:
A container filled with hot water to cook or to hold at a temperature.

BAKE BLIND:
To cook a pastry shell before adding the filling; 'bake the pastry blind'.

BAKING BEANS:
Weights to keep a pie shell from shrinking, see Bake Blind.

BECHAMEL SAUCE:
A white sauce made with milk.

BEIGNET:
A pastry that is deep fried, can be sweet or savoury.

BLANCH:
To transfer food to ice water to stop the cooking process; 'blanch the vegetables'.

BOUILLON:
A broth made from cooking meat or vegetables in water.

BOUQUET GARNI:
A selection of herbs contained in a cheesecloth bag.

BURRATA:
A fresh Italian cheese, made from mozzarella and cream. The shell is solid mozzarella while the inside holds mozzarella and cream.

BUTTERFLY:
To cut a food down the centre but not cutting all the way through and then to open out in the shape of a butterly; 'butterfly the chicken'.

CANELLE KNIFE:
A small kitchen tool similar to a vegetable peeler.

CARAMELISE:
To convert sugar to caramel; 'caramelise the sauce'.

CARAPACE:
The hard shell-like covering of a crustacean.

CHINOIS:
A conical sieve with an extremely fine mesh.

CLARIFIED BUTTER:
Butter that has been melted, evaporating the water and separating the milk solids.

CO_2 SIPHON:
A siphon charged with CO_2 cartridges to add air to creams and desserts.

CONFIT:
Food immersed in a substance for flavour and preservation.

COULIS:
A thick sauce made of puréed fruit or vegetables.

COURT BOUILLON:
A flavoured liquid for poaching or quick-cooking foods.

CREME ANGLAIS:
A rich vanilla-flavoured sauce that can be served hot or cold with cake, fruit, or another dessert.

CROUSTILLANT:
From the French meaning crisp.

CUTLET BAT:
A heavy tool used to thin out food by striking on a work surface or chopping board.

DEGLAZE:
To use a liquid to remove cooked-on residue from a pan and reduce until syrup-like.

DICE:
To cut into small cubes; 'dice the onions'.

DOUBLE BOILER:
Two pots in which one sits inside the other, the lower pot is used to hold water heating the food in the upper pot.

EMULSIFY:
To combine two liquids together which normally don't mix easily; 'emulsify the water and oil'.

FONDANT:
1. A paste made by mixing together boiled sugar and water.

2. A smooth creamy mixture, often used as an accompaniment of filling.

GANACHE:
A glaze, icing or filling.

GENOISE:
A light, rich cake similar to a sponge cake.

GLAZE:
To thinly coat with a mixture; 'glaze the pastry with the mixture'.

HEAVY-BOTTOMED PAN:
A pan similar to a skillet, often made from cast iron.

JOCONDE:
An type of sponge cake.

JULIENNE:
To cut into thin strips; 'carrots, Julienne'.

MANDOLINE:
Kitchen utensil used for slicing and cutting, especially into julienne (long and thin) strips.

MANTECATURA:
The final step, when butter or olive oil are stirred into the risotto. This step binds the ingredients together and makes the risotto creamy.

MARINATE/MACERATE:
To soak a meat, fish or vegetables in a seasoned liquid mixture to absorb the flavours of the marinade or to tenderise. When fruits are soaked in liquid it is referred to as macerate; 'marinade the steak in the stock', 'macerate the strawberries in water and sugar'.

MIREPOX:
A combination of chopped carrots, celery and onions used to add flavour and aroma to stocks, sauces, soups and other foods.

MOULI:
A french rotary grater for grating chocolate or nuts.

MOULIS:
A type of sieve.

OXIDISING:
To chemically react when exposed to oxygen; 'add lemon juice to the apple to stop it oxidising and changing colour'.

PALETTE KNIFE:
A knife with a flat flexible blade and a blunt end for smoothing icings and toppings.

PANNA COTTA:
An Italian dish often using cream and milk.

PANETTONE:
A sweet bread with orange peel, raisins and nuts originating from Italy.

POACH:
To cook in boiling or simmering liquid.

PULSE:
To use an on-off mixing method; 'pulse the vegetables in a blender'.

PUREE:
To blend or strain cooked food until a thick consistency; 'blend until a purée'.

QUENELLE:
To shape with two spoons into small round or oval dumplings; 'add a quenelle of sorbet'.

RAMEKIN:
A small individual circular, porcelain, glass or earthenware oven-proof dish.

REDUCE:
To simmer or boil a liquid until much of it evaporates, making it more concentrated; 'reduce the sauce'.

RESERVE:
To keep to one side; 'reserve until serving'.

SABAYON:
A dessert made by mixing egg yolks and sugar over simmering water. Also known as a zabaglione.

SALAMANDER:
A piece of equipment used to brown the top of foods.

SAUTE:
To fry briefly over high heat; 'sauté the onions'.

SEAR:
To brown quickly over very high heat, 'sear the meat'.

SILPAT:
A popular silicone mat used in baking to provide a non-stick surface without fat.

SIMMER
To cook food in hot liquid just below boiling point, 'simmer the potatoes'.

SOFT BALL STAGE:
A stage in sugar cooking where sugar becomes a soft ball.

SOUFFLE:
A light, fluffy baked dish made with egg yolks and beaten egg.

SPRAY GUN:
A tool to lightly spray food with oil or decorate plates.

SPRINGFORM PAN:
A baking pan with a detachable rim to release baked contents.

SWEAT:
To cook slowly over a low heat; 'sweat the onions'.

TRIMOLINE:
Inverted sugar syrup made from splitting sucrose into glucose and fructose.

TUILE:
A thin, crisp cookie that is placed over a rounded object to mould into shape.

WATER BATH:
See Bain Marie.

VAC-PAC MACHINE:
A piece of equipment to seal food in a plastic airless vacuum to either cook or store.

⬎ INDEX

↘ RESTAURANT DIRECTORY

GIORGIO LOCATELLI
LOCANDA LOCATELLI
Marylebone, London
020 7935 9088
www.locandalocatelli.com

JEREMY BLOOR
OXO TOWER
South Bank, London
020 7803 3888
www.harveynichols.com

TOM AIKENS
CHELSEA, LONDON
Tom Aikens
020 7584 2003
www.tomaikens.co.uk

ALAIN ROUX
THE WATERSIDE INN
Bray-on-Thames
01628 620691
www.waterside-inn.co.uk

CYRUS TODIWALA
CAFE SPICE NAMASTE
London
020 7488 9242
www.cafespice.co.uk

NIGEL HAWORTH
NORTHCOTE
Blackburn
01254 240555
www.northcotemanor.com

MARTIN BURGE
THE DINING ROOM AT WHATLEY MANOR
Malmesbury
01666 822888
www.whatleymanor.com

CLIVE DIXON
KOFFMANN'S
Knightsbridge, London
020 7235 1010
www.the-berkeley.co.uk/koffmanns

THEO RANDALL
THEO RANDALL AT THE INTERCONTINENTAL
Park Lane, London
020 7318 8747
www.theorandall.com

RAYMOND BLANC
LE MANOIR AUX QUAT' SAISONS
Oxford
01844 278881
www.manoir.com

ARMAND SABLON
BISTRO K
South Kensington, London
020 7373 7774
www.bistro-k.co.uk

MICHEL ROUX JR
LE GAVROCHE
Mayfair, London
020 7408 0881
www.le-gavroche.co.uk

GALTON BLACKISTON
MORSTON HALL
Blakeney
01263 741041
www.morstonhall.com

SAT BAINS
RESTAURANT SAT BAINS
Nottingham
01159 866566
www.restaurantsatbains.com

PHIL THOMPSON
AUBERGE DU LAC
Welwyn Garden City
01707 368888
www.aubergedulac.co.uk

PIERRE KOFFMANN
KOFFMANN'S
Knightsbridge, London
020 7235 1010
www.the-berkeley.co.uk/koffmanns

HYWEL JONES
THE PARK (AT LUCKNAM PARK HOTEL)
Bath
01225 742777
www.lucknampark.co.uk

ALAN MURCHISON
L'ORTOLAN
Reading
01189 888500
www.lortolan.com

MARCUS WAREING
MARCUS WAREING AT THE BERKELEY
The Berkeley Hotel, London
020 7235 1200
www.the-berkeley.co.uk

FRANCESCO MAZZEI
L'ANIMA
Broadgate West
London
0207 422 7000
www.lanima.co.uk

JONAS KARLSSON
FIFTH FLOOR RESTAURANT, HARVEY NICHOLS
Knightsbridge, London
020 7235 5250
www.harveynichols.com

ANDRE GARRETT
GALVIN AT WINDOWS
Park Lane, London
020 7208 4021
www.galvinatwindows.com

MARK JORDAN
ATLANTIC
Jersey
01534 744101
www.theatlantichotel.com

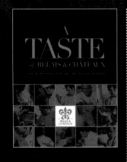
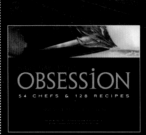
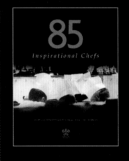